T0310465

GLOBAL
BEST PRACTICES
FOR CSO, NGO,
AND OTHER NONPROFIT BOARDS

EDITED BY
PENELOPE CAGNEY

GLOBAL
BEST PRACTICES
FOR CSO, NGO,
AND OTHER NONPROFIT BOARDS

Lessons From Around the World

BoardSource®   WILEY

Copyright © 2018 by BoardSource. All rights reserved.

Published by John Wiley & Sons, Inc., Hoboken, New Jersey.

Published simultaneously in Canada.

No part of this publication may be reproduced, stored in a retrieval system, or transmitted in any form or by any means, electronic, mechanical, photocopying, recording, scanning, or otherwise, except as permitted under Section 107 or 108 of the 1976 United States Copyright Act, without either the prior written permission of the Publisher, or authorization through payment of the appropriate per-copy fee to the Copyright Clearance Center, Inc., 222 Rosewood Drive, Danvers, MA 01923, (978) 750-8400, fax (978) 646-8600, or on the Web at www.copyright.com. Requests to the Publisher for permission should be addressed to the Permissions Department, John Wiley & Sons, Inc., 111 River Street, Hoboken, NJ 07030, (201) 748-6011, fax (201) 748-6008, or online at http://www.wiley.com/go/permissions.

Limit of Liability/Disclaimer of Warranty: While the publisher and author have used their best efforts in preparing this book, they make no representations or warranties with respect to the accuracy or completeness of the contents of this book and specifically disclaim any implied warranties of merchantability or fitness for a particular purpose. No warranty may be created or extended by sales representatives or written sales materials. The advice and strategies contained herein may not be suitable for your situation. You should consult with a professional where appropriate. Neither the publisher nor author shall be liable for any loss of profit or any other commercial damages, including but not limited to special, incidental, consequential, or other damages.

For general information on our other products and services or for technical support, please contact our Customer Care Department within the United States at (800) 762-2974, outside the United States at (317) 572-3993 or fax (317) 572-4002.

Wiley publishes in a variety of print and electronic formats and by print-on-demand. Some material included with standard print versions of this book may not be included in e-books or in print-on-demand. If this book refers to media such as a CD or DVD that is not included in the version you purchased, you may download this material at http://booksupport.wiley.com. For more information about Wiley products, visit www.wiley.com.

Library of Congress Cataloging-in-Publication Data

Names: Cagney, Penelope, 1956- editor.
Title: Global best practices for CSO, NGO, and other nonprofit boards :
  lessons from around the world / Penelope Cagney, editor.
Description: Hoboken, New Jersey : John Wiley & Sons, Inc., [2018] | Includes
  bibliographical references and index. |
Identifiers: LCCN 2017057988 (print) | LCCN 2018010696 (ebook) | ISBN
  9781119423201 (epub) | ISBN 9781119423287 (pdf) | ISBN 9781119423270
  (cloth)
Subjects: LCSH: Nonprofit organizations—Management. | Nongovernmental
  organizations—Management. | Boards of directors. | Corporate governance.
Classification: LCC HD2769.15 (ebook) | LCC HD2769.15 .G57 2018 (print) | DDC
  658.4/22—dc23
LC record available at https://lccn.loc.gov/2017057988

Cover Design: Wiley
Cover Image: © wektorygrafika/iStockphoto

Printed in the United States of America

10 9 8 7 6 5 4 3 2 1

This book is dedicated with love to my family: Helen, Nate, Jay, Candy, Jimmy, Kemper, Naomi, and Joey.

Contents

Acknowledgments

My thanks to BoardSource first for supporting this exploration of global governance; and to my publishing team—Anne Atwood Mead at BoardSource and Brian Neill at John Wiley & Sons. I would also like to thank especially Usha Menon (Singapore and Philippines) who edited the ambitious Asia Chapter; and the contributors: Bekay Ahn (Korea); Consuelo Castro (Latin America); Tariq Cheema (MENA); Louise Coventry (Southeast Asia); Noshir Dadrawala (India); Naila Farouky (MENA); Burkhard Gnärig (ICSOs); Alan Hough (Australia); Miho Ito (Japan); Oma Lee (China); Yinglu Li (China); Krishan Mehta (Canada); Velario Melandri (Europe); Mike Muchilwa (Africa); Darmawan Triwibowo (Indonesia); Garth Nowland-Foreman (New Zealand); Paloma Raggo (United States); Masataka Uo (Japan); and Marilyn Wyatt (Central and Eastern Europe and Eurasia).

—Penelope Cagney

CHAPTER 1

Overview

Penelope Cagney

This chapter provides an overview of the book—who it is for and why it is needed, who the contributors are, the context and framework for the book's content, and an outline of chapters.

WHO THIS BOOK IS FOR

Nonprofits are entrusted with some of the world's most important work, and the scope and size of this sector has expanded tremendously in the past few decades. These organizations seek to solve, often in partnership with other sectors, the biggest problems of the planet—namely, climate change, poverty, hunger and the need for clean water, resolution of war and protection of rights, and promotion of education and health. They are charged, too, with the preservation and promotion of arts and culture and other important issues relating to quality of life.

The need for responsible, informed, and well-equipped governance for nonprofit organizations is critical. This book is intended for those who seek to prepare themselves to provide it. Boards everywhere, composed of impassioned grassroots volunteers, concerned philanthropists, and accomplished community and business leaders, seek guidance on providing quality leadership to nonprofits. This book is also for capacity-building organizations that strive to equip nonprofits in the best way possible to carry out their important tasks. It is also for CEOs and executive directors intending to assist their boards with working at optimal performance levels and for those who teach in, and study, our sector.

1

INTRODUCTION

While there are political and societal forces tugging us in different directions today, technological innovations, such as social media, have undeniably brought us closer together. Whether we are talking about the nonprofit food bank around the corner that serves the neighborhood or a colossal nongovernmental organization (NGO) that spans continents, the need for good governance is universal. But do we all agree on what constitutes "best practice"? Little is known about how NGO governance is practiced around the world.

New wealth everywhere is encouraging nations to view their cultures and traditions as the compasses guiding the direction of their philanthropy and civil society. This has value for us all.

> There is much to be gained from setting aside preconceived ideas and looking intently for what really works for local people.
>
> *Coventry (2017), 55*

Even those of us whose interests go no further than our own borders need to examine our preconceived ideas about what is "best," because we live in increasingly diverse societies that call for more nuanced approaches to what works. To understand, serve, and include, we need to first confront the limitations of our own cultural biases.

What we hope to accomplish here is to open the discussion about governance to the dazzling diversity of perspectives and practices around the world that can enrich our common knowledge of how *our* boards, wherever they are, can do their jobs well.

ABOUT THE BOOK'S TITLE

As Chapter 4's authors Alan Hough and Garth Nowland-Foreman wisely point out, *best* is a relative term. As shown in the case study of Oxfam Australia (see Chapter 4), what is best varies even for a single board, based on circumstances, where the organization is in its life cycle, or what the organization's current understanding of what *best* is.

So then why does this book's title include the term *best practices*? It was deliberately chosen, both so that those seeking advice on how to improve their governance could easily find the book and as a point of departure for the book's contributors' discussions about governance in their specific countries or regions.

The book's title also references CSOs (civil society organizations), NGOs, and other nonprofits. There is little agreement on the nomenclature for these kinds of organizations (see the glossary for some commonly used terms). While inexact, the title was chosen, again, to ensure that those who might possibly benefit from this book would recognize that it is intended to address their needs. We do not differentiate between CSOs, NGOs, and nonprofits throughout, as they are common terms.

ORGANIZATION OF CONTENTS

Chapter 2 through Chapter 9 cover specific geographic regions or countries, organized alphabetically. Chapter 10 looks at international civil society organizations (ICSOs) and Chapter 11 concludes with some thoughts on the future of boards.

FRAMEWORK

BoardSource has developed a knowledge base over decades through its work with many thousands of boards. It has distilled its experience into several publications. Two of them, *Ten Basic Responsibilities of Nonprofit Boards* and *The Source: Twelve Principles of Governance That Power Exceptional Boards* (see the appendix), have been used to aid our exploration of what constitutes good governance around the world. Each contributor to this book was asked to examine the applicability of the 10 roles and responsibilities and to consider the 12 principles in the light of their experience and knowledge specific to their own country or region.

APOLOGIES

I offer my sincere apologies to any countries or regions overlooked in this survey. This book is by no means encyclopedic, and presents instead a broad sampling of governance as practiced around the world. My hope is that readers will be able to draw useful insights from the material and even be inspired to adapt some of the practices described to their own boards.

I also ask the reader's indulgence with respect to my own (American) cultural biases. I have done my best to compensate for them.

CULTURE

Contributors have also been asked to identify the significant character-istics of, and trends in, their locations. Each chapter is intended to con-tain the elements of NGO governance specific to a particular place (i.e. current political and legal environment, historical origins). Each author has also been invited to consider the cultural dimensions of governance.

Culture is a complex business. We certainly do not want to over-simplify, create or reinforce national stereotypes, or suggest that one culture's way of doing things is better than another's. Not attempting to address culture at all, however, would seem a serious omission in a book of this type.

> Humans are deeply social animals. Our beliefs, desires, and behaviors are affected by social preferences, our rela-tionships, and the social contexts in which we live and make decisions.
>
> *World Bank (2015), 42*

The means of thinking about culture that is outlined in Fons Trompenaars and Charles Hampden-Turner's 1997 book, *Riding the Waves of Culture*, is therefore offered as a conceptual framework. The research database used therein included 50,000 cases in 100 countries studied over a period of 15 years. The results were intended to help dispel the notion that there is one best way of doing things in business (Trompenaars and Hampden-Turner 1997, 2) but can also help shed light on the civil sector.

Trompenaars and Hampden-Turner developed a means to help people understand organizational management in the context of culture, which they define as the way people solve problems. Their model entails five ways in which people deal with each other (universalism vs. particularism, individualism vs. communitarianism, neutral vs. affective, specific vs. diffuse, ascription vs. achievement); their perspective on time (sequential vs. synchronic); and how they relate to the environment (internal vs. external control). We will discuss each of these in turn next.

Universalism Versus Particularism

Are rules or relationships more important? Universalism is the belief that ideas and practices should be applied without modification in all circumstances, while particularism is the belief that circumstances should dictate how ideas and practices are applied. Cultures with a strong belief in universalism hold board meetings that are characterized by rational, professional arguments and a businesslike attitude. At the opposite end of the spectrum, particularists consider it highly unethical to disregard relationships in favor of rules.

Individualism Versus Communitarianism

Individualism is the principle that individuals are valued over the group, while communitarianism holds that the welfare of the group is primary.

Dissent is expressed carefully on boards in communitarian societies. Some in Asia, for instance, place a high value on social harmony, based in the tenets of Confucianism. The emphasis on saving face may mean that it is advisable to criticize individual members privately, rather than in a group forum. This has obvious implications when evaluating individual boards.

Neutral Versus Affective

In neutral boardrooms emotional restraint is prized. In other boardrooms (those in affective cultures), more expressive behaviors may be the norm.

Specific Versus Diffuse

A specific culture is one in which an individual board member has a large public space that is readily shared with others and a small private space that is guarded closely and shared only with close friends and associates.

A diffuse culture is one in which public spaces and private spaces are similar in size and individuals guard their public spaces carefully, because entry into public space affords entry into private space as well. Formality is respected in diffuse cultures.

Ascription Versus Achievement

In an ascription culture, status is based on who or what a person is. Older board members—elders—may be highly valued in ascription cultures (for instance, in Africa, Cambodia, Central Europe, and Eurasia). Inherited titles, position, or caste may affect social status.

In an achievement culture, status is based on performance, and what a person has done matters most. Board members are respected for the knowledge and influence they bring to the table.

Wealth (inherited or earned) can be viewed as a powerful asset in either type of culture.

Synchronic Versus Sequential

Different cultures occupy different positions along a spectrum of perspectives on time, and each puts its own emphasis on the past, future, and present. How one thinks about time affects decision-making.

In cultures that treasure their history, boards might pose generative questions that reference historic precedence, such as, How can we resurrect our glorious past? Boards oriented to the present may stress the need for immediate action in their decisions, as in, What do we need to do right now for today's problem? Future-focused boards will ask themselves how their decisions will impact future generations.

Boards in synchronic cultures see the past, present, and future as interwoven or may see them as a continuous loop. For some, the concept of karma is used to frame board accountability—what one does in this life will affect the next (e.g., Cambodia). Karma is key in several religions.

Punctuality, planning, and adherence to schedule are important in sequential cultures. Sequential cultures tend to see time as spooling out in front of one in a straight line (e.g., Australia and New Zealand and the United States).

Internal Versus External Control

Some Eastern philosophies emphasize living in harmony with the environment and hold that there are forces that cannot be controlled or influenced (karma is an important element in several religions, including Buddhism and Hinduism, for example), and that therefore you must adapt yourself to these external circumstances. Attitudes about control are often rooted in religious beliefs. For some, the acceptance of circumstances is necessary to the transcendence of them.

Westerners seek to control their environments as much as possible. This has its roots in religion too: Judeo-Christian orthodoxy gives man dominion over all on earth (Gen. 1:26). As an example, America's drive to master the environment is rooted in a pioneering past, and lives today in the innovation of its technological industries.

Culture is dynamic. There are degrees of each of these seven dimensions of culture across categories of, and even individual, NGOs, and cultures differ widely not only across global regions and across nations, but within nations, and even within cities. There are other determinants of culture besides geography, which are described next.

Size and Maturity

Size and organizational maturity matter. Most nonprofit organizations are small, with few (if any) staff members and typically many more volunteers. New organizations often have hands-on boards doing double duty as both board directors and staff, while more mature organizations may have many staff who tend to managerial matters, leaving boards freer to concentrate on governance. Age is not the only determinant of the roles of board members; some boards never move beyond the working-board stage. Often, though, as organizations get larger and staff are added, the need to reconcile these roles usually becomes apparent and important.

Sector

Any corporate leader in a first-time NGO board role can attest: Culture is also sectoral. There are distinct ways of conducting business within each of the three sectors: public (government), corporate (business), and civil (NGOs). Interestingly, however, there is a trend towards the borders between the business and civil sectors becoming less distinct.

There are also distinct cultural differences in governance practices from one kind of nonprofit to another kind. For instance, nonprofits of a religious nature may be more communitarian than the culture surrounding them. An example: While Quakers are a Christian denomination that originated in individualistic England, they make decisions by group consensus. Issues will be debated until unanimous agreement is reached.

GLOBAL TRENDS

For context, readers should also keep in mind five important larger trends affecting this sector everywhere: (1) threats to civil society, (2) growing pains of civil society, (3) pressure to be more transparent and accountable, (4) boards' needs for greater diversity and inclusiveness, and (5) the emergence of new kinds of organizations that straddle the for- and not-for-profit models.

Threats to Civil Society

It is becoming increasingly hard to operate independently as an NGO in certain parts of the world. Restrictions on foreign funding, barriers to registration, intervention in internal affairs, and other forms of harassment are rampant. There have been serious threats to civic freedoms in at least 96 countries around the world (CIVICUS 2015).

Growing Pains

The civil sector is growing by leaps and bounds in some regions. Dramatic growth is accompanied by inevitable growing pains, with the sector experiencing excessive regulation in some countries (Indonesia), contending with uneven regulation in others (India), and seeing the need for more infrastructure and capacity building in still others (Africa, Korea). While many countries/regions have discussed and articulated standards for governance, these standards may not yet have been recognized or embraced in the sector.

Pressure for Transparency and Accountability

A growing demand for transparency and accountability and a greater emphasis on the board's role is another trend. Neglect of oversight, questionable financial and fundraising practices, lack of internal controls, inadequate CEO supervision, poor and shortsighted decision-making, improper stewardship of assets, failure to include representatives of the community—not to mention outright fraud and corruption—are all betrayals of the public trust by boards.

A recent, though by no means isolated example, is a scandal concerning the fundraising practices of some NGOs that roiled the United Kingdom during the years 2015 and 2016. The resultant public uproar led to changes in the UK's Charity Governance Code, created in 2004 to help charities strengthen and develop their governance. The 2017 changes raised the bar for charities and placed greater emphasis on board leadership. They intentionally pushed trustees "to excel in their role and provide strong leadership." (Good Governance Steering Group 2017).

As other nations inevitably grapple with similar crises of public trust (or proactively try to avoid them), the changes in the United Kingdom may point a way forward to establish greater levels of board performance and accountability.

Need for Greater Diversity

Diversity can be defined differently, depending upon the context and who is doing the defining. For our purposes, it means bringing a broader range of perspectives to boards. Diversity can be reflected in differing socioeconomic backgrounds, ethnicities, genders, ages, physical abilities, geographies, and experience.

Diversity is important, and in many places progressive social agendas underscore this. There are also large historical and cultural factors driving towards social justice. In India, for instance, Gandhi's theory of trusteeship, which included abolishing untouchability and empowering women and the poor (through rural development), remains influential (Bhaduri and Selarka 2016, 46). Today women outnumber men on India's NGO boards, and there, enhancing diversity means getting more men on boards, especially when the conversation is about human rights for women or violence against women (Keidan 2017, 48).

Some nations are especially successful in living with diversity. Indonesia's cultural diversity remains unmatched in Southeast Asia and even in the world. The nation is home to more than 500 ethnic groups, each with their own language and dialect. The Muslim majority (quite diverse in itself) coexists peacefully and productively with fellow citizens having Hindu, Buddhist, Confucian, Christian, and a variety of Indigenous belief systems (Just Landed, n.d.).

It is a challenge to embrace diversity on our boards when our own societies may fall short of the ideal. Even with the general agreement that our boards need to be more diverse, boards everywhere tend to recruit those from the same class, educational background, ethnicity, and values.

A troubled recognition that we have made little progress in the direction of inclusion has emerged recently:

- BoardSource, in *Leading with Intent 2017*, its most recent biannual report on governance in the United States showed that 84% of board members and 90% of board chairs were white, and that few boards were actively working to address racial imbalances and lack of diversity in general (BoardSource 2017, 10).
- In a survey undertaken in 2017 of International Civil Society Centre members, the most significant change over previous surveys was that 56% of the respondents wanted "to increase the involvement of their beneficiaries" and outside experts in governance. The recommendations included that the composition of international boards should reflect an organization's global presence, that there should be more board members from the Global South (experts and/or partner representatives), that a better gender balance in governance was needed, and that local ownership should be strengthened and that the most marginalized should be included (see Chapter 10).
- A 2017 survey by Getting on Board in the United Kingdom showed that 59% of the nonprofits that responded admitted that their charity was not representative of their community and service users. Even so, 45% of charities were not actively working to improve the diversity of their boards. Ninety percent said they recruited through word of mouth and existing networks, a practice that tends to maintain the status quo, limiting diversity (Getting on Board 2017, 1).

Recruiting from a wider, more diverse pool of candidates would help to address the common complaint that it is difficult to attract qualified candidates. More purposeful recruitment methods would improve diversity, as would strict adherence to term limitations.

> If the role of philanthropy is to move us toward social justice, we should require the boards of its institutions to be ahead of the curve ensuring progress, not behind.
> *Mishra and Seay (2017)*

We must begin by looking within ourselves. Open and courageous conversations in the boardroom can be a catalyst for confronting the lack of diversity in the boardroom.

New Entrants to Civil Society

Social enterprises are stirring excitement (for example, in Korea, India, Japan, China, and Europe). While these organizations don't introduce new legal structures, the globally recognized B Corp certification in the United States is also an actual legal form of incorporation available in several states (B Lab 2017). Another US hybrid of for- and not-for-profit entities is the low-profit limited liability company, or L3C, which raises some interesting questions about governance (Wikipedia 2017).

A heartening discovery in the course of our research was that there are examples of outstanding boards in every corner of the globe, and that we share many common challenges. We have much to learn from one another.

REFERENCES

Bhaduri, Saumitra N., and Ekta Selarka. 2016. *Corporate Governance and Corporate Social Responsibility of Indian Companies*. Singapore: Springer.

B Lab. 2017. "Certified B Corps and Benefit Corporations." www.bcorporation.net/what-are-b-corps/certified-b-corps-and-benefit-corporations (accessed October 22, 2017).

BoardSource. 2017. *Leading with Intent: 2017 National Index of Nonprofit Board Practices*. Washington, DC: BoardSource.

CIVICUS. 2015. "Civil Society Rights Violated In 96 Countries." CIVICUS, June 18, 2015. www.civicus.org/index.php/media-resources/news/962-new-civicus-report-Dcivil-society-rights-violated-in-96-countries (accessed October 5, 2017).

Coventry, Louise. 2017. "Want to Improve Governance? Context Matters." *Nonprofit Quarterly* 24, no. 1 (Spring): 55–58.

Getting on Board. 2017. *The Looming Crisis in Charity Trustee Recruitment*. London, UK: Getting on Board.

Good Governance Steering Group. 2017. *Charity Governance Code*. www.charitygovernancecode.org/en/5-board-effectiveness (accessed October 15, 2017).

Just Landed. n.d. "Diversity, Religion and Values: An Introduction to the Cultural Variety of Indonesia." Guides. www.justlanded.com/english/Indonesia/Indonesia-Guide/Culture/Diversity-religion-and-values (accessed October 22, 2017).

Keidan, Charles. 2017. "Interview with Priya Paul." *Alliance* 22, no. 3 (September): 48.

Mishra, Sumitra and Angela Seay. 2017. "Nothing about Us without Us—Philanthropy's Diversity Challenge." *Alliance* 22, no. 3 (September): 33.

Trompenaars, Fons and Hampden-Turner, Charles. 1997. *Riding the Waves of Culture: Understanding Cultural Diversity in Business*. London, UK: Nicholas Brealey.

Wikipedia. 2017. "Low-Profit Limited Liability Company." www.en.wikipedia.org/wiki/Low-profit_limited_liability_company (accessed October 22, 2017).

World Bank. 2015. *World Development Report 2015: Mind, Society, and Behavior*. Washington, DC: World Bank.

CHAPTER 2

Africa

Mike Muchilwa

Mike Muchilwa offers an overview of the context for governance in Africa.

HISTORICAL AND CULTURAL CONTEXT FOR GOVERNANCE

History

The roots of CSOs in Africa can be traced to the colonial era. Given colonial governments' reluctance to provide services such as education and health to Africans, Western missionaries stepped in. The assistance paradigm was one of charity, in line with the religious convictions of the missions. The continent still has many schools and hospitals that have their origin in the work of missionaries. Following independence in many African countries, the focus of many of these early faith-based CSOs moved to development, which was also the agenda of various governments and secular donors of the 1960s and 1970s. These donors funded the development projects of Western CSOs such as Save the Children, Plan International, Christian Aid, and Oxfam, and also set up programs of their own. Some of these projects and programs later become institutionalized and morphed into present-day CSOs. The availability of donor funding to support development activities targeting poverty also created a conducive environment for the establishment of new CSOs. Thousands of CSOs were established on the continent in the 1970s, 1980s, and 1990s.

Culture

CSOs have been influenced by governance practices in the diverse cultures across the African continent. In many African cultures—for example, in the Buganda Kingdom in Uganda and the Swazi Kingdom in Swaziland—those in positions of authority have rarely been challenged. The kings and chiefs usually have had their way and their word has been law. There have been some cultures in which a council of elders also held sway over the community—sometimes even over the dictates of the king or chief. The *Njuri Ncheke* of the Ameru people of Kenya to this day exercise great influence over the local community.[1] Elders serving on the Njuri Ncheke are awarded a high status.

Status also comes from wealth. In a continent where more than half the population survives on less than US$1 a day, people with money and in positions of authority are often looked up to. The affluent are considered "big men and women," and wield influence over poorer and more humble citizens. This is also seen in CSOs with significant resources that work with the poor. Those who run CSOs are often placed on the same high level as government officials and donors. Venerated by beneficiaries, and having huge resources at their disposal, those who govern and run CSOs run the risk of developing the so-called big-man mentality. As a result, some boards and CEOs feel that they are not accountable to anyone but their donors and the government.

CHALLENGES TO CSO GOVERNANCE

Need for Capacity Building

The majority of the boards and management of African NGOs have never been trained on how to govern well. There are a handful of African capacity-building organizations that focus on improving governance in Africa. Pact, an organization active in Kenya and Zimbabwe, is one. Act (once a part of Pact, and which we will discuss later) focuses on capacity building for Kenya. Donors have also sponsored governance programs. For example, the United States Agency for International Development previously supported the Faniksha Institutional Strengthening Project, which worked with large health CSOs to improve their governance practices, systems, and resource mobilization activities. The development of voluntary codes is also helping to promote good governance. For example, the Civil Society Working Group in South Africa developed the independent *Code of Governance for Non-Profit Organisations in South Africa.* The code is a statement of values, principles, and recommended practices to which nonprofits in South Africa can voluntarily subscribe. The standards that some countries are establishing will help to raise the bar across the continent.

Defining and Balancing Governance and Management Roles

Balancing the governance and policy-making roles of the board with the operational and programmatic roles of the management is another challenge African boards face. Some weak boards act as virtual rubber stamps for decisions made by the organization's management. Other boards are far too powerful, and intimidate management and micromanage operations.

There are several reasons for this role confusion, but it can often be traced back to the organization's roots. The law in many African countries demands that an organization seeking registration provide the names of its founders, which often end up being the names of friends and relatives. Once established, these founding board members can end up serving the organization in perpetuity, resulting in stagnant leadership. Some founders remain indefinitely as board chairs. Furthermore, many founders become CEOs, resulting in a real imbalance of power and authority, with boards being dominated by the founder/CEO. In these boards, one either toes the line or is quietly pushed out!

When founders overstay their term, dominate the board, or step over into management roles, all power becomes concentrated within the founding board. This concentration of power tempts some to capitalize on their positions of privilege and benefit themselves rather than serve their constituents.

On the other hand, sometimes the power imbalance is on management's side instead of the board's. Some management structures regard the board as a necessary evil at best—a legal requirement that they must comply with, but would rather do without.

Honoring Constitutions

A third challenge is that some boards ignore their constitutions by disregarding term limits, failing to hold annual general meetings, and neglecting to submit annual reports to the authorities. Across the continent, the CSO sector has traditionally operated with a free hand. Few governments are interested in the oversight of CSO affairs, except when they pose a political threat. CSO governance, however, has increasingly become an issue in East and southern Africa, and authorities are paying greater attention to the civil society sector. One motivating factor for the increased interest has been the large amounts of money being funneled into these CSOs. In Kenya, for example, NGOs managed more than US\$852 million[2] in 2013/2014 from the 74% of the NGOs reporting (NGOs Coordination Board, 6).[3] This does not include the funds spent by other CSOs, such as societies, trusts, community-based organizations (CBOs), and NGOs registered as companies limited by guarantee without share capital. The other factor has been the increased demand for good governance in the business sector, which in turn has also shone the spotlight on the boards of CSOs.

The authorities ignore poor CSO governance until it becomes an issue. Little investment is made, from within or from outside of the organization, into strengthening the capacity of the board to identify these kinds of problems and to seek their resolution.

GOVERNANCE SUCCESSES

Some African CSOs practice exemplary governance. These organizations, though few, are great models for others. Following are the principles these boards live by:

- Respect constitutional term limits set by the organization and have orderly transitions from one board to another.
- Guard the organization's mission, vision, and values.
- Offer direction and spearhead the development of strategic plans.
- Govern rather than micromanage the organization.
- Develop effective policies and ensure their implementation by management.

- Contribute resources to the organization (rather than take resources from it).
- Support resource mobilization activities, ensuring that the organization has sufficient resources to operate and implement its programs.
- Declare conflicts of interest.
- Comply with the legal requirements governing their organizations.
- Serve the beneficiaries and other stakeholders (and not themselves).

For example, the Eastern Arc Mountains Conservation Endowment Fund (EAMCEF) in Tanzania has a strong, policy-oriented board. This nine-member board of trustees is appointed from a range of stakeholders, including government, the corporate sector, the civil society sector, and the academic and research sphere, as well as from beneficiary communities. The board meets twice annually to review the annual plan and budget, hear annual reports on capital investments, and evaluate the performance of the organization, as well as to make key decisions, formulate policy, and agree on strategic direction. Term limits are respected, and members are replaced when their terms are up. The board sticks strictly to its governance and policy-making agenda and does not engage in micromanagement.

Though few, the boards that strive to honor these principles are growing in number in response to improved recruitment practices and increased organizational investments in building the capacity for governance by the CSOs themselves, and also by donors who have initiated programs to promote good practices. It will, however, be many years before the majority rather than minority of CSO organizations embrace the fundamental principles of good governance.

CHARACTERISTICS OF AFRICAN CSO BOARDS

Hakuna Matata Board

Some boards can be categorized as *Hakuna Matata* Boards (hakuna matata is a Swahili term that translates to "there is no problem—everything is okay"). These boards tend to believe the CEO's assurances that all is well. They therefore do not look too closely into issues concerning the organization. Board meetings are therefore a mere formality. These boards are common when the CEO and members of the management are founders and have largely recruited friends and family to serve on the board. The founders maintain control over the organization even when there is a board in place that is supposed to carry out specific legal responsibilities.[4]

Hakuna Matata Boards are also common when the organization seems to be doing very well—attracting abundant funding, implementing impressive programs, and employing significant numbers of staff. The board complacently accepts management's positive reports and neglects to look deeply into the organization's finances or otherwise does not exercise due diligence. It is only when things start going wrong that it panics and starts to pay attention, but by then it is usually too late. One organization that focused on livelihoods and economic empowerment had a board that happily met and had superficial discussions about issues for years, but never really scrutinized reports. When the founding CEO left the organization, his replacement was not as astute in mobilizing resources. Once resources began to decline and prospects dimmed, the second CEO also left the organization. The next CEO was also unable to mobilize resources, leading to increased staff turnover and the termination of key programs. Rent and staff salary arrears began to accumulate, leaving the board in a difficult situation. The CSO is now facing imminent collapse.

Aloof Board

The Aloof Board cares little about the organization, which results in dysfunctional governance. Members often skip meetings or show up late. Board meetings frequently suffer from a lack of a quorum. Members do not bother to read through the material that they receive that is critical to decisions they must make.

This situation often is the case for organizations that are facing financial challenges or are in decline. Board members in these scenarios may believe the organization at best has little potential for growth, and at worst, that it is doomed to extinction. They are resigned to this grim fate.

The Aloof Board may also be present in organizations that have failed to take off after their establishment, despite the grand dreams of their founders. Founding board members may stubbornly resist reality, hoping for a miracle that could turn the organization's fortunes around. Some members hang on because they do not want to disappoint the

CEO. Others are reluctant to give up the social status they get from being on the board. This kind of board is common in many of the organizations that fail to attract donor resources to implement their missions, making it a fairly common type of board!

Star Board

A board that recruits well-known personalities can become a Star Board. This board is characterized by people recruited because of their social status, wealth, and influence, rather than their skills. The result is often a board that is ill equipped to govern the organization. Members are hard to control or discipline because of the power and influence they have in society. These boards are common in organizations started by leading politicians, top civil servants, members of prominent families, and powerful business people. The organizations will usually go into decline once the key benefactor passes away or loses power, influence, and money.

Intimidated Board

The Intimidated Board lives in awe and fear of the management. Members do not dare challenge or question the organization's CEO. The board is often handpicked by the CEO to meet statutory obligations. CEOs tend to pick compliant or weak board members who will not question their authority. Many of the board members stay on because they enjoy their privileges. This board is common in small NGOs and CBOs, which are often dominated by an individual.

Policing Board

The Policing Board acts like a police force and concerns itself with every little thing that goes on—meddling in everything from the recruitment of junior staff to the procurement of inconsequential supplies. It does not trust staff leaders and members mistakenly believe that their role is to police the CEO. The CEO is even asked to leave meetings to enable the board to deliberate on very minor issues. Terrified of losing their jobs, CEOs toe the line even when the board invades managerial turf. These boards are common when powerful founding board members will not allow management to play its proper role. In other instances, this type of board results when a powerful chairperson is bent on implementing his or her ideas, irrespective of what everyone else thinks. This type of chair may lord it over other board members and not just management. In one extreme case, a chair who had been a powerful minister in the past and was an influential lawyer belittled his board colleagues. He deliberately failed to remember their names in public and referred to them as "little girls" and "little boys"—and even sought to employ his daughter as the CEO. Fortunately, after two years of this abuse, the other board members gathered their courage, and with the support of the key donor, threw him off the board.

Swamped Board

In the case of the Swamped Board, management overrelies on its members to make decisions on every minor issue—recruitment of junior staff, staff disciplinary matters, projects, small equipment purchases, and so on. The board's calendar is crowded with frequent (even monthly) committee or full board meetings.[5] Management overwhelms the board with volumes of information. Distracted by operational issues, the board has little time to think strategically. Stressed out board members are less productive and may even suffer decisional paralysis. These boards are common when the organization has a weak and understaffed secretariat or management team that relies on the board to support its operations. Membership-based organizations, such as associations and societies, organizations that are in the early stages of their development, and those that have a weak CEO or management team (and a more competent board) can have this problem.

Board of Professionals

A board composed of professionals, may, in truth, know much more about an organization's programs than the management does. They may be highly respected and competent lawyers, accountants, or professors who are experts in the organization's area of interest and thus intimidate those in management who may not be as accomplished. Contributions by management may be belittled and management may retreat into a shell. Management simply takes orders, denying the organization the dynamic exchange of ideas that supports good governance. This kind of board may also develop when founding members still play key roles on the board or when a former CEO joins the board.

Board of Impunity

The Board of Impunity is only interested in what it can get, not what it can give. Members see business and employment opportunities for themselves, their friends, and their relatives. The result is a board that exhausts the resources of the organization, and in extreme cases, causes its closure. In one case, in a society in Tanzania, the board's six-month allowance for board expenses exceeded staff salaries! Meetings would be convened and pushed to the next day so that members could collect twice the allowance. Members significantly raised their own allowances, resulting in severe cash-flow challenges for the society. Staff and suppliers remained unpaid as the board literally ran amok. Members of the society reacted by throwing out the entire board during a special annual general meeting. In another case, in Kenya, the chair passed all the funds received from donors to his firm. Anyone who questioned this practice was shown the door. Fortunately, the key donor noticed the irregular practice and insisted on changing the way things were done. This happened during the 1990s and early 2000s, when there were several instances of funds being redirected by boards to purposes outside a donor's intention. Several donors then forced out boards that did not have good governance practices in a bid to protect their funds and ensure better service to beneficiaries.

Hybrid Board

Hybrid Boards include members of management (usually founders) on the board. They often result from situations where founder members are registered as subscribers or promoters during the registration process. Many African countries require that organizations submit the names of founder members. This facilitates checks by security agencies to establish qualification for operation. Some founders who began in dual board/staff roles fail to relinquish their positions because they want to maintain control. It becomes a problem when, for instance, the blurred lines between governance and management make it difficult to fire an incompetent manager or change strategic direction.

Model Board

The Model Board is a rarity. It focuses on governance rather than micromanagement. It formulates policy to guide the governance of the organization. Members are trained on their responsibilities, usually on an annual basis at a retreat that may include a performance appraisal. While some organizations may handle training and performance appraisals internally, others use consultants to facilitate training and self-appraisals. The organization will normally have a board charter that is respected by the board. Members of the board go through a careful recruitment process that considers the skills that are required. Members retire when their time is up. The board and management enjoy a great relationship that is based on mutual respect and understanding of each other's roles and responsibilities. The Kenya Community Development Foundation (KCDF) has such a Model Board. It appraises its board members every year, provides capacity building when required, and has clear boundaries between management and board functions.

Of course, boards will display more than one character type. It's also useful to keep in mind that the character of a board changes over time. Today's Model Board could become an underperformer tomorrow.

To further understand good board practices in Africa, the rest of this chapter will focus on Kenya as a national case study.

CASE STUDY: KENYA

As with any other country, Kenya is home to many different types of boards, some exhibiting good governance practices and some exhibiting less admirable leadership. In the final analysis, only a very few achieve so-called model status. We will now look at some of the determinants for exceptional board performance.

Chairperson

One determinant is the influence of the personalities of individual members, but especially that of the chairperson. Desirable skills for a chair include the ability to make decisions, the ability to lead and build teams, and excellent communication abilities. Personal qualities include integrity, respectability, and commitment to the organization's vision and mission. A good chairperson plays a crucial role in enabling the board to perform well in its governance role.

Recruitment of Board Members

Board recruitment in Africa varies according to the type of CSO and its constitution. A key recruitment concern is diversity, including diversity in gender, age, and representation of marginalized groups (i.e., those with disabilities), as well as adequate inclusion of members of the communities that the organization serves. African boards are becoming increasingly more diverse with regard to women, youth, and community beneficiaries, sometimes in response to donor requirements and government mandates.

Common approaches to board recruitment include selection, election, and competitive process. The approach used is often stipulated in either the organization's constitution, registration, bylaws, board charter, or board manual.

Selection

When the CEO identifies and proposes potential board members to the board, it can be difficult to ensure professionalism and objectivity. Having the board propose candidates is better practice, but it may not necessarily result in a better choice. Some boards strengthen this process by requesting the CVs of potential members and conducting interviews. Those who qualify are then nominated to the board. This has been an approach used by Act, a capacity-building CSO in Kenya.

Election

Elections are more common in member-based CSOs and NGOs with strong beneficiary engagement. For example, Action Aid Kenya elects its board through a vote of the general council during the annual general meeting. The challenge is that democracy does not always produce the best board members. The candidates who are skilled in politicking and campaigning and are well resourced will usually carry the day. Ethnicity may also be a factor, with people voting for leaders from their own ethnic communities. While it has its drawbacks, this approach is the most democratic.

Competitive Process

In the competitive-process approach, the organization advertises board vacancies, describing attributes it is seeking in the candidates. The candidates are vetted, resulting in a short list that allows for a reasonable number of candidates to be interviewed. The interviews are conducted by a subcommittee of the board, or alternatively, by an independent organization. The candidates are then vetted by the full board and the selected candidates invited to join.

VSO Jitolee (which has now been dissolved and replaced by VSO International) used to advertise vacancies on its board.[6] Applicants had to write a letter explaining why they wanted to join the board and submit a CV. The human resource department would then review the applications and prepare a short list. Candidates would then be interviewed by the department to establish whether they had the skills, expertise, and attributes that the organization required. The short list of candidates would then be shared with the board recruitment committee for further interviews. The board would make the final decision based on the results. This stringent process produced a professional and committed board. This approach has inspired others to seek board members through more competitive processes.

Some CSOs use an outside independent party for competitive selection. The Micro Enterprises Support Programme Trust has used PricewaterhouseCoopers to identify potential candidates in a competitive process. Potential directors/members must apply for the positions and go through a rigorous interview process conducted by the firm. This ensures an objective process for attracting the very best candidates. After a final round of interviews, the final decision is made by the board.

Competitive recruitment is an emerging practice that enables organizations to tap into a larger pool of potential candidates that it would not have been able to identify on its own. It supports better governance because candidates know what is expected of them right from the beginning.

Supporting the Organization's Resource Mobilization Efforts

While management plays a key role in resource mobilization, the overall responsibility for financial sustainability is with the board. Many boards, however, shy away from resource mobilization, preferring to leave this function with management. Few are willing to donate. Even when the organization is facing financial challenges, board members may not act to ensure organizational viability and sustainability.

Some boards do actively play a role in mobilizing resources—making regular contributions, lending their contacts, identifying potential donors, and using their networks and expertise to support management's efforts. Several boards have established resource-mobilization committees. One of these is the One Shilling Foundation's board. The foundation seeks to alleviate poverty within the Kenyan Muslim community in the areas of health, water, education, and energy. The board of Community Asset Building Development Action (CABDA) is another example of a board that has established a resource-mobilization committee. CABDA is a leading NGO in western Kenya with a mandate of transforming lives through community health care, women's empowerment, water, sanitation and hygiene, and support of orphans and vulnerable children. Members of the board contribute funds annually based on their ability to give. Along with the boards of these two CSOs, the boards of Action Aid, Act, and the KCDF have also established resource-mobilization committees.

Remuneration of Board Members

The question of whether board members should be paid or not is a thorny one. Many organizations consider board service voluntary and therefore do not pay allowances or salaries. Some, however, pay a token allowance to board members for various purposes. Sometimes it is a given amount to reimburse any board-related costs. At other times, it's considered to be a token of appreciation. CSOs such as KCDF, Action Aid, Act, KICK Trading, Ufadhili, and the Kenya Association of Fundraising Professionals do not pay allowances, but do reimburse justified travel and accommodation expenses. The constitution and bylaws set the framework by stating whether the board's work is voluntary or paid. More detailed reimbursement policies may be stipulated in the organization's personnel policy and procedures manual.

The practice of paying allowances can be abused. For example, for six years one board maintained the practice of paying a token allowance of US$25 per quarterly board meeting, an amount equal to US$100 per member every year; this in a country where half the population earns less than US$2 per day. When some board members retired from their regular full-time jobs, they exerted pressure on their colleagues to double the allowance, which they now claimed was too low. Committees were formed and several meetings held in order to justify the hikes in allowance. It was increased again a year later. Eventually, what had started off as a token of appreciation for the board's service became an avenue for generating a salary through the back door! In short, CSO boards need to be careful about allowances, as they can easily lose control over their board budgets.

BEST PRACTICES OF KENYAN BOARDS

Conducting Board Appraisals

Annual appraisals or reviews are important in pushing the board to attain and maintain high standards of governance. Reviews make individual members, as well as the whole board, accountable to the organization and its stakeholders. Regular appraisals support the board in regulating its performance by identifying strengths as well as shortcomings and setting targets for improvement. Appraisals identify gaps in performance that can then be addressed through training. In some cases appraisals can indicate the need for new blood, to bring new expertise, skills, and competencies to the board.

High-performing Kenyan boards conduct regular board performance evaluations. Because Act is a leading provider of board capacity building, it must practice what it preaches. The Act board employs both individual and collective evaluation tools. Action Aid Kenya also appraises its board as a whole in a peer-review process led by two members from another Action Aid country. KCDF also conducts annual reviews of its board. In short, board appraisal is emerging as a good governance practice in Africa.

Investing in Building the Capacity of the Board

Little if any investment is made in the boards of most organizations. Few have a board-orientation process. Training is minimal or nonexistent, as it's assumed that directors come equipped with all the requisite skills. Some CSOs would like to train their board members but lack the resources to do so.

An exception is the African Capacity Alliance, a health-focused and membership-based CBO headquartered in Nairobi and operating across sub-Saharan Africa. Board members receive training at least once annually. Another exception is Nuru, based in Migori County in Kenya, which also provides training for its board annually. Nuru organizes retreats centered around a training agenda that includes such topics as best practices in governance and the board's role in resource mobilization. Budgeting for and investing in building the capacity of boards is essential if they are to achieve high standards of governance.

Operating with a Board Charter

Board charters (or board policy manuals) are the exception rather than the rule. Few CSOs know what they are, let alone have them! As a result, board members are in the dark about their actual roles and responsibilities. Some have never even seen the constitution of the organizations that they lead. While board charters will vary, they should contain the values, principles, mandates, roles and responsibilities, and terms of service of the board. They also should include guidance on recruitment, transition, removal of members, and more. The charter should clearly state what is expected of the board, as well as how it should relate to management.

Leading CSOs in Kenya have charters. For instance, Act's charter was developed by the board itself with the support of management and a consultant. Action Aid Kenya and KCDF also have charters to guide the operations of their boards.

Charters enable boards to uphold values and principles and maintain the high standards of governance expected of them. It also supports the appraisal and review process by establishing benchmarks.

Developing the Organization's Strategic Plan

Setting strategic direction and strategic planning are critical functions of the board. Strategic plans provide the framework under which the organization rolls out its programs and activities over a specific period of time, usually three to five years.

The board needs to own the strategic-planning process and resultant document right from the beginning, although management and a consultant can assist with development of a plan. CABDA uses a joint approach in the development of its strategic plan, but the board is involved right from the beginning, beginning with participating in stakeholder workshops tasked with developing the key aspects of the plan and ending with board approval of the final document. The board is also involved in regular and end-term evaluation of the plan. The board's involvement in strategic planning has contributed to the organization's growth over time.

Having a strategic plan reduces the chances that the board will interfere in the organization's day-to-day operations and programs. It also gives management a clear road map of the direction the organization should take, the programs it should focus on, the resources that will be needed to move forward, and the beneficiaries to be served in achieving its vision and mission. Boards ensure that the plan is implemented, review it at least annually to keep it relevant, and make sure that it is adequately resourced.

Few African CSOs have strategic plans. For those that do, a key problem is that the plan is forgotten once it has been developed and is only used as a fundraising tool for donors. Thus programs are dictated by donor interests and funding needs rather than by strategic imperatives. Staffing, infrastructure, and even beneficiaries are overly influenced by donor interests. Management assumes de facto governance through the board's abdication of its proper role in planning.

Creating Accountability and Transparency

Accountability and transparency are challenges for many African CSOs. Even the staff can be unaware of how much money has been collected, where it has come from, or how it has been expended. Yet accountability and transparency are sorely needed in an environment where corruption is a concern and donor confidence can be compromised.

International nongovernmental organizations, also known as international civil society organizations, influence the governance of their affiliates in Africa, usually getting them to emulate the high standards of accountability and transparency in their Western-based offices. The Kenya Red Cross has excelled in this, becoming a role model to other countries in which the Red Cross operates on the continent. Audited accounts going back many years are available on its website.

The organization declares the sources of its revenue, including large donations from individuals. It has a reputation for informing donors of the amounts of money raised during various stages of its campaigns. This was the case in the well-known Kenyans for Kenya Campaign in 2011, which was organized with various corporate and media partners. The campaign raised about US$11.8 million for famine relief over a period of one month during a severe drought. It was the same with the We Are One Campaign, organized following the 2013 West Gate Attack in which unidentified gunmen killed and injured several dozen persons in an upscale mall in Nairobi. Not only does the Kenya Red Cross dutifully make regular reports to the public at different stages of its campaigns, it informs them of what it intends to do with any surplus raised. This high degree of accountability and transparency has made the Kenya Red Cross one of the most trusted CSOs in Kenya.

The Rhino Ark Charitable Trust is another organization that publishes audited accounts on its website. A high degree of transparency and accountability has helped it run the most successful special event in the county and region: the Rhino Charge. This is an extremely popular international off-road 4×4 competition that takes place over approximately 100 kilometers of rough terrain in Kenya within a 10-hour period. The trust works to conserve and protect Kenya's spectacular mountain range ecosystems. The event raised US$1.39 million in 2016 alone. Another conservation NGO, the David Sheldrick Wildlife Trust, which secures safe havens for endangered and/or orphaned species, such as elephants and black rhinos, also posts its annual report and accounts on its website.

Transparency and accountability is not only sound practice; it can be a competitive advantage. Unfortunately, most CSOs in Kenya and Africa do not share annual reports and accounts with key stakeholders, except at the demand of donors and government agencies. Leading CSOs are finding, however, that transparency and accountability is not only sound practice, it can be an advantage in an environment in which corruption has discouraged many potential donors.

Respecting Term Limits and Ensuring Smooth Board Transition

Board transition continues to be a problem for many CSOs. Few board members adhere to the term limits outlined in governance documents. It is not uncommon to find boards that have overstayed their terms of office; several have even been fixed in place since the establishment of the organization and beyond the constitutional limits of renewable terms (usually one to three years).

Who does honor board term limits? An examples of good practices is the VSO Jitolee board, whose members serve for a renewable term of three years, after which they leave the board. The vacancies are then advertised. The Act and Action Aid boards also honor their renewable terms of service. The KCDF is governed by a board of trustees and a board of directors. The board of trustees appoints a nine-member board of directors whose members are selected based on their integrity, expertise, and qualities of diversity. The board of directors oversees the organization's activities and programs. Its members leave office when their terms are up.

Respecting the organization's establishing documents, such as the constitution, is key to good governance. Organizations that do are among the few on the continent whose board members heed their terms of service and do so without disrupting the organization's governance, thus ensuring the smooth and continual growth and development of the organization.

Developing Effective Policies to Guide the Organization's Operations and Programs

The development of strong and effective policies to guide the operations of the organization is a key role of the board. It enables the board to ensure that the organization's operations and programs are being effectively and professionally implemented. KCDF has a board that focuses on the development of effective policies. Its board members bring different skills, including financial, legal, resource mobilization, and community development acumen, that inform policy. The KCDF board knows that without good policies, there are risks that the board will stray into management's domain.

TRENDS

Improving National Governance Standards

CSO governance does not operate in a vacuum. The larger national governance culture and environment influences the governance of various kinds of institutions operating within its boundaries, including CSOs. Unfortunately, Africa is sometimes better known for bad governance rather than good governance practices. On the other hand, leaders such as the late Nelson Mandela have been a beacon of hope among many on the continent and a model of leadership for the world. Countries have come together to promote better governance across Africa. The adoption of the African Peer Review Mechanism has increased the spotlight on the governance practices of leaders on the continent. Initiated under the New Partnership for Africa's Development, the mechanism seeks to improve the governance practices of African presidents and their governments. The improving governance practices in many African countries will slowly impact on the governance of the NGOs operating in them.

Growing Awareness of Need for Good Governance

According to an African Development Bank Report, the number of people in the middle class was 313 million in 2010.[7] That number was expected to increase to 1.1 billion by 2060. Additionally, there were 100,000 people with at least US$1 million to invest. A growing and better educated middle class, equipped with improved access to information via the Internet, better understands the value of good governance. This has already been seen in the political sphere, as more countries are being forced to open the democratic space and adopt good governance practices. Donors, too, have played their part, by supporting various domestic groups to push for better governance practices at the country level. CSOs are also feeling pressure to adopt good governance practices for their organizations.

CONCLUSION

The demand for good governance in Africa has grown over time. At one point in the continent's history, only Western donors were demanding better governance from their CSO partners. Better governance then became an issue for corporations doing business with authorities and shareholders who expected better corporate governance. The trend today is for better CSO governance, and it is driven by governmental authorities, donors, and other stakeholders. For many CSOs in Africa it will not be business as usual. They will either have to improve their governance practices or risk extinction.

NOTES

1. Since the seventeenth century the Ameru have been governed by elected and carefully selected councils of elders. This governance structure is hierarchical, with the first rank of elders dealing with matters at the clan level (*Kiama*), then comes the middle rank (*Njuri*), and finally the supreme *Njuri Ncheke* council. Their edicts apply across the entire community. The Njuri Ncheke make and execute community laws, settle disputes, oversee and enforce regulations controlling the use and conservation of open grasslands and forests and the preservation of sacred sites, and act as the custodians of tradition and culture. They also influence socioeconomic and political decisions; for instance, the decision in 1983 to donate 64 acres of the community's land to serve as the site of the College of Science and Technology. In early 2013, the college was renamed the Meru University of Science and Technology. The Njuri Ncheke today are represented on the University's Council. www.en.wikipedia.org/wiki/Meru_people (accessed November 3, 2017).
2. Currency referenced in this chapter is in US dollars as converted from Kenyan shillings on October 5, 2017.
3. NGOs Coordination Board. *NGOs Sector Report 2013–2014 Popular Version* (p. 6).
4. In most African countries, the board is legally responsible for the governance of the organization and determines its vision, mission, strategic direction, and general programs.
5. Committees are set up by the board to specifically address governance issues. Some will be established by the organization's constitution while others are set up by the board. Examples of committees include the Executive Committee, Finance Committee, and Resource Mobilization Committee. The names and functions of these committees will vary from one organization to another.
6. *Jitolee* means "volunteer" in Swahili.
7. African Development Bank. 2011. *The Middle of the Pyramid: Dynamics of the Middle Class in Africa*. www.afdb.org/fileadmin/uploads/afdb/Documents/Publications/The%20Middle%20of%20the%20Pyramid_The%20Middle%20of%20the%20Pyramid.pdf (accessed March 2, 2018).

CHAPTER **3**

Asia

OVERVIEW

Usha Menon

The 21st century will be the Asian century. This also means
that Asia will be expected to provide greater leadership to
solve global challenges.

Kishore Mahbubani, Dean at Lee Kuan Yew School of
Public Policy, n.d.[1]

Asia as a region is characterized by diversity in culture and in
socioeconomic and political systems, which results in each nation taking
different measures to build and enhance accountability, transparency,
and organizational effectiveness of nonprofits. Across Asia NGOs are
engaged in a range of services, from social services, health, education,
the arts, and national development to more complex areas, such as
environmental protection, saving and credit, advocacy, and human and
land rights. Governments and the market have started to recognize
and accept the role of NGOs as policy and community partners, and in
improving the governance of societies and nations. With this increased
prominence, greater influence, and greater interaction with the state
and the market, comes the heightened need for higher standards of
accountability from stakeholders, such as government, regulators,
donors, civil society networks and partners, beneficiaries, and the
community. That being said, there are still some governments that
are attempting to shut down NGO activities related to areas deemed
sensitive and that are using state-controlled media to tarnish the public
image of rights and advocacy NGOs.

The NGO sector across Asia has transformed over recent decades. Factors driving these changes include:

Exponential economic growth. The dynamic growth in Asia has resulted in the fastest wealth generation in the world. This has lifted Asian countries to middle-income country levels and above, resulting in foreign aid and donors shifting their support away from Asia. The decline in foreign funding and the ill-conceived exit plans of these funders have resulted in many NGOs having to cease operations or to reevaluate their missions and whether the organizations are sustainable. Additionally, many governments have tightened the rules on the free flow of foreign funding through NGOs as related to issues that are seen as unfavorable to the public interest and to religious NGOs using foreign funding for conversion/evangelical purposes.

Realization of the need for constituency building. In the past, constituency and capabilities building were hindered by a dependence on foreign-aid funding, which drove NGOs in many Asian developing countries to follow donor priorities rather than those of the local constituency. The short-term nature of foreign funding also discouraged NGOs from creating long-term strategic plans. Most NGOs in Asia do not have codes of conduct or publish annual reports, unless required by donors or the government. However, self-regulation is gradually getting better, with improvements in NGO accounting systems and more transparent reporting to key stakeholders. The Cooperation Committee for Cambodia is collaborating with international NGOs to encourage their local NGO partners to go through an NGO governance and professional practice certification program. NGOs in the Philippines and India are skilled in community organizing which, despite the vastness of these countries, allows them to reach target beneficiary groups and build effective constituencies to support policy advocacy and service delivery.

Role in disaster response. Natural disasters since the mid-2000s, such as the Asian tsunami (2004), the Shenzhen earthquake in China (2008), Typhoon Haiyan in the Philippines (2013), the Nepal earthquake (2015), and many others, have forced local NGOs to diversify their skills and services in order to engage in relief and recovery efforts. The government's image of NGOs has improved, resulting in the recognition of the importance of the NGO engagement and collaboration in national efforts and with social issues. The public image of the nonprofit sector has improved due to their visible role in disaster response, relief, and rebuilding efforts. Disasters have also triggered a surge of local volunteerism, thus increasing engagement with, and hence trust in, the sector.

Engagement with the state and the market. As is the case in many places around the globe, the civic space in many Asian countries is subject to strict monitoring and control. Governments use their constitution and laws to suppress freedom of expression and have shut down NGOs advocating for land and environmental rights.

Other Asian countries, however, such as Sri Lanka, have seen a dramatic opening of the civic space, and CSOs have gained the ability to work freely in-country. Likewise, the military government in Thailand has begun to open up in certain areas and engage CSOs on policy formulation, and has launched a campaign to raise national awareness of the tax benefits of donating to NGOs. The Government Procurement Reform Act in the Philippines mandates the participation of CSOs as observers in all phases of the procurement process. Some Asian nations, such as China, are working to create environments conducive to the growth and health of the civil sector in terms of tax exemption, special registration, and reduced administrative processes.

The business sector, too, has opened up. While nascent, engagement with the corporate sector and citizens is on the rise. In the Philippines, nonprofit consortiums of over 200 corporations have been mobilizing resources for various social projects. New regulations promoting corporate social responsibility (CSR) in India, Indonesia, and Thailand are encouraging enhanced cooperation between NGOs and the corporate sector. In Nepal, financial contributions from the corporate sector are supporting advocacy initiatives on corruption, human trafficking, and other issues out of the mainstream.

Innovations in service and resource mobilization models. New social service models that have CSOs engaging in economic activity, micro credit and lending programs, and social enterprise have created sustainable and local funding models. In 2017, the Singapore social enterprise sector saw growth of 32%. The use of social media to disseminate information and engage with the community has also increased the effectiveness of the service provision. Mobilization of citizens for advocacy campaigns through greater use of social media has impacted outreach as well as trust in the nonprofit sector.

Scandals. Scandals involving laundering of public funds through fake CSOs and misappropriation of funds have impacted public trust. As many of these scandals involve tax issues and public funding, the tax authorities in the Philippines, the government in India, and the charity regulator in Singapore have had to become involved. In response to these scandals, several reform efforts have been undertaken. Standardization of operating procedures, the publication of annual reports as a means of increasing transparency, and in Singapore as an incentive for the charities to maintain their ability to provide 250% tax-exemption benefits to their donors, and the construction of self-regulatory frameworks that focus on locally developed codes of ethics and certification are being put in place.

As with many models emerging out of Asia, which take a pragmatic and hybrid format, the transformation of the nonprofit sector across the region has resulted in a strategic alliance between the state, the market, and civil society. This has increased the need for more effective governance to improve internal and external accountability, transparency, and organizational effectiveness.

NGOs that receive state subsidies or enter into contracts with governments to provide social welfare, health, and education services are already subject to regulatory standards and policies. The private sector has also been exerting pressures for improved internal and public accountability through increased reporting requirements.

These pressures—along with increased outreach to and interaction with the local population in the post foreign-aid era, resulting in greater public expectations of the sector—and the ready availability of virtual tools to make financial and operational information public have resulted in increased attention to self-regulation, codes of ethics, and certification processes from the sector itself.

Asia's growth dynamic is reflected in the region's approach to its civil sector, with emphasis being placed on building a dynamic and effective civil society, rather than on establishing checks and balances. Most NGOs lack the ability to link accountability and transparency to management structures and board responsibilities. Fortunately, some coalitions and intersectoral partnerships have been formed to improve the sector's infrastructure so that nonprofits have opportunities to acquire the strategies and skills that they need to improve their governance. There is also a growth of intermediary support organizations that are providing training, funds, research, consultancy, and other services to help. Asia is so vast, its population so widely dispersed, and its cultures and languages so diverse, that many of these resources are only available in major cities.

Because the region is so far-flung, this chapter includes perspectives from several countries. This tour of Asia—with stops along the way in Cambodia, China, India, Indonesia, Japan, Korea, the Philippines, and Singapore—will offer insights into nonprofit governance in this part of the world today.

ASIA OVERVIEW NOTES

1. Mahbubani, Kishore. Human Leadership Capital Institute website. n.d. https://www.hcli.org/hcli-advantage/summary (accessed December 28, 2017).

CAMBODIA

Louise Coventry

The concept of governance is unfamiliar to most Cambodians; it is a concept without local historical roots that are comparable to the understanding found in the Global North. To the extent that the concept of governance can be found in Cambodia historically, it has been deemed to be more rightly the work of others: either royalty or the state, depending on political viewpoint (Noren-Nilsson 2016). Either way, governance is not understood to be the responsibility of citizens. Similarly, accountability is a new, and mostly unfamiliar, term in Cambodia. Fewer than 5% of 583 villagers surveyed had ever heard the term *accountability*, and none knew its meaning (Kim 2012). The term *accountability*, like *governance*, formally entered the Khmer language in the 1990s, coinciding with the influence of the United Nations Transitional Authority in Cambodia and the political rehabilitation of Cambodia after an extended period of civil war and the disastrous Khmer Rouge regime.

Conceptual challenges notwithstanding, the greater challenge to governance and accountability in Cambodia is the failure of donors from the Global North to take Cambodia-specific conditions into account when introducing governance and accountability reforms (Pak et al. 2007). In the absence of well-articulated indigenous conceptions of governance acceptable to powerful international donors, CSOs in Cambodia have mostly embraced donor interpretations of what constitutes good governance. However, implementation of these ideas is patchy at best and deeply dysfunctional at worst. Moreover, models of so-called good governance from the Global North sit uneasily and awkwardly with local models of patronage, creating a complex dual system of governance that does not ultimately serve organizations' beneficiaries.

Civil society leaders navigate this duality with creativity. Civil society leaders are skilled in matching new governance concepts to local requirements. Yet the process of navigation and adaptation is complex and nonlinear. Sometimes civil society leaders feel the need to resist the first model and embrace the second; on other occasions they may favor the first model over the second, depending on what seems most practicable. This practicality demonstrates Trompenaars and Hampden-Turner's (1997) explanation of particularism: Relationships are more important than rules. According to their model of differences across national cultures, Cambodia is characterized by particularism (people tend to value relationships over rules), neutrality (emotions are not readily displayed), specificity (personal space is closely guarded and there is more formality), communitarianism (group membership is valued over personal identities), ascription (status is ascribed more than achieved), synchronicity (the past, present, and future are seen as interwoven), and external control (people tend to believe that nature or their environment controls them and that they must work with their environment to achieve their goals). Of course, great care must be taken in assigning such labels as culture is amenable to change, and even within nations cultures can be highly variable.

Most registered NGOs in Cambodia have a board and attempt to follow the corporate model of governance: Nearly 80% of respondents to the most recent census of NGOs (2011) report that they have a governing body, such as a board of directors or trustees (Cooperation Committee for Cambodia 2012). Another survey (Suárez and Marshall 2014) found that almost all organizations have a board of directors (88% of Cambodian NGOs and 93% of international NGOs). Most boards are quite small, with an average of six members, and boards meet approximately three times a year, but boards of international NGOs have more members and meet more regularly than boards of Cambodian NGOs. Alarmingly, another more recent study (Henke 2015) found that one-quarter of sampled Cambodian NGOs had serious financial system weaknesses and weak governance: One in five to seven Cambodian NGOs is affected by fraud. The fact that 20% of surveyed NGO leaders did not know how many members were on their boards or how frequently the boards met is similarly troubling (Suárez and Marshall 2014).

Underscoring the potentially tokenistic role of the board, the Royal Government of Cambodia, while requiring NGOs to have a board, in practice does not accord legal authority to the board.[1] This sets the legal environment for NGOs in Cambodia apart from most jurisdictions across the developed world. In instances in which the board has attempted to remove an executive director, the Royal Government of Cambodia has taken the side of the director against the board. Indeed, there are some local examples of directors of NGOs sacking the entire board. Yet donor oversight mostly does not account for compromises to the legal authority of boards and donors continue to require, for the most part, only the presence of a board and audited statements as evidence of good governance. In Cambodia, these indicators are poor proxies for good governance.

Many NGOs have only tenuous and tokenistic connections to a membership base, if one exists, and accountability to service users or other constituents is low. NGOs are more likely to regard donors as their primary stakeholders than beneficiaries. When asked to name their three main stakeholders, NGOs participating in the 2011 NGO Census named, in order, donors (65%), beneficiaries (48 %), and local authorities (39%) (Cooperation Committee for Cambodia 2012).

In contrast to downward accountability, peer accountability is well established in Cambodia. An important response of Cambodian NGOs to increased demand for accountability and governance is the self-certification system introduced by the Cooperation Committee for Cambodia, a key peak body within the sector. The self-certification system is part of the national Governance and Professional Practice program that aims to strengthen standards of governance among NGOs. It is based on the Code of Ethical Principles and Minimum Standards for NGOs developed through a large-scale participatory process, which has been increasingly implemented since 2007 but has had a low take-up rate. As of June 23, 2017, 24 organizations have been certified as compliant with the code and the minimum standards and a further 35 organizations are pending certification.[2] However, this represents a decrease in interest from previous years.

While NGOs themselves report relatively high capacity for governance (Yin and Sok 2012), others identify governance as one of the more significant capacity challenges for NGOs.[3] Key (self-identified) areas for improvement include long-term monitoring and evaluation planning, interpretation of vision and mission statements, functioning of boards, strategic planning, and managing diversions from plans in response to donor agendas and objectives. Significant funds have been invested in capacity development in Cambodia over past decades with limited success (Ou and Kim 2013), and this continues. In July 2016, the United States Agency for International Development announced a five-year, US$9 million project to strengthen the organizational and technical capacity of Cambodian CSOs.[4]

Among other, less formal, CSOs, it is often a respected elder who is the founder and who makes all key decisions associated with the organization's management. Some organizations may be founded by well-meaning expatriates or local elites, including returnees. Visitors may return to their home country and raise funds to start an organization in Cambodia, or long-term residents may identify, and then seek to fill, a particular need within Cambodian society (Coventry 2016). Examples abound across the spectrum of excellence, and include Sunrise Cambodia, Empowering Youth in Cambodia, VBNK, Social Services Cambodia, Kaleb, and the Somaly Mam Foundation. Expatriate-founded organizations may quickly become formal and resemble NGOs described above, but in smaller and less formal organizations initiated by local elders, different characteristics may be observed. For example, membership may be understood as a given, and not subject to change. While elite sponsorship, as an approach to governance, is open to abuse and corruption, it rests on time-honored traditions of personal integrity, tradition, and maintenance of social harmony. Governance frameworks are often adopted that allow the founder to continue to be influential, consistent with the role of a patron. The founder may collect a mix of expatriate and local individuals to assist in the governance, perhaps forming a board; however, organizational ownership is unlikely to rest with that group. Rather, the sense of ownership stays with the founder, or at least is perceived as being with the founder. While many founders seek to empower others and act with enormous integrity, the recent negative publicity about Somaly Mam (Marks 2014 and Wofford 2014) and her subsequent resignation from her eponymous foundation illustrates some of the dangers of reliance on a single charismatic individual.

Remembering that boards simultaneously attend and respond to international donor standards and conform to broader societal expectations of noninterference, respect for elites, and limited involvement in decision-making, it becomes possible to nominate some potential good practices for governance in Cambodia. Such practices hinge on:

- Building sophisticated and shared critiques of governance models from the Global North.
- Deepening community understandings of governance.
- Using patron-client relationships as the foundation and starting point for learning more about governance.
- Exploring options for creating hybrid models of patronage and corporate governance.

Specific examples follow.

To critique governance concepts introduced by international donors, it is wise to examine how these can be practiced in a manner consistent with traditional practices and informal structures and relationships within the society (Bañez-Ockelford and Catalla 2010). For example, it may be useful to use the lens of patronage to examine how affection-based connections between networks, such as friendship, kinship, and loyalty, or how the Buddhist concept of karma, can be used to enhance accountability and how alternatives to the Western-centric ideas of independence and conflicts of interest can be unearthed and supported.

Increased success in promoting an understanding of governance may come from using simple words, drawings, and metaphors, giving clear examples drawn from local experiences, connecting issues of governance to other preexisting priorities within organizations, asking questions of each other such as Why do we have a board? or What would a good board look like?, and, in instances in which a board already exists and is eager to improve its practice, working systematically through a process of collectively developing an accountability framework, outlining, step by step, to whom the board is accountable, and for what, and then how these accountabilities can be demonstrated.

Taking account of the history and culture of patronage in Cambodia, boards could consider appointing a meeting facilitator rather than a chairperson, thereby disrupting the hierarchical power relations typical of patronage. Boards may also choose to rewrite bylaws to confirm that the chairperson (or equivalent) cannot make decisions on the board's behalf. Alternatively, boards may draw relationships between organizational stakeholders and examine how these connect to the board members and potentially also connect individual board members to a personal constituency or client base, thereby creating a functional form of patronage for organizational stakeholders who may otherwise be overlooked.

According to the corporate/policy model of governance followed—and preferred—by most NGOs in Cambodia, the board leads recruitment of new board members unless there is an election of board members by ordinary members (as is common among membership organizations). A good process for recruitment—learned from the current practice of Banteay Srei, a Cambodian NGO focused on women's civil and political participation—could involve two formal interviews, the first as a background check, and to ensure that there are no obvious conflicts of interest, the second for a discussion of roles and responsibilities. Clear, written instructions about expectations, roles, and responsibilities could sensibly be provided to each potential new board member, as well as detailed information about the NGO. Board members can be asked to visit projects within the first year of their membership on the board and be asked to sign a contract or similar document to this effect.

Board members may need a capacity development plan, separate from staff. Remembering that capacity for governance is values based, it is useful to meet with individual board members, one by one, to find a change agent on the inside if possible, and to identify a trigger to start the conversation about improving governance. Then board members can be invited to a planning event at which a strengths-based, empowering approach can be used to facilitate discussions. In Cambodia, it seems that board members are willing to learn more. In planning for developing their capacity, boards will likely need extra support to find ways to hear and engage voices of beneficiaries in decision-making.

Mindful reflection and critical thinking about governance, peer-supported learning, and a sustained commitment to improving outcomes for a range of organizational stakeholders, especially beneficiaries, offer hope for the expansion and articulation of culturally sensitive and functional models of governance in Cambodia.

CAMBODIA REFERENCES

Bañez-Ockelford, Jane, and A. P. Catalla. 2010. *Reflections, Challenges and Choices: 2010 Review of NGO Sector in Cambodia*. Phnom Penh, Cambodia: Cooperation Committee for Cambodia.

Cooperation Committee for Cambodia. 2012. *CSO Contributions to the Development of Cambodia, 2011*. Phnom Penh, Cambodia: Cooperation Committee for Cambodia.

Coventry, Louise. 2016. "Civil Society in Cambodia: Challenges and Contestations." In *Handbook of Contemporary Cambodia*, edited by Katherine Brickell and Simon Springer, 53–63. Milton Park, UK: Routledge.

Henke, R. 2015. *NGO Governance in Cambodia: Service and Support Options For Improving Financial Management*. Phnom Penh, Cambodia: Southeast Asia Development Program.

Kim, S. 2012. "Democracy in Action: Decentralisation in Post-conflict Cambodia" (PhD thesis, School of Global Studies, University of Gothenburg).

Marks, Simon. 2014. "Somaly Mam: The Holy Saint (And Sinner) Of Sex Trafficking." *Newsweek*. www.newsweek.com/2014/05/30/somaly-mam-holy-saint-and-sinner-sex-trafficking-251642.html (accessed July 11, 2017).

Noren-Nilsson, A. 2016. *Cambodia's Second Kingdom: Nation, Imagination and Democracy*. Ithaca, NY: Cornell University.

Ou, S., and S. Kim. 2013. "20 Years' Strengthening of Cambodian Civil Society: Time for Reflection." Working Paper Series No. 85. Phnom Penh, Cambodia: Cambodia Development Resource Institute.

Pak, K., V. Horng, N. Eng, et al. 2007. "Accountability and Neo-patrimonialism in Cambodia: A Critical Literature Review." Working Paper 34. Phnom Penh, Cambodia: Cambodia Development Resource Institute.

Suárez, D., and J. H. Marshall. 2014. "Capacity in the NGO Sector: Results from a National Survey in Cambodia." *VOLUNTAS* 15, no. 1: 176–200.

Trompenaars, Fons, and Charles Hampden-Turner. 1997. *C.* Riding the Waves of Culture: Understanding Cultural Diversity in Business. London, UK: Nicholas Brealey.

Wofford, Taylor. 2014. "Somaly Mam Foundation Closes." *Newsweek*. www.newsweek.com/somaly-mam-foundation-closes-278657 (accessed July 11, 2017).

Yin, S., and S. Sok. 2012. Needs Assessment on Capacity Development and Learning of Civil Society Organizations (CSOs) in Cambodia. Phnom Penh, Cambodia: Cooperation Committee for Cambodia.

CAMBODIA NOTES

1. 2015. "General Provisions." Law Of Associations And Non-Governmental Organizations. www.sithi.org/admin/upload/law/Unofficial-Translation-LANGO.pdf (accessed October 21, 2017).
2. Cooperation Committee for Cambodia (website). www.ccc-cambodia.org/en/what-we-do/governance-system-and-tools (accessed October 23, 2017).
3. See, for example, K. Un, "Cambodia: Moving Away from Democracy?" *International Political Science Review* 32, no. 5: 46–562 (2011); Sophal Ear, *Aid Dependence in Cambodia: How Foreign Assistance Undermines Democracy* (New York, NY: Columbia University Press, 2013); and S. Springer, *Violent Neoliberalism: Development, Discourse and Dispossession in Cambodia* (New York, NY: Palgrave Macmillan, 2015).
4. "Assisting Civil Society in Cambodia," 2016. www.editorials.voa.gov/a/assisting-civil-society-in-cambodia/3434018.html (accessed July 12, 2017).

CHINA

Yinglu Li and Oma Lee

Historical Context for Governance in China

The emergence of nonprofits in China began in the 1970s, when the country underwent major economic, political, and social reforms. The rapid urbanization process in the 1980s propelled the development of nonprofits and the expansion of their work in diverse fields and areas. The 2000s saw a spike in the number of grassroots nonprofits covering a wide range of social issues. Natural disasters and subsequent social media spotlights also helped catalyze the growth of the sector. Unfortunately, China's nonprofit sector has also been plagued by a plunge in public confidence, instigated by a few widely spread public scandals that precipitated a drop in donations and an increased call for accountability. As the sector has become more sophisticated, nonprofit good governance and a streamlined regulatory framework have become increasingly necessary.

After China transitioned from a central-planning economy to a market economy in 1978, the NGO sector gained more room for development economically, socially, and politically. Major foundations, such as the China Children and Teenagers' Fund, the Amity Foundation, the China Women's Development Foundation, and the China Youth Development Foundation were founded in the 1980s, reflecting the NGO sector's accelerating growth and government support. In the 1990s, the rapid growth of NGOs led to increasing charitable activities among citizens. The China Charity Federation, the first comprehensive NGO, was founded in 1994, with 375 membership organizations in mainland China currently. The Donation for Public Welfare Law was passed in 1999 as China's first law regulating donations. It provided more structured governance of NGO donations' use and management, and encouraged greater public generosity. The 2000s experienced a new level of public philanthropic engagement, reaching more than US$15 billion[1] in 2008 as charitable activities became popular among the ultrarich, and as the media's and the public's attention on philanthropy strengthened. Starting in 2012, the expanding use and influence of smartphones and online giving made donations easier and quicker than ever before. Thus, the governance of digital NGO activities has become one of the major NGO governance issues in China as the country has been experiencing the ever-increasing impact of technology on NGOs and philanthropy.

A Governance Regulatory Milestone

The introduction of China's first Charity Law in September 2016 was the single most important milestone in recent nonprofit governance history. The law has greatly shaped how these organizations operate in China. In addition, the Overseas NGO Law was also introduced to govern foreign nonprofits in China. The stated goal of the new Charity Law is to build a single, comprehensive regime for the regulation and management of charity organizations in China. The Charity Law improves nonprofit governance in a few key ways.

First, the Charity Law regulates public fundraising qualifications for nonprofits and sets a high bar for their governance. The new law offers clarity and structure—a solid legislative basis for fundraising. Only charitable organizations that have applied for and received public fundraising certification may raise funds, and these certificates are only issued to charities deemed to have sound internal governance and a good record of legal compliance. Those without such qualifications can only fundraise publicly if they do so in cooperation with an entity approved for public fundraising. The law also explicitly provides for online fundraising—good governance is necessary for charities to meet the minimum requirements to engage in online activities. These activities must be published on an online platform designated by civil affairs authorities, and operators of public fundraising platforms must verify the charitable status of organizations using this platform and must report illicit behavior in a timely manner.

Transparency and Accountability

The Charity Law also requires high standards of transparency. According to the Charity Law, nonprofits must publish their fundraising activities and programs every three months, and public foundations are also required to submit an audited annual report. Although some say these regulations are unclear and pose an administrative burden, informational transparency can help restore public confidence in the governance of nonprofits in China.

Chinese nonprofits are responding to the Charity Law in various ways to maximize their efficacy. As the law makes information more available and reliable and public confidence grows, nonprofits can even more effectively mobilize philanthropy through innovative online charitable efforts, such as September 9th Charity Day, to promote both fundraising and volunteer recruitment nationally. Greater accountability and openness will also encourage participation in competitions that catalyze innovative nonprofit programs and collective actions. Moreover, because the law has different regulations for foundations' and social organizations' management of the ratio of annual income to expenses, nonprofits will set different annual priorities to manage their spending on programs strategically.

The law sets different limits to administrative costs for charities based on their legal classifications, net assets, and public fundraising qualifications. For example, public foundations are required to keep their administrative costs at a level no greater than 10% of overall expenditures for a given year. The law also regulates volunteer management and requires a detailed registration of the identities of volunteer and other information about them.

Additional regulation is coming that will help to promote good governance. China is currently drafting specific regulations on asset management, credit records, and further information transparency requirements. For example, there will be regulations on annual reports and selective supervision, regulations on the management of charitable properties, regulations on credit records of charities, and so forth. When published, these regulations will set a high standard for governance models. In addition to compulsory submission of annual reports, special examinations of select social enterprises will take place every year.

The Charity Law today paves the way for the growth of philanthropy tomorrow by reinforcing the public's right to monitor nonprofit behavior and to mandate reporting to local governments. Public trust and understanding will grow in response to a more ethical charity system, and there will be greater appreciation of nonprofits as asset investments as well as an environment conducive to sustainability. China's regulatory environment for nonprofits is fast becoming one in which internal transparency, accountability, and good governance will be expected.

Need for Capacity Building

As China's civil sector develops and becomes better regulated and more professional, many in the sector are calling for better working environments, organizational structure design, job design, and staff development and training. In response, various organizations have emerged to focus on improving governance and other aspects of nonprofit performance. For example, the China NPO Network is one of the first to offer nonprofit professional training.

Interestingly, there has been a lot of crossover training and capacity building between the Chinese nonprofit scene and the up-and-coming social entrepreneurship space. The past several years have witnessed the creation of social enterprise membership organizations, incubators, training sessions, and teaching curricula. Among the providers of related services are the China Social Entrepreneur Foundation, which develops social entrepreneurial skills training workshops, and the Nonprofit Incubator. A lot of these trainings also serve nonprofit professionals and lend methodologies that are applicable to better governance, human resources management, and other areas of practice.

Research institutes and universities are also playing an important role in the development of the philanthropy system in China. For instance, China Philanthropy Research Institute, the first of its kind here, conducts research into social philanthropy and governance models and also provides a philanthropic consulting service. The China Global Philanthropy Institute specializes in training philanthropists and senior public-welfare management personnel, with the ultimate objective of building a team of professionals to assist in the formation of a new philanthropic paradigm for China.

Trends

In addition to the introduction of the Charity Law, there are other reforms underway. This strong government push to advance the sector will continue to help shape better governance in the field.

Corporate Philanthropy

Momentum is also coming from the private sector. Attention from the media that spotlights corporate giving has helped to advance this giving from CSR to a more sophisticated philanthropy. An increasing number of philanthropic organizations are being established to encourage entrepreneurs to take collective action—together with nonprofits, social enterprises, and corporations—in pursuit of common philanthropic objectives.

Social Enterprise

The global trend of social enterprises has spread to China, leading to questions about what organizational models are best for sustainable and ethical business here. The B-Corp movement stands out as one of the most watch-worthy developments, as companies in China try to achieve certification by changing their practices to fit a better business governance model. There are an increasing number of B Corps certified in China, and the embrace of these more ethical and sustainable business models will encourage nonprofits to borrow the best management practices from industry.

All in all, the future of the philanthropic sector in China is promising. The sector will continue to improve in governance and professionalization, and the synergetic exchange between nonprofit corporations and social enterprises, along with better laws and regulations, bodes well for nonprofits and their governance.

CHINA NOTES

1. Currency referenced in this chapter is in US dollars, converted from Chinese yuan renminbi on October 31, 2017.

INDIA

Noshir H. Dadrawala

The governance of voluntary/NPOs becomes increasingly important as they grow and develop. Although most have governing boards, motivating and channeling them wisely is often a challenge. As nonprofits establish themselves and diversify operations and programs, the work of the board takes on new meaning. An engaged and purposeful board can make the difference between an organization that is merely surviving from day to day and one that approaches the future with vision and determination.

In recent years, there has been a growing awareness in India concerning the governance of nonprofits. With increasing resources (both regional and international) available in the civil sector, and greater public attention to nonprofits, the functioning and effectiveness of these organizations draws more scrutiny. Of late there have been many critiques and questions raised in the media by social and political commentators and from within the nonprofit sector itself.

These questions have prompted national-level workshops and conferences to strengthen the overall capacity of nonprofits, including their governance. Some of the concerns surfaced at these events are a lack of standardization due to uneven regulation and the variety of forms of legal incorporation, a lack of agreement on the remuneration of board members, a lack of understanding of the board's relationship to the CEO, a need for greater transparency and accountability, and common board behaviors that do not contribute to good governance. These concerns are discussed in more detail next.

Uneven Regulatory Environment

In India, charities are under state, not federal, jurisdiction. Some states have excessive regulations while others have virtually none.

There are some 400,000 trusts and societies registered in the State of Maharashtra alone. They are regulated by the Office of the Charity

Commissioner under the Maharashtra Public Trusts Act of 1950. However, several states, including neighboring Karnataka and the national capital, Delhi, do not have a charity commissioner or a public trusts act in place. This means that a new nonprofit could legally and officially bypass one state-regulating authority by registering the trust deed with the Registrar of Deeds or the subregistrar's office in Delhi or Bangalore, which are mere registering, not regulating, authorities.

Although trusts registered in Delhi, Bangalore, and the northeastern states are regulated by the Ministry of Home Affairs only for tax purposes, if the NGO receives foreign funds and is registered under the Foreign Contribution Regulation Act, it receives more stringent oversight. NGOs in Maharashtra and Gujarat are regulated rather excessively by the Charity Commissioner. For example, in these states the Charity Commissioner requires regular so-called change reports to be filed. Permission must be obtained to buy and sell immovable property. Budgets must be filed. Prior approval must be granted even for obtaining a bank loan or an overdraft. Some entities choose to register with the Registrar of Companies as Section 8 companies, but compliance under the India Companies Act of 2013 is even more onerous.

Options for Legal Incorporation

Another issue is the diversity of legal choices for incorporation, each with differing requirements for accountability. While societies and nonprofit companies are subject to a modicum of accountability, including holding annual general meetings and issuing annual reports to members, trusts are legally exempt from these requirements. Also, while societies and nonprofit companies are required to rotate board membership periodically using a process of nomination and election, the boards of trusts are not. Trusteeship is usually for life and new trustees are appointed by surviving trustees. Below are descriptions of the three options for incorporation.

Trusts

Generally, two or more trustees may manage a trust. The charter or trust deed generally specifies the minimum and maximum number of trustees the trust may have. Unless specified otherwise in the trust deed, the trustees may remain trustees for life.

Societies

Seven or more members may form a society and serve as its first managing committee or governing council. A society is structurally more democratic than a trust. A society usually has a general body of members with the power to vote at general meetings of the body, elect members of the managing committee or remove them if their performance is unsatisfactory, call for special meetings, and demand to examine accounts and other records.

Companies

The internal governance of a nonprofit company resembles that of a society; however, legal compliance under the Indian Companies Act is much more elaborate.

The boards of these organizations go by different names, as follows:

- *Trustees*, in the case of a charitable or religious trust.
- *Managing committee* or *governing council*, in the case of a society.
- *Board of directors* or *managing committee*, in the case of a nonprofit company.

These boards do have the following six legal obligations in common:

1. Funds, properties, and assets of the organization vest in the board.
2. The onus of advancing the organization's aims and objects is on the board, often through the CEO.
3. Board members cannot derive personal benefit from the organization, and their involvement in the organization is fiduciary.
4. Boards are jointly and individually responsible, hence duties and responsibility are shared by the team.
5. Boards are required to approve and sign the audited accounts and annual report.
6. Policy is set by the board through process of periodic meetings and resolutions.

Remuneration of Board Members

In India it is not uncommon to find boards whose members are remunerated for their service. The law generally allows "reasonable" remuneration. However, this raises ethical questions and debate.

Boards' Relationships with the CEO

The relationship between an organization's board and its chief executive is also an issue that merits deeper attention and understanding. Sometimes it is the CEO that drives the organization and at other times it is the board. Both situations are undesirable. There should be healthy respect, communication, and interaction, as well as a system of checks and balances.

Transparency and Accountability

Trustees of trusts are not bound by law to provide copies of the trust's annual accounts and returns to stakeholders other than registering authorities, such as the Charity Commissioner, Registrar of Societies, Home Ministry, and the like. Societies and nonprofit companies are required by law to provide these details only to their subscribing members. Obtaining these details from even the registering authorities is difficult. Additionally, internal standards for excellence, including policies on conflicts of interest, human resources, financial accountability, fundraising, and public affairs, are still unheard of among many Indian nonprofits.

Board Culture and Behaviors

Beyond legal classifications, boards fall into different categories according to different scenarios. Rajesh Tandon, executive director of Delhi-based Participatory Research in Asia (PRIA), a capacity-building organization, characterizes boards as four common types, based on a range of observed behavior that he terms "board games":

1. *Family Board.* The NGO founder's family members are recruited as members and the board takes on an informal, closed character.
2. *Invisible Board.* The founder convenes a token board from time to time with little real function.
3. *Staff Board.* The staff themselves form the board, with the result that wider governance becomes indistinguishable from day-to-day management.
4. *Professional Board.* Individual board members are recruited for their special professional skills and sometimes remunerated. But, it is often difficult to generate a shared vision and sustain commitment.

These characterizations resonate strikingly with the findings of Margaret Harris, former director of the Centre for Voluntary Organizations at the London School of Economics, though independently researched from them, as well as with other research in the United Kingdom and United States.

Another common concern is the culture created by self-important board members who view their service as doing the organization a favor. The general refrain from these types is: "Look—I have such a full and busy life and yet I am giving my time for free to this cause rather than to my family. I volunteer my time at great self-sacrifice, and now you also want me to be accountable for the nonprofit's practices and give you *hisab* (an account) of what we do, where we spent, how we spent, how often we meet? Of course we spent the money well! Is our word not enough, or is our name not enough to invoke confidence?"

Many Indian board members tend to think that their commitment and competence should be accepted at face value, and that asking for further accountability is indirectly doubting or questioning their personal integrity.

Some spend years on the board. They are affronted if politely asked to make way for others, and are likely to respond along these lines: "I have given my best years to this organization, I have been so loyal, so involved, raised so much money ... I am lending my name and credibility to the organization! Will someone coming in my place have the same level of commitment as I do?"

Investing in Building the Capacity of the Board

Today, thanks to corporate and overseas donors, there is a growing awareness regarding the need for good governance and for strict compliance with not just legal and fiscal regulations, but in reporting and accountability to stakeholders.

In 2016 the Centre for Advancement of Philanthropy (CAP) introduced the very detailed and robust Compliance Complete Certificate Program. Through this program, NGOs use CAP to work towards compliance in eight core areas—legal, financial, human resources (HR), board governance, communication, strategy, fundraising, and volunteer management. A structured series of workshops are held throughout the year, each following a defined syllabus. Every workshop is followed by a one-on-one consultancy with the NGO. NGOs that are part of this program depute designated personnel working in the program's core areas to attend the workshops and consultancy sessions. Each such representative then works towards fixing the compliance required within that area. For example, an HR employee attends HR workshops to build his or her organization's HR resources and ensures that the division remains compliant in this area. At the end of the year, if the NGO successfully fulfills the requirements of CAP's proprietary Compliance Checklist and has instituted systems to ensure that it remains compliant, it is awarded a Compliance Complete Certificate by CAP.

GuideStar India's certification program also validates NGOs based on their legal and financial compliance as well as their level of public disclosure of information. NGOs opt for certification levels based on their interest and capacity for transparency. NGOs that are found to be compliant (having undergone due diligence by experts) are certified for one year based on the level of compliance. This ranges from GuideStar India Platinum (Champion Level) to GuideStar India Gold (Advanced Level) to Transparency Badge (Intermediate Level) and finally to Transparency Key (Foundation Level).

Since 2008, the Delhi-based Financial Management Services Foundation has also run online courses on good governance. Dasra[1], which works with high-impact NGOs to enhance scale and outreach, also stresses good governance as the foundation on which all else is built.

In other words, there are resources here. The challenge is in reaching grassroots nonprofits in remote districts and towns across India as well as all of the 3.3 million NGOs registered in the country. Even GuideStar India's database of 7,000 NGOs is a mere fraction of the whole.

Good governance is the price we pay for the freedom to exercise power and authority in an enlightened and democratic society. In Dasra's 2014–2015 annual report Rohini Nilekani reiterates: "Addressing governance issues is important because whichever silo you work in, be it education, sanitation, food or health, you would eventually hit the governance deficit" (Dasra 2015, 20).

Trends

Social enterprises are new entrants to the civil sector. A social enterprise is an organization that applies commercial strategies to maximize improvements in human and environmental well-being. This may include maximizing social impact along with profits for external share-holders. A social enterprise is not a legally defined entity and there is neither a separate statutory nor a regulatory body for it. Thus, a social enterprise could be a for-profit entity registered as either a sole propri-etorship, a private limited company, or a limited liability partnership. If structured as a nonprofit, it would be registered as either a trust, a society, or a Section 8 company. Hence, where governance is concerned, social enterprises do not introduce any new or special governance models. They may have innovative approaches and solutions for social problems, but that innovation does not apply to their governance structures. The oldest for-profit social enterprise in India is Tata Steel, located in Jamshedpur. It built schools, hospitals, and places of worship, and created a sustain-able environment and then said in all humility: "We also make steel."

While government regulation is one method to assure accountability and transparency in the third sector, nonprofits and philanthropies should minimize government involvement. They can do this by establishing their own self-regulatory systems in addition to heeding government's requirements. Self-regulation has also become even more important in recent years in the battle against terrorism and money laundering.

> NGOs fill gaps in the government's delivery systems and do a lot of good work, but that does not take away the fact that these NGOs must function transparently and in an account-able manner. Doing good work is no excuse for shabby governance. Awards and certifications are not merely an exercise in validating an entity, it involves building capacity of our key human resource, reviewing all our legal docu-ments, systems, processes and policies, periodic interac-tion with our staff and board, and finally providing us with the assurance that we were compliance complete.[2]

Conclusion

If your linen is clean, hang it out to dry for all to see.

Most of us, beginning from our school days, have grown up to dislike rules and regulations. Why would we like them any more as grown, responsible adults? Rules are made, however, when we are not self-disciplined, and regulations are enforced when we fail to exercise self-control. As a sector we should be looking out for each other's best interests and well-being.

While self-governance may seem simple, loose, and unstructured in comparison to externally imposed regulation, it is actually just the opposite. As practitioners of self-governance we quickly learn how hard it is to operate openly, responsibly, and accountably, and also how much better it is for us to do this on our own before regulators or stakeholders push it on us, often in a manner we do not quite appreciate.

In the times that we live in, self-regulation is the way forward. Set your own house in order before law enforcers and other stakeholders compel you to do it in a manner that may cause you greater discomfort!

As a sector, committing to maintenance of a shared set of values can be a great tool for creating a positive, sector-based experience, enhancing our collective self-respect, and earning the respect of all stakeholders. My personal theory is simple: If your linen is clean, hang it out to dry for all to see.

INDIA REFERENCES

Dasra. 2015. "Catalyst for Social Change." *Annual Report 2014-2015.* 20.

INDIA NOTES

1. Dasra is a strategic philanthropy shaping the process of social change by forming partnerships with funders and social enterprises.
2. Source quote is Mrs. Annabel Mehta, who currently serves on the Board of Give India, and is a member of the Accreditation Committee of Credibility Alliance. She founded Apnalaya 40 years back, a charity enabling underserved people to improve health, livelihood and gender relations. Apnalaya has won multiple NGO governance awards, including GuideStar India's Platinum Award and CAP's Compliance Complete Certification.

INDONESIA

Darmawan Triwibowo

Darmawan Triwibowo, CEO of the TIFA Foundation[1], explains how Indonesian nonprofits are navigating their way through an excessive regulatory framework.

Indonesia's civil sector came into being in the early 1970s with the establishment of various community development projects addressing widespread poverty and in response to the need for nongovernmental initiatives to promote socioeconomic development at the grassroots level. The New Order authoritarian regime, which ruled the country from 1965 to 1998, recognized the value of collaborating with nonprofits to share the cost of development. However, it maintained tight control on their activities by restricting their activities to the implementation of government-approved development programs, primarily in the areas of health services, water and sanitation, poverty alleviation, and education (Anand and Hayling 2014; Vandendael et al. 2013). The weakening of the regime in the mid-1990s, followed by its collapse and subsequent political reforms, restored basic freedoms of speech and assembly and eased repressive regulations, enabling nonprofits to expand their scope of work and participate in policy advocacy and political decision-making (Anand and Hayling 2014; Lowry 2008).

The nonprofit sector is rapidly developing in Indonesia. The government defines *nonprofit* as a NGO having "an organizational structure and the existence of common purpose; the autonomy to govern itself; voluntary nature of its establishment; clear orientation to give benefits for the public; its distinction from political party function; and not for profit nature of its activities" (Local Assesment Team 2010). Although determining the exact number of nonprofits currently operating in Indonesia is challenging, the 2010 NPO Domestic Review report recorded 21,699 nonprofits registered by the Ministry of Law and Human Rights in 2009 (Local Assessment Team 2010)—a dramatic jump from the estimation of 8,300 nonprofits in 2000 (Lowry 2008). The survey discovered that only 11,468 of the 21,699 could be recorded based on their location. Nearly half of those 11,468 were located on Java Island, which is the most populated area in Indonesia. The islands with smallest number of nonprofits are Maluku and Papua Island. The provinces with the most are DKI Jakarta (the capital city of Indonesia) and East Java. Based on the findings of the report and a review of available literature, the primary thematic areas of focus of these organizations can be classified as law and human rights, religious affairs, community development (including health and social services, infrastructure development, education, and economic empowerment), environmental management and preservation, and gender equality (Anand and Hayling 2014; Local Assessment Team 2010).

Regulatory Environment

The Ministry of Home Affairs classifies nonprofits into six categories: foundations, associations, mass organizations, assemblies, NGOs, and community gatherings. In general, however, the laws and regulations in Indonesia only cover two types: foundations (*yayasan*) and associations (*perkumpulan*) (Local Assessment Team 2010). Nonprofits can choose between the two legal incorporation structures. An association is defined by law as a membership organization, whereas a foundation is not. A foundation has a collection of assets and is formed with the intention to achieve certain objectives (Anand and Hayling 2014; Lowry 2008).

Tax deductions for individuals and corporations are recognized for only a limited number of activities, namely, national disaster management, research and development, education facilities (including education related to sports, art, and culture), sports activities, and the development of public facilities (legally known as "social infrastructure," which includes religious buildings, cultural centers, and health clinics).

In 2010, the Indonesian government instituted a regulation stipulating that the amount of a donation that can be deducted from gross income in a year may not be more than 5% of the net income of the previous year. In addition, contributions must not be provided for parties that have conflicts of interest under tax law.

Challenges

The sprawling regulatory framework in Indonesia is excessive. The nonprofit sector is regulated by 26 laws and regulations: 15 laws, 4 government regulations, and 7 ministerial decrees (Local Assessment Team 2010). The implementation of such laws and regulations is conducted by 10 government institutions (8 ministries and 2 ministerial-level institutions). The issuance of the new regulation in lieu of law (*Perppu*), No. 2/2017 on Mass Organizations (*Ormas*), which grants government the sweeping power to disband mass organizations without judicial process (if deemed to pose a threat to state ideology and the constitution), added another layer to the already thick structure of nonprofit regulation. The TIFA Foundation is currently working with five nonprofit coalitions nationwide to prepare a judicial-review application to the Constitutional Court to annul the *Perppu*.

The law permits foreign citizens, together with Indonesians and others, to establish philanthropic organizations, but they must adhere to an additional set of stringent requirements. In a similar fashion, international NGOs must also comply with additional criteria in order to operate in Indonesia, including the obligation not to engage in political, missionary, commercial, and fundraising activities in Indonesia (Anand and Hayling 2014).

Not all of those regulations are effective. As an example, although nonprofits are required to register with the Ministry of Law and Human Rights in Jakarta (as per the Law on Foundations as amended in 2004), many nonprofits, especially those located in rural areas, do not comply with the law and are not officially registered. Those in remote or rural areas see the registration process as expensive and lengthy, so they escape through a loophole that allows them to operate based solely on a certificate of registration (*Surat Keterangan Terdaftar*) from the local branch of the Ministry of Home Affairs (Anand and Hayling 2014). Consequently, the number of nonprofits officially registered with the Ministry of Law and Human Rights is far below the number actually in operation. The 2010 NPO Domestic Review report concludes that the existing regulatory framework is only "partially effective," as the government's effort to develop interagency coordination related to nonprofit supervision, including the sanctioning of lawbreakers, has not been optimized yet (Local Assessment Team 2010).

To be fair, not all of those regulations are detrimental—some of them could potentially benefit the nonprofit sector by creating a sustainable source of domestic philanthropic support (Anand and Hayling 2014). Law No. 40/2007, for example, serves to encourage responsible business practices, particularly among mining companies and those utilizing Indonesia's natural resources, by mandating that they spend at least 2% of their profits on CSR programs. Clear guidelines from the government linking mandatory CSR spending to Indonesia's future social spending (on education, health, and conservation) could bridge the fiscal gap in national and local government budgets and create a sustainable revenue stream for nonprofits working in these areas. Moreover, Law No. 36/2008 provides income tax exemptions related to religious donations, the income of nonprofits working on education and research and development (as long as profits are reinvested in said programs or in supporting public infrastructure), and income used for scholarships, in addition to those listed earlier in this section.

Promoting Accountability and Strengthening Sustainability

Accountability, transparency, and financial sustainability have long been the Achilles heel of Indonesian nonprofit governance. These serve as entry points for the government to question nonprofit credibility and exercise strict control of the sector. During the New Order era, for example, Soeharto's regime used many foundations to cover their corruption and money-laundering practices (Vandendael et al. 2013; Ashman et al. 2011; PRIA 2012).

Cultural factors might contribute to this situation. In Indonesia, traditional decision-making, called *musyawarah untuk mufakat* (unanimity in decision-making) and *gotong-royong* (in-group solidarity), is still dominant in the sector (Radyati 2008). These practices reflect the ethical values of harmony towards other *(tepo-slira)* that might lead to widespread conflict-avoidance and permissive behavior in organization. In many organizations, people tend to tolerate bad governance practice in order to avoid conflict among colleagues. These values are deeply ingrained in Indonesian traditions and customs, and are still practiced in both rural and urban areas (Radyati 2008).

Trends

A positive trend is the series of initiatives that have been introduced to improve governance. Since 2002, for example, the Agency for Research, Education, Economic and Social Development, a national organization, has prepared and implemented a code of ethics (Lowry 2008). The code, signed by 252 organizations from eight provinces, addressses integrity, accountability, and transparency; independence; antiviolence; gender equality; and financial management, including accountability to external parties such as beneficiaries, government, donors, other organizations, and the public at large (Lowry 2008). Satunama, a Yogyakarta-based organization that is active in education, training, and management consultancy, has launched a certification program for nonprofits. The program aims to improve public accountability and management performance in order to strengthen public trust (Lowry 2008). Twelve organizations made up a task force to formulate certification criteria for the program. The task force, as of 2005, has developed solid instruments, procedures, and certification standards; initiated a public campaign for certification; and established a certification agency. It also has created an advocacy campaigns for tax-law reform and laws for the nonprofit sector (Lowry 2008).

The Women's Fund (*Pundi Perempuan*) is an initiative to strengthen nonprofit financial sustainability. The National Commission on Violence against Women (*Komnas Perempuan*) set up the fund in collaboration with Indonesia for Humanity (*Indonesia untuk Kemanusiaan*/IKa), a Jakarta-based national nonprofit, to help women's crisis centers, other NGOs, and grassroots and community-based organizations working in the field. The fund was needed to counter declining support from donor agencies.[2] IKa uses the fund to facilitate multiple fundraising efforts at the national level (such as music concerts, art auctions and performances, book publishing, community bazaars, individual donations, and CSR) in cooperation with various stakeholders. The money is then distributed to select grantees all over the country. IKa also provides capacity-building services to its grantees as an integrated component of its partnerships, so that the grantees can develop accountability and independence.

A troubling trend at the global level could impose an additional burden on the sector, which is already overwhelmed with regulation. Indonesia, along with 204 other countries in the world, upholds a global standard to combat money laundering, the financing of terrorists, and the proliferation of weapons of mass destruction, and other threats related to the integrity of the international financial system developed by an intergovernmental body named the Financial Action Task Force (FATF).

Through the development of Recommendation 8, FATF aims to ensure that nonprofits are not misused by terrorist organizations by:

- Posing as legitimate entities
- Exploiting legitimate entities as conduits for terrorist financing, including for the purpose of escaping asset-freezing measures
- Concealing or obscuring the clandestine diversion of funds intended for legitimate purposes but diverted for terrorist purposes

As a member of FATF, Indonesia will undergo a mutual evaluation (ME) process late in 2017 to assess its compliance to the standard. The government is devoting significant effort to improving its compliance with the 40 FATF standards prior to its ME. This process is being led by the Center for Reporting and Analysis of Financial Transaction (*Pusat Pelaporan dan Analisa Transaksi Keuangan,* or PPATK), Indonesia's financial intelligence unit (FIU). FIUs are financial intelligence agencies specializing in financial transactions, but having no specialist understanding of the nonprofit sector. The role of PPATK as FIU is based on Law No. 15/2002 regarding the crime of money laundering and amended by Law No. 25/2003.

PPATK recently completed a process to identify high-risk nonprofits in line with the first part of FATF Recommendation 8. Alarmingly, no nonprofits were consulted during the implementation of the National Risk Assessment, Regional Risk Assessment, and Assessment of Nonprofits in 2016, and the results are confidential. As part of the next stage, PPATK will review the laws and regulations that apply to these so-called high-risk nonprofits and propose further mitigating measures. TIFA is supporting a group of nonprofits' engagement with PPATK and related government agencies to open up the process, discuss the results of PPATK's risk assessments of the civil society sector in a more transparent manner, and ensure the participation of nonprofits in the upcoming Indonesia's ME process. Nevertheless, the secrecy that underpins its work is consistent with PPATK's recent history of a nonconsultative and confidential approach to the development of terrorist financing policy, with troubling implications for nonprofits.

Nonprofits act as societal watchdogs in Indonesia—criticizing the government's work, actively promoting public participation in various sectors, and encouraging the establishment and implementation of policies for the welfare of the poor. It is imperative that they achieve the support of the public and at the same time, independence from the State.

INDONESIA REFERENCES

Anand, Prapti Upadhyay, and Crystal Hayling. 2014. "Levers for Change—Philanthropy in Select South East Asian Countries." Social Insight Research Series report. Lien Centre for Social Innovation, Singapore Management University.

Ashman, D., L. Carter, J. Goodin, and D. Timberman. 2011. *Intermediate Support Organizations (ISOs): Partners in Strengthening Local Civil Society.* Management Systems International. 1qswp72wn11q9smtq15ccbuo.wpengine.netdna-cdn.com/wp-content/uploads/Intermediate-Support-Organizations.pdf (accessed October 29, 2017).

FATF. 2012. *International Standards on Combating Money Laundering and the Financing of Terrorism & Proliferation: The FATF Recommendations.* Paris, France: FATF.

FATF/OECD. 2015. Best Practices: Combating the Abuse of Nonprofit Organizations (Recommendation 8). Paris, France: FATF/OECD.

Local Assessment Team. 2010. *NPO Domestic Review (Nonprofit Organizations): Indonesia's Report.* Coordinating Minister for Political, Legal and Security Affairs of the Republic of Indonesia.

Lowry, Cameron. 2008. *Civil Society Engagement in Asia: Six Country Profiles (Japan, South Korea, The Philippines, Indonesia, India, Thailand).* Asia Pacific Governance and Democracy Initiative (AGDI), East-West Center.

Radyati, Maria R. Nindita. 2008. "Third Sector Organisation Governance in Indonesia: Regulations, Initiatives and Models." *In* Comparative Third Sector Governance in Asia: Structure, Process, and Political Economy, edited by Samiul Hasan and Jenny Onyx. Springer Science+Business Media.

Scanlon, Megan McGlynn and Tuti Alawiyah. 2015. *The NGO Sector in Indonesia: Context, Concepts and Updated Profile.* Prepared by Cardno for the [Australian] Department of Foreign Affairs and Trade.

Society for Participatory Research in Asia (PRIA). 2012. *Civil Society at Crossroads: Shift, Challenges, Options?* www.intrac.org/wpcms/wp-content/uploads/2016/09/Civil-society-at-a-Crossroads-Global-Synthesis-Report.pdf (accessed October 29, 2017).

Vandendael, Anouk, Bas Hagoort, Jelle van Balen, and Joppe Ter Meer. 2013. *Stimulating Civil Society from the Perspective of an INGO: An Explorative Study of Indonesia* (research study, Rotterdam School of Management, Erasmus University).

INDONESIA NOTES

1. The TIFA Foundation was established on December 8, 2000, as a grant-making institution that supports national and local NGOs promoting an open society in Indonesia. Globally, TIFA is part of the Open Society Foundation network in the Asia-Pacific region.

2. See the section on *Pundi Perempuan* on the IKa website at http://indonesiauntukkemanusiaan.org/pundi-perempuan/ (accesssed on January 3, 2018).

JAPAN

Masataka Uo and Miho Ito

Given a limited understanding of public-interest activities by citizens, it has not been easy for organizations engaged in civic activities to incorporate as legal entities in Japan. In the 1980s the nation's civil society groups began seriously discussing and deliberating about the need for a system that would make incorporating NPOs easier. The Great Hanshin earthquake of 1995, with a direct impact on Kobe City, a major urban center, played a catalytical role in creating an awareness of the importance of volunteerism and civic action among both politicians and ordinary people.

The Japan NPO Law, which came into force in 1998, allows CSOs to acquire nonprofit corporation status. The law, together with the 2008 reform of public-interest corporation laws, enabled Japanese society to realize the pivotal role of citizens' engagement in supporting the public interest.

There are many types of classifications for nonprofit corporations, including Specified Nonprofit Corporation (Tokutei Hieiri Katsudo Hojin) and Public Interest Corporation (Koeki Hojin), which includes Public Interest Incorporated Foundation and Public Interest Incorporated Association. Public Interest Corporations are approved by the Public-Interest Approval Councils (Charity Commissions), which make public-interest approval judgments based on whether an organization fulfills certain criteria. Other nonprofit corporation classification types include Social Welfare Corporation (Shakai Fukushi Hojin), Religious Organization (Syukyo Hojin), Incorporated Educational Institution (Gakko Hojin) and Medical Corporation (Iryo Hojin).

The Specified Nonprofit Corporations that meet standard conditions and received approval from the Cabinet Secretariat, prefectural governments, or designated cities become Certified Specified Nonprofit Corporations. Donors to the Certified Specified Nonprofit Corporations receive income-tax deductions. Tax incentives and the registration process were improved significantly in 2011. However, there are still very few Certified Specified Nonprofit Corporations (less than 2% of nearly 50,000 NPO corporations in Japan). Public Interest Corporations and other nonprofit corporations also receive preferential treatment under the current tax system.

Governance rules vary slightly for these different types of corporations. For example, Public Interest Corporations are legally required to have over half of their directors physically present at their board meetings. On the other hand, Specified Nonprofit Corporations are allowed to count proxy letters for the attendance requirement.

The governance of NPOs is monitored by different ministries according to the jurisdiction of their particular nonprofit corporate status. For example, the Cabinet Office and local governments are responsible for overseeing the legal compliance of Specified Nonprofit Corporations and Public Interest Corporations; the Ministry of Health, Labour and Welfare has jurisdiction over Social Welfare Corporations and Medical Corporations. The governance of Incorporated Educational Institutions is overseen by the Ministry of Education, Culture, Sports, Science and Technology. Religious Organizations are overseen by the Agency for Cultural Affairs. The specifics of governance and taxation vary for each type of nonprofit corporate status as set forth by the law.

In Japan, people often think the main role of an organization's board is to act in an advisory capacity to its administration. It is common for boards of directors to not see themselves as being responsible for the governance of the organization. Some directors are even asked to be on the board for their names, not to actively participate. It is still rare to see a board that is actively engaged in fundraising activities, as the administration plays the main role in moving things forward and the board is secondary to the administration.

Investing in Building the Capacity of the Board

One can find many training classes on subjects such as strategic planning and accounting, and a very limited number of training courses on nonprofit finance for auditors, but it is hard to find any classes on board management or courses designed especially for board members.

Some key initiatives for strengthening board performance do exist. As transparency and accountability are important elements of good governance, an online platform called the CANPAN Center was established in 2007. CANPAN rates nonprofits on the extent of information they disclose to the public. Approximately 13,000 organizations are registered on this website. CANPAN, along with the others, is taking a leading role in increasing transparency of NPOs through online initiatives. The Citizen Advisory Board for Excellent NPOs has been formed and identifies three criteria—"citizenship", "social innovation" and "organizational stability"—as key indicators of NPO excellence. This effort has also led to the inaugural Excellent NPO Award in 2012.

Further, based on a study of international best practices for nonprofits undertaken by the BBB Wise Giving Alliance and Charity Navigator, the Japan Center for NPO Evaluation was founded in April of 2016 by some leading grant-making foundations and intermediaries. This is the first third-party certification authority in Japan to evaluate the governance of NPOs. The Center has established five criteria for excellence: Mission and Performance, Governance, Compliance, Transparency, and Management.

In addition, there are about 300 intermediary organizations in Japan that support NPOs in strengthening their accountability and management skills in general.

Trends

Japan's nonprofit sector is at a turning point. Today's Japan faces a huge financial deficit and many social challenges, including decreasing birth rate and aging population. Expectations for the nonprofit sector have been growing.

Tax Code Changes

This trend is supported by two symbolic events: First, the Great East Japan Earthquake of 2011, which compelled 76% of the Japanese people to give for disaster relief. As a result of this event, the tax incentives for giving improved significantly. Second, the Dormant Account Utilizing Law was enacted in December 2016. Because of this law, it will be possible to utilize over US$500 million of dormant deposits annually to invest in efforts and activities to solve social issues. In order to utilize the financial resources made available by these changes as efficiently as possible, the frameworks to discern and select appropriate grantees are urgently needed.

Social Enterprises

Another trend is the introduction of a new business model—the social enterprise, or social business—whose operational success is gauged not only by its bottom line, but also by its contribution to the public interest and the resolution of society's problems. It has drawn considerable attention and has created a new breed of social entrepreneurs eager to launch such businesses. The interest this trend has generated among talented men and women of all ages, especially among the young, is cause for genuine hope for the future.

As of now, there is no certification system for social enterprises, but the need for such a certification system has been expressed and discussed. The Ministry of Economy, Trade and Industry has recently compiled a study on this topic. Social businesses are widely recognized as an important vehicle for making social change, but tax incentives are still under discussion.

In addition to policy measures at the State and local levels, private corporations and NPOs themselves have undertaken a number of related initiatives. A business daily Nihon Keizai Shimbun has instituted the Nikkei Social Initiative Award to honor the achievements of Japanese social enterprises and NPOs. An NPO called ETIC (Entrepreneurial Training for Innovative Communities) has played a key role over the last 20 years in training social entrepreneurs and assisting them in developing new business models.

In addition, the first benchmarks for Japan's Social Impact Measurement Initiative have been established. In 2016, over 150 organizations including corporations, government, nonprofits, and universities announced the Road Map to 2020. The road map's three main themes outline the necessary approaches to achieve the vision. They are cultivation of a social-impact measurement culture, developing an enabling environment of social-impact measurement, and best practices in the collection and application of social-impact measurements.

KOREA

Bekay Ahn

Organizations that are nonprofit, or tax-exempt voluntary, and independent organizations in Korea are known as NPOs (*biyoungri danche*), NGOs (*mingan danche*), CSOs (*simin danche*), civic movement organizations (*simin woondong danche*), and public-interest corporations (*gongick bubin*). These are not clearly differentiated terms, are frequently used interchangeably, and confuse even local practitioners. The terms NGO and CSO are widely used in the field of academia as well as in the media. The term *public-interest corporations* is commonly used only in a governmental or legal context. South Korea's nonprofit sector has been invisible due to the deep-rooted tradition of a government-centered society. Little is known about the sector, and interest and investment at the national level is needed to raise awareness of nonprofits and to fund research.

Korea does not yet have an entity like the Charity Commission in the United Kingdom, the Australian Charities and Not-for-profits Commission in Australia, or the Charity Council and the Commissioner of Charities in Singapore. National commissions such as these promote and encourage the adoption of good governance and best practices, as well as help enhance public confidence and promote self-regulation in the sector. Even without such a resource, Korean civil society is flourishing because of a favorable political and social regulative environment. The restoration of a democratic government following the mass movement in 2016 galvanized public support for CSOs, which had played a significant and positive role in the movement. Interest in NGO governance (Kim 2003) and the operational effectiveness of nonprofits is growing, culminating in a public outcry for government to establish a Korean charity commission.

At the same time, systematic and independent self-regulation is needed in the sector, and would be preferred over the current situation in which government regulation ensures financial transparency in CSOs.

Board Recruitment

With the exception of social welfare organizations, boards often function poorly and sow seeds of governance dysfunction. Korean civil society still faces the problem of charismatic founders (in the case of philanthropies and educational medical institutions) wielding undue influence, and boards consisting of societal leaders who do not take their fiduciary roles seriously. Checks and balances for boards are needed, and more emphasis needs to be placed on internal constituents beyond founders and their friends. Otherwise, so-called founder's syndrome or good old boy syndrome results. Another unhappy outcome in these situations is the so-called usual suspect syndrome—recruitment of the same person (or type of person) to join the board, which impedes organizational development and possibly breaches ethics (as in failure to avoid conflict of interest). The number-one organizational concern expressed by both boards and CEOs is succession planning (Better Future 2016). If this issue was properly addressed, it would encourage better board composition and should be a consideration in recruitment.

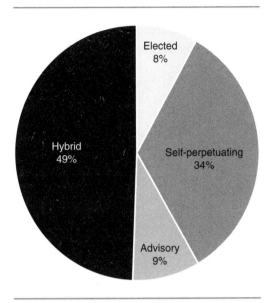

FIGURE 3.1 Recruitment of Korean Boards

The selection process should also take into account the agendas, priorities, and pressure that individual candidates may bring to their work on the board. CEOs must carefully attend to recruitment. It is critical to them, because a CEO is appointed and evaluated by an organization's board. A survey conducted of 45 NPOs (Ahn 2014) revealed how the recruitment methods employed determine the nature of the board (see Figure 3.1):

Hybrid. Selection is through appointment by some authority outside the organization, but the board may also have some seats that are held ex officio—that is, designated to be held by the individual who holds a certain office or position (for example, the vice president of development). In Korea the CEO (or executive director) is an ex officio board member. Half of Korean boards are selected in this way.

Self-perpetuation. Selection is by the existing members of boards. Thirty-four percent of Korean boards self-select.

Election. In some cases, this is election by the membership of the organization and in other cases, it is by a pro forma vote. Eight percent of Korean boards are voted in.

Appointment. Advisory boards and councils may have influence but no legal responsibility or authority for governance of the organization. Nine percent of Korean boards are in this category (Ahn 2014).

The Board and the CEO

In some organizations the CEO may be dominant with the board playing a passive role. The CEO may manipulate the board, orchestrate board meetings, and relegate the board to the role of a rubber stamp for his or her initiatives. The danger in such a scenario is that the CEO could lead the board and the organization in directions that are inappropriate or risky, and thus the board may fail in its responsibilities for ensuring adherence to mission, fiscal soundness, and optimal performance.

Board Development

According to a mobile survey conducted by the International Council for Nonprofit Management (2017), a significant portion (43%) of respondents indicated that qualified leadership and board-member and CEO training was the most effective way to improve fundraising. This highlights the importance of governance and leadership training.

Culture

Overall, the culture of large nonprofits resembles what is found in corporations. It can be characterized in the following terms: clan management; top down decision-making; paternalistic leadership; bureaucratic conflict resolution; very bureaucratic systems, yet a low degree of formally standardized systems; and a close government-business relationship. Loyalty and a Confucian work ethic are prized.

New Kinds of Organizations Pose Questions for Governance

Korea has progressively adapted some innovative organizational forms that share characteristics of both corporations and nonprofits. These hybrids pose new and interesting questions about governance.

B Corps

B Corps are for-profit companies certified by the nonprofit B Lab to meet rigorous standards of social and environmental performance, accountability, and transparency. Ten companies have been awarded the designation in Korea since 2012. Companies are awarded the designation based on meeting the criteria of the Global Impact Investing Rating System. One of the four categories evaluated includes corporate governance. An example of a Korean B Corp is SoCar. By bringing a car-sharing platform to a densely populated country, SoCar has helped alleviate parking problems and lessen pollution.

Social Enterprise

South Korea is the only country in East Asia to have a legal definition for *social enterprise*. It was part of the 2006 Social Enterprise Promotion Act (SEPA), which went into effect in 2007. SEPA was influenced in part by British law and in part by a social cooperative law passed in Italy in 1991. The government defines a social enterprise as "a company or organization which performs business activities while putting priority on the pursuit of social purposes." It can be for- or not-for-profit. The seven-step certification process mandates addressing any governance issues. As of September 2017, there are 1,814 certified social enterprises in South Korea. The government aims to have more than 3,000 certified social enterprises by 2018.

Capacity Builders

The major players for building governance capacity in the nonprofit ecosystem have yet to emerge, but there are already some on the playing field. An intermediary organization is needed to link and coordinate information collection and the sharing of resources, technology, and service. A survey has shown that such an intermediary organization is quite necessary (Park 2015).

GuideStar Korea is one of the leading sources for information on the sector. While it provides analysis of financial statements and performance measurements, and establishes accreditation criteria for transparency and accountability, it has not yet focused on governance issues.

The Korea Society of Philanthropy (KSoP) has developed a code of governance for its nonprofit members. All nonprofits are strongly encouraged to apply the principles and practices of this code. Recognizing that nonprofits differ greatly in size, activities, and circumstances, KSoP acknowledges that not all of the guidelines will apply to everyone, but does recommend that all organizations should at least review the code and adopt what applies (see Table 3.1).

TABLE 3.1 Korea Society of Philanthropy's Code of Governance

Ensuring Adherence to Values	Exercising Leadership	Ensuring Fiscal and Legal Compliance
1. Fidelity to Purpose	1. Vision, Purpose, and Values	1. Establishment and Incorporation
The fundamental responsibility of the board of an NPO is to endorse, practice, and require a commitment to the core values that are inherent in the Korean philosophy described as *Nanum*.	It is the responsibility of a board to ensure that the vision, purpose, and values of the organization are clearly defined.	The form of legal structure (in terms of which an NPO is established under) may determine how and when the responsibilities of governance arise.
2. Altruism and Benevolence	2. Accountability and Transparency	2. Administrative and Procedural Requirements
An NPO's resources, energies, and activities must be devoted to promoting its public benefit purpose and not to any personal or private objective.	A critical responsibility of the board is to ensure commitment to accountability and transparency.	Each form of alternative legal structure has its own specific reporting obligations to comply with applicable laws and regulations.
3. Integrity	3. Fundraising, Sustainability, and Risk	3. Other Legislative and Regulatory Compliance
The underlying motivation must be one of public interest, not self-interest.	It is the board's responsibility not only to monitor expenditures and appropriation of funds, but also to ensure that an organization continues to be adequately funded.	The board's responsibility for governance includes a responsibility to ensure that the organization remains compliant with all its statutory duties and obligations.

4. Optimizing Resources

The board must act responsibly and effectively in ensuring that valuable and limited resources are spent in an appropriate manner.

5. Conflicts of Interest and Self-Dealing

A fundamental principle and value of NPO governance is the avoidance of conflicts that arise when people in a position of trust make a decision or enter into a contract from which they themselves, or friends, relatives, and associates, stand to benefit.

6. Equality and Nondiscrimination

It is the responsibility of the board to take proactive steps to prevent unfair discrimination in the conduct of an organization, including discrimination that may be based on grounds of race, gender, or disability.

4. Collaboration and Synergy

NPOs should act collaboratively and cooperate with other similar entities—including official government welfare agencies.

5. The Board and Other Governance Structures

Board members should be recruited with due regard to a number of relevant factors, including their knowledge, skills, diversity, and availability.

6. Procedural Formalities

Procedural formalities prescribed in founding documents (the constitution) must be thoroughly observed.

4. NPO Status—Fiscal Benefits and Conditions

It is a fundamental responsibility of the board to ensure that such privileges are not squandered or abused.

TABLE 3.1 *(continued)*

Ensuring Adherence to Values	Exercising Leadership	Ensuring Fiscal and Legal Compliance
7. Democracy and Empowerment		
In the conduct of its affairs and in its relationships with each of its stakeholders, an NPO must demonstrate a clear commitment to the democratic process and decision-making.		
8. Independence and Impartiality		
A public-benefit purpose implies that all eligible beneficiaries must be treated equally and fairly, without special favor or prejudice.		

Source: Adapted from the Independent Code of Governance for NGOs in South Africa.

Conclusion

We should focus on principles, not just best practice, because Korea's nonprofits are not fully developed yet. We also need to avoid the pitfall of borrowing or adapting processes and tools without full leadership support and commitment. Tools alone will not generate the desired results. All too often Korean nonprofits have little tolerance for mistakes, which leads many organizations to become risk averse. And when mistakes are made, the tendency is to sweep them under the carpet—depriving the sector of important lessons. We need to try new things and take risks.

KOREA REFERENCES

Ahn, Bekay. 2017. *Governance Study for Korea Community Foundation.* International Council for Nonprofit Management.

Ahn, Bekay. 2014. *Asian Hospital Feasibility Study.* International Council for Nonprofit Management.

Better Future. 2016. *Korean Nonprofits Governance Study* [in Korean]. www.futurechosun.com/archives/15518 (accessed November 2, 2017).

International Council for Nonprofit Management, 2017.

Kim, Junki. 2003. "Accountability Governance and Non-governmental Organization: A Comparative Study of Twelve Asia-Pacific Nations." Paper. Seoul National University.

Park, Se Hoon. 2015. "The Role of Intermediary Organizations in Community Planning in Korea: A Government-Civil Society Relation Perspective." *Journal of the Korean Urban Management Association* 28 (September): 75–104.

KOREA FURTHER READING

Hasan, Samiul, and Jennifer Onyx, eds. 2007. *Comparative Third Sector Governance in Asia: Structure, Process, and Political Economy.* New York: Springer.

Kim, Inchoon, and Changsoon Hwang. 2002. "Defining the Nonprofit Sector: South Korea." Working Paper No. 41, Johns Hopkins Comparative Nonprofit Sector Project. Johns Hopkins Center for Civil Society Studies.

Panas, Jerold. 1991. *Boardroom Verities.* Precept Press.

Renz, David O., ed. 2010. *The Jossey-Bass Handbook of Nonprofit Leadership and Management,* 3rd ed. San Francisco, CA: Jossey-Bass.

PHILIPPINES

Usha Menon

Philippine CSOs are widely seen as some of the most vibrant and advanced in the world. The Philippines has the largest number of NGOs per capita in Asia, and civil society has contributed to democratization of the country.

The basis for civil society in the Philippines comes from the Filipino concepts *of pakikipagkapwa* (holistic interaction with others) and *kapwa* (shared inner self). Voluntary assistance or charity connotes for Filipinos an equal status between the provider of assistance and the recipient, which is embodied in the terms *damayan* (assistance of peers in periods of crisis) and *pagtutulungan* (mutual self-help). The Western notion of charity (*kawanggawa*) may have been introduced to the Philippines by Catholic missionaries.

NGOs in the Philippines engage in a broad range of activities, the most common being in:

- Education, training, and human resource development
- Community development
- Enterprise development and employment generation
- Health and nutrition
- Law, advocacy, and politics
- Sustainable development

Political activism takes on a larger role in Filipino CSOs than elsewhere. Indeed, CSOs played major roles in achieving Filipino independence from the Spanish and the Americans, in toppling the Marcos regime, and in ending the administration of President Joseph Estrada.

Regulation

There is no single government agency that is in charge of registering, certifying, and monitoring NGOs in the Philippines; however, the following requirements need to be met:

Registration. NGOs must be registered as a non-stock, nonprofit corporation and in compliance with regulatory and reportorial requirements, with the Securities and Exchange Commission (SEC), and with the Bureau of Internal Revenue (BIR), and have a permit to operate from the local government unit.

Governance. A minimum number of five members is required for the board; annual elections must take place and no board member may have any administrative case filed against him or her. There are no other limitations.

Income Tax Exemption. NGOs registered as non-stock NPOs may be entitled to an income-tax exemption for donations and contributions received. They can apply for donee institution status, which exempts their local donors from paying the 30% donor's tax and allows them to enjoy 100% deductibility of donations made from gross taxable income. The main requirement for this status is the inclusion of the following provisions in the articles of incorporation and bylaws:

- No part of the net income or asset of the organization shall belong to or inure to the benefit of any member, organize, officer, or any specific person.
- Administrative expenses shall, on an annual basis, not exceed 30% of the total donations received and of total expenses for the taxable year.
- In the event of dissolution, the assets of the organization should be distributed to another accredited NGO organized for similar purposes, or to the State for public purposes.
- Board members may not receive compensation or remuneration for their service to the organization.

Ongoing Annual Report. NGOs are required to submit audited financial statements/reports and a general information sheet regarding the board, and to report on sources and amounts of donations received and how these were utilized. The BIR also requires the submission of audited financial statement/reports, income tax returns, types and amounts of taxes paid, and amounts and sources of donations received.

Tax on Earnings. NGOs are allowed to engage in income-generating activities. However, corresponding taxes, similar to those paid by for-profit companies, should be paid relative to its for-profit operations.

In addition, there is a national voluntary certification program, the Philippine Council for NGO Certification (PCNC).

Philippine Council for NGO Certification

In 1995, when the Comprehensive Tax Reform Program was being crafted, one of the amendments considered was the elimination of the granting of donee institution status (see income tax exemption, above) to qualified NGOs as a means of increasing government revenues. This would have meant that local donors to donee institutions would have lost the incentives of exemption. Recognizing the detrimental effects that this action would have had on NGOs dependent on local donors, the NGO community lobbied the Department of Finance (DOF) to retain the tax incentives given to local donors. In response, DOF challenged the NGO community to establish a self-regulatory body to certify non-stock NPOs that qualified for donee institution status. The community saw this as an opportunity to complement the efforts of the government to ensure that resources gifted to NGOs were used for their intended purposes, and that only donors to qualified NGOs would be provided with tax incentives.

Six of the largest NGO networks in the Philippines rose to meet the DOF's challenge—the Association of Foundations (AF), the League of Corporate Foundations, Philippine Business for Social Progress, the Bishops-Businessmen's Conference for Human Development, the National Council for Social Development, and the Caucus of Development NGO Networks (CODE-NGO)—and organized the PCNC. It was registered with the SEC as a non-stock, nonprofit corporation in January, 1997, and launched publicy in 1999. PCNC's main purpose is to serve to "certify NPOs that meet established minimum criteria for financial management and accountability in the service to underprivileged Filipinos.[1]"

In early 1998, the PCNC and the DOF signed a memorandum of agreement authorizing the newly formed council to certify NGOs' applications for donee institution status granted by the BIR. The first years of PCNC were devoted to the development and refinement of a certification system that was to be characterized by integrity and professionalism, the national promotion of its services, and the training of volunteer peer evaluators. Certification criteria was developed with assistance from experts, referencing the certification systems used by other disciplines, and in consultation with NGOs from different parts of the country. The Ford Foundation, Sasakawa Peace Foundation, and the United States Agency for International Development (USAID) generously provided funding for this start-up phase.

Documentation of compliance with basic government regulatory and reportorial requirements is required before a nonprofit can begin the evaluation process. Volunteer peer evaluators, who are senior management personnel of PCNC-certified organizations or members of the Philippine Institute for Certified Public Accountants, then score the organization in key areas: vision, mission and goals, governance, administration, program operations, financial management, and networking capabilities.

In 2009, the purpose of PCNC was expanded to improve the effectiveness of Philippine NGOs. Now PCNC not only measures compliance with standards of good governance and management, but also makes recommendation on how certified organizations may improve efficiency and effectiveness. Further, management courses are offered to help in implementing recommendations. Training is funded by the World Bank, the Spanish Cooperation Agency for International Development, and USAID.

NGOs are often started by small groups of good-hearted people or families wanting to help to the disadvantaged. As their reach and funding increase, many formally organize into non-stock NPOs, duly registered with the SEC and the BIR.

New nonprofits typically have few or no staff to implement programs, so board members and volunteers perform this function. This informal structure suits many organizations well—everything is under control and they are able to pursue the purpose for which they got together. They are able to help those in need, although on a limited scale.

These small nonprofits, however, are unprepared for the rigorous registration requirements of the SEC and BIR. In addition, they must meet the accreditation standards of the government agency that oversees the type of programs they conduct. The most common reason NGOs fail to pursue PCNC certification is that they cannot meet the requirements of the SEC and BIR.

For others, however, incorporation is only the beginning. They grow in operational capacity, extend their reach, and seek and attract more funding so they can deliver even more services to greater numbers of beneficiaries. Along the way, they "professionalize" their operations and hire more staff. These larger organizations are better equipped to meet all standards and qualify for PCNC certification, and this helps them grow stronger as they get bigger.

PCNC Guidance for Governance

PCNC routinely advises assessed NGOs on how to develop the capabilities and improve the functioning of their boards. One of PCNC's governance policies encourages diversity on boards that are usually more closed by their nature (family and corporate foundations) by recommending outside representation.

Family foundations are usually organized to share their blessings, and programs are often based on the advocacy nearest the heart of the patriarch or matriarch of the family. Funds of the foundation are usually sourced only from family members. These boards are, most of the time, composed of immediate family members.

Several companies in the Philippines have set up their own corporate foundations to pursue CSR. Many of them, however, go beyond traditional CSR, and provide assistance to communities outside of their places of operation. Members of the board of these corporate foundations are usually executives from its affiliate for-profit companies. Only for-profit corporations are mandated by the government to have independent directors on the board.

PCNC has adopted a policy that NGOs organized by family, corporations, and religious congregations have at least one independent, third-party member serve on the board. This is to ensure that funds given to the NGO are used for the intended purpose(s) of the NGO, and are not used to benefit organizers/incorporators, management, and staff. Violation of any of the above provisions can lead to cancellation of tax exemption and loss of donee institution status.

PCNC has also developed two handbooks on NGO management that include sections on governance. Governance is also covered in PCNC's management training for NGOs.

PCNC's Challenge

The greatest challenge for PCNC is that very few NGOs are interested in certification. They do not view it as beneficial for improvements in their efficiency and effectiveness. The number of PCNC-certified organizations ranges from 410 to 450 at any given time, plus another 60 whose certification or recertification is in process. PCNC reaches only 1% of the nation's estimated 45,000 active NGOs. Most of them are small.

In addition to what PCNC provides, three networks—CODE-NGO, AF, and the League of Corporate Foundations—conduct board development training courses if funds are available.

Trends

Filipino organizations registered as non-stock NPOs may engage in direct service, grant-making, advocacy, and/or research programs. They may engage in for-profit activities. However, profits cannot be distributed to members of the board, management, and staff, or to any individual. All income must be used for the programs and operations of the organization. Thus, a social enterprise that is directed towards generating income for the owners/board cannot register as a non-stock NPO.

There is a bill in Congress that would amend the tax code of the Philippines. Among the amendments are the lowering of donor's tax from 30% to 6% and raising the maximum amount of donations not subject to donor's tax to US$1,931.[2] It is said that the bill will most likely be passed into law. The implications for revenue, especially for small NGOs that have not attempted PCNC certification, are significant.

Conclusion

The Philippines' civil sector has achieved some exceptional success. In proactively working together to meet the threat of loss of tax-exemption privileges for donors, the nonprofit community here has fashioned a self-regulatory system that also promotes best practices in governance.

PHILIPPINES NOTES

1. Philippine Council for NGO Certification website. http://www.pcnc.com.ph/ (accessed December 28, 2017).
2. US dollars were converted from Philippine pesos on October 24, 2017.

SINGAPORE

Usha Menon

As a nation, Singapore has always rated among the top on all global indices related to governance—rule of law, regulatory quality, government effectiveness, and control of corruption. These high standards have helped strengthen the nonprofit ecosystem in the area of governance. The Charities Act, enacted in 1995, made provision for the registration of charities, the administration of charities and their affairs, the regulation of charities and institutions of a public character (IPCs are nonprofit entities that are able to issue tax-deductible receipts for qualifying donations to donors), and the regulation of fundraising and the conduct of fundraising appeals by charities.

Despite the supportive infrastructure, there was a governance breach in 2005 at one of the biggest charities, which resulted in its CEO and chairman being investigated and jailed for malpractices. This episode stunned many Singaporeans and caused a loss of public confidence. It provided, however, the impetus for the government and the sector to review and rejuvenate charity sector governance.

In 2007, the new Charities Act was brought into operation and the Charity Council set up to establish and enhance governance standards of the charity sector in Singapore by playing the following roles:

Promoter. Promoting and encouraging the adoption of good governance standards and best practices to enhance public confidence in the charity sector.

Enabler. Helping to build the governance capabilities of charities to enable them to comply with regulatory requirements and be more accountable to the public.

Advisor. Advising the Commissioner of Charities (COC) on key regulatory issues that may have broad-ranging impact on the charity sector.

The office of the COC, with support from the Charity Council, works to maintain trust in charities, promote compliance to legal obligations and effective use of charitable resources, and enhance the accountability of charities to all their stakeholders.

The COC is further supported in overseeing charities and IPCs in their respective sectors by five sector administrators. They are:

Ministry of Education. Overseeing charitable objectives related to the advancement of education.

Ministry of Health. Overseeing charitable objectives related to the promotion of health.

Ministry of Social and Family Development. Overseeing charitable objectives related to the relief of poverty or those in need by reason of youth, age, ill health, disability, financial hardship, or other disadvantages.

People's Association. Overseeing charitable objectives related to the advancement of citizenship or community development.

Sport Singapore. Overseeing charitable objectives related to the advancement of sport.

Additionally, the COC directly oversees charities related to the arts and heritage, animal welfare, environmental protection, and religion. The three priority areas that the COC currently focuses on are strengthening the sector's governance capabilities, promoting the importance of informed giving, and moving towards coregulation.

While the office of the COC takes on the role as the regulator of the sector, as part of the coregulation efforts, the Code of Governance for charities has been developed and refined with extensive consultations with various stakeholders. The code operates on the so-called principle of comply or explain and is not mandatory. To help with the process, a governance evaluation checklist (GEC) has been designed to help IPCs self-evaluate the extent of their compliance to the Code of Governance. All charities and IPCs are required to submit a report on their compliance to their respective sector administrators online via the charity portal within six months after the end of each financial year. The full responsibility for providing accurate and updated checklist information rests with the respective charity boards. If a charity is unable to comply fully, the governing board is responsible for documenting the circumstances and either indicating the steps it plans to take to address the noncompliance or explaining why it cannot or is deciding not to comply.

The code is organized into nine sections and the guidelines are tiered according to the charity or to IPC status and size based on total operating expenditure of the entity:

- Board Governance
- Conflict of Interest
- Strategic Planning
- Program Management
- Human Resource Management
- Financial Management and Controls
- Fundraising Practices
- Disclosure and Transparency
- Public Image

The Sector

Organizations established exclusively for charitable purposes and carrying out activities to achieve these purposes are legally required to apply for charity registration with the COC. All registered charities get to enjoy income and property-tax exemption on premises used exclusively for charitable purposes. As of 2016, there were 2,247 registered charities in Singapore. Only 179 of them had annual receipts above US$7.5 million in 2015.[1]

Registered charities that have IPC status can issue tax-deductible receipts of 250% of the donated amount to donors who want to claim tax relief based on the amount of qualifying donations made (for every $1 donated to a registered charity, $2.50 is deducted from the donor's taxable income for the year). Under the Income Tax Act, outright cash donations, donations of shares by individual donors, donations of computers (including hardware, software, accessories, and peripherals) by corporations, donations of artifacts, donations under the Public Art Tax Incentive Scheme, and gifts of land and buildings all qualify for a tax deduction.

Charities are required to register for the goods and services tax if their annual taxable supplies exceed US$740,000, even if they are engaged mostly in nonbusiness activities.

Capability-Building Efforts

In the effort to develop the governance capabilities of board members so that they can exercise sound and responsible stewardship of public resources in fulfilling the objectives of the charities, various capability-building training and incentives have been put in place.

The Charity Transparency and Governance Awards

These annual national awards recognize nonprofits for their exemplary disclosure and transparency practices. Award candidates are tiered into the small, medium, and large categories for the qualifying standards of governance, based on their gross annual receipts. A charity transparency scorecard helps the charities to evaluate themselves in nine areas of disclosure. Annual reports, financial statements, GECs posted on the charity portal, websites, and social media presence are examined to determine levels of transparency.

Town Hall Meetings

Since 2015, the Charity Council and the Centre for Social Development Asia have coorganized a series of town hall meetings. These serve as platforms to raise the sector's awareness of the need to enhance core competencies and practices in financial management, accountability, and disclosure. The sessions allow board members and staff of charities to discuss and explore practical solutions to address common issues and challenges.

Charity Governance Conference

The office of the COC and the Charity Council organize the annual charity governance conference. The most recent conference's theme was Purpose, Values, and Culture—How Does It Drive Governance in Charities? The previous conference peered into the future and sustainability with the theme Governance for Charities in the 21st Century.

Voluntary Welfare Organizations' Charities Capability Fund

Introduced in 2007, the Voluntary Welfare Organizations' Charities Capability Fund (VCF) aims to enhance governance and management capabilities of charities and IPCs through the following grants:

- The VCF training grant provides cofunding for local training courses to help charities comply with regulatory requirements and build good governance standards.
- The VCF consultancy grant provides cofunding for the engagement of external consultants for governance and management consultancy projects.

- The VCF shared services grant provides cofunding for charities that outsource their payroll, finance, and accounting functions to a third-party service provider.
- The VCF info-communications technology grant provides cofunding for small and medium-sized charities to harness information and communication technology to facilitate the submission of annual returns and transactions on the charity portal.

Nonprofit Directors Program

This annual program designed and curated by Usha Menon is a collaboration between the Singapore Institute of Directors and the Social Service Institute of the National Council of Social Service. Designed around the learning needs of board members of NPOs, the faculty is made up of practitioners and leaders in the nonprofit field who combine their insights and knowledge of the sector with case studies to showcase the real life struggles of boards.

BoardMatch

The National Volunteer and Philanthropy Centre (NVPC), through the Centre for Nonprofit Leadership (CNPL), helps the nonprofit sector by creating a leadership pipeline, building effective boards, and partnering with nonprofit leaders and corporate professionals. BoardMatch is CNPL's flagship program, designed to address and build leadership capacity, diversity, continuity, and renewal at the board level of NPOs.

Work in Progress

While much has been done and achieved to enhance the board skills and quality of nonprofit governance, good governance is a continuous journey and there is still room for improvement, particularly in the standard of reporting. In 2016, the inaugural Board Leadership Survey was carried out by the NVPC to gain an understanding of board practices, policies, and activities of charities and IPCs. Some of the key findings related to areas for improvement were term limit policies for the positions of chair and treasurer, improvement in board diversity, and a formalized process for board succession/renewal.

The survey also highlighted that women make up 31% of board members, which is higher than the percentage in the for-profit sector in Singapore.

With emerging global risks that impact charity governance, protective measures have been put in place for Singapore's civil sector in the areas of anti–money laundering initiatives and countering of the financing of terrorism. The office of the COC has developed a guide aimed at board members, trustees, and key executives. The guide serves to help charities familiarize themselves with the measure. It also provides examples of good practices to reduce and manage exposure to such risks, as well as advice on actions to take if they spot any suspicious transactions.

Trends

Singapore is home to many family offices, foundations, and wealthy individuals who are looking at alternate social-finance models in addition to their philanthropic giving. Hence Singapore now has many regional impact investing intermediaries, such as the Asian Venture Philanthropy Network and Impact Investing Exchange, as well as international impact investing funds. Local initiatives such as the DBS Foundation and the Singapore Centre for Social Enterprise focus on expanding the social enterprise and social entrepreneurship segment.

With this growing segment comes exploration of emergent governance models and board responsibilities. Questions abound: Who can qualify as an impact investor? How are investees selected? How do investors and investees find each other? How is social impact measured? What financial returns are acceptable?

Conclusion

Thanks to the COC, the Charity Council (composed of volunteers with expertise in accountancy, corporate governance, entrepreneurship, and law, together with representatives from the nonprofit sector and government ministries), the use of technology to ensure sector transparency and to promote informed giving, and boards willing to hold themselves up to scrutiny through self-assessment and external reporting, the nonprofit sector is seeing many positive outcomes.

SINGAPORE REFERENCES

Charity Council (charity portal) https://www.charities.gov.sg/Pages/Home.aspx (accessed December 23, 2017).

Office of the Commissioner of Charities. 2015. *Protecting Your Charity Against Money Laundering and Terrorist Financing*. Guide.

Commissioner of Charities. 2017. *Commissioner of Charities Annual Report for the Year Ended December 31 2016*. Ministry of Culture, Community and Youth.

National Volunteer and Philanthropy Centre (NVPC). 2017. *Board Leadership Survey 2016 Findings*. www.nvpc.org.sg/resources/board-leadership-survey-2016-survey-findings (accessed October 18, 2017).

Šoštarić, Maja. 2015. "Singapore, the Impact Investing Hub of Asia? A Comparison with Hong Kong." White Paper. Lien Centre for Social Innovation, Singapore Management University. csi.smu.edu.sg/sites/lcsi.smu.edu.sg/files/lcsi/files/2012/03/Singapore-the-Impact-Investing-Hub-of-Asia.pdf (accessed October 18, 2017).

SINGAPORE NOTES

1. Currency referenced in this section is in US dollars converted from Singapore dollars on October 18, 2017.

CHAPTER 4

Australia and Aotearoa New Zealand

Alan Hough and Garth Nowland-Foreman

Alan Hough and Garth Nowland-Foreman highlight similarities and differences between the NGO sectors in Australia and Aotearoa New Zealand, including in the laws relevant to their governance and in the practice of governance in particular settings. In relation to the available data, the writers identify significant limitations in our understanding of NGO boards due to the limited research on governance, with the available research being systemically biased in favor of medium and large organizations. In part because of these limitations, and in part on conceptual grounds, the authors argue for caution in assertions about so-called best-practice NGO governance.

HISTORICAL AND CULTURAL CONTEXT FOR GOVERNANCE

Australia and New Zealand—or to use New Zealand's Māori name, *Aotearoa*—share much in common. Both countries were colonies of Britain, and their main languages, much of their law, significant elements of their political processes, and some social customs are derived from Britain. However, the cultures of both countries are diverse and enriched by the traditions of their first peoples and by waves of immigration. In both countries, the belief that government is responsible for providing health, welfare, and education services to its citizens is common, but there is an increasing trend towards government divesting these services (at least in the first two areas) in favor of both the not-for-profit and for-profit sectors. Indeed, the histories and cultures of the two countries

89

have so much in common that the Australian constitution recognizes Aotearoa New Zealand as a potential state of Australia.

Points of difference include the fact that Australia is much larger and more economically prosperous than Aotearoa New Zealand. Australia's population is over 24 million, almost five times that of Aotearoa New Zealand, with its largest city more populous than the whole of its neighbor. Australia has a land mass almost 30 times that of Aotearoa New Zealand. It has about eight times the gross domestic product of its neighbor. Historically, some Australian states were first established under military rule as penal colonies of Britain, whereas European settlement in Aotearoa New Zealand was motivated by a strange mix of seeking personal wealth, escaping a past, and establishing a morally ideal society. Reflecting its geographical size, Australia is a federation of states. Thus, legal and tax arrangements for Australian NGOs can vary by state of operation, whereas Aotearoa New Zealand has a unitary legal system.

The relationship between the dominant cultures and the two countries' first peoples is markedly different, in part for reasons of demographics and in part for reasons of history. Australia's Aboriginal and Torres Strait Islander people constitute 2.8% of its current population (Australian Bureau of Statistics 2017), whereas just over one in seven (14.9%) of the Aotearoa-New Zealand population identify as Māori (Statistics New Zealand 2014). A treaty (the Treaty of Waitangi, or *Te Tiriti o Waitangi*) was reached between representatives of the British Crown and Māori hapu (sub-tribes), but there is as of yet no treaty with Australia's Aboriginal and Torres Strait Islander peoples.

The dominant cultures of the two countries are similar. To use Fons Trompenaars's *Riding the Waves of Culture* framework that was introduced in Chapter 1, the dominant culture in both countries can be characterized as:

- Believing in common approaches and solutions (universalism)
- Thinking and relating more from an individual than group perspective (individualism)
- Giving a limited place to the expression of emotion (neutral)
- Relating based on the specific role and context more than on the basis of the whole person (specific)
- According social status to an individual based more on her/his achievements and less on matters such as age or family (achievement)

- Placing a high emphasis on planning and staying on schedule (sequential)
- Believing in one's ability to control the external environment (internal control)

Whether part of the dominant or other cultures, the work of boards necessitates directors making decisions more as a group than as individuals. Further sources of diversion from the dominant cultural traits are the diversity among individual directors, boards, and organizations. Matters such as ethnicity, gender, socioeconomic status, religious beliefs, and political beliefs are likely to impact how governance is practiced in a particular organization. For example, the cultures of both countries' first peoples feature cultural attributes that are almost the polar opposite to those identified above. In particular, Māori kin-based associational forms have been identified as one of three key historic influences on the NGO sector in Aotearoa New Zealand (Sanders et al. 2008), which shape something of a broader sector subculture that edges away from the dominant culture—at least among those who see themselves as "community" organizations.

It is in these broader contexts that governance in Australian and Aotearoa New Zealand NGOs occurs, and in which boards of directors perform their work.

UNDERSTANDING THE NGO SECTOR

One of the challenges in writing about the two countries' NGOs and their boards is that there is much less data available compared to countries such as the United States. The latest general nonprofit data for both countries relates to 2012–2013, with a considerable lag in publication (Australian Bureau of Statistics 2015; Statistics New Zealand 2016). The published data on Australian charities, one form of NGO, is for 2015 and more recent (Cortis et al. 2016). Reporting data for both NGOs and charities leads to apparent contradictions, but this relates to the difference in time periods reported.

There are estimated to be some 600000 NGOs in Australia (Productivity Commission 2010). This includes an estimated 440000 NGOs (73%) that are not incorporated (Productivity Commission 2010). However, given the challenge of identifying unincorporated organizations, which tend to be informal groups such as tennis clubs or card clubs, such projections involve considerable speculation. The latest available data suggests that of the incorporated organizations, 136000 were incorporated associations and 11700 were "companies limited by guarantee" (Productivity Commission 2010). For economically significant NGOs, there were 56,894 identified in 2012–2013, with a contribution to gross domestic product of US$45.56 billion.[1] It is estimated that there are some 20,000 social enterprises in Australia, many of which are of recent origin (Barraket et al. 2010).

More contemporary data is available for registered Australian charities, of which there were 50908 in Australia in 2015 (Cortis et al. 2016). They had a total income of US$106.18 billion. The latest estimate for total giving in Australia is US$6.79 billion (Scaife et al. 2016).

For Aotearoa New Zealand, 114110 economically significant NGOs were identified, which contributed US$4.36 billion (2.7%) to gross domestic product, excluding voluntary labor. Twenty-two percent of these were incorporated societies, with a further 15% incorporated as boards or societies under the Charitable Trusts Act. Like Australia, the majority (60%) of NGOs are not incorporated under any law (Statistics New Zealand 2007).

There are currently just under 28,000 registered charities in Aotearoa New Zealand.

In both countries, the last 30 years has seen increased interest in governance generally and the governance of NGOs in particular. There is now a host of guidance on NGO governance—from regulators, standards and accreditation bodies, academic centers, peak bodies, professional organizations for directors, lawyers, and consultants—that simply did not exist 30 years ago (for examples, see Australian Institute of Company Directors (AICD) 2013; NZ Navigator 2017; Standards Australia International 2003; Te Puni Kōkiri 2017). However, there is an imbalance between the quantity of advice and the research that justifies that advice. It is not unusual to find a gap between the prescriptive literature (the sometimes heroic "how-to" advice) and the descriptive literature that is based on researching what actually happens in boards (Cornforth 1996).

For studies of NGO governance practices, this chapter must draw on a limited and eclectic research base:

1. The useful but nonetheless nonrepresentative annual surveys by the Australian Institute of Company Directors (the latest survey results being from 2014, 2015, and 2016) and those by accounting

and consulting firm Grant Thornton that cover New Zealand, and more recently, Australian NGOs (the most recent being from 2014 and 2016)

2. One-off convenience samples (see Chelliah, Boersma, and Klettmer 2016; Grant Thornton 2015)

3. A survey for which it is unclear whether respondents were randomly selected or were part of a convenience sample (Erakovic and McMorland 2009)

4. Censuses or stratified random samples of particular types of NGOs taken at particular times, namely:
   - Queensland NGOs registered to fundraise (McDonald 1993)
   - Community-managed welfare organizations in two South East Queensland electoral districts (Wiseman 2002)
   - Companies limited by guarantee in Australia (Woodward and Marshall 2004)
   - New South Wales incorporated associations (Passey 2004)
   - Members of a NGO health and disability network in Aotearoa New Zealand (Rowe 2014)

5. Observation studies of boards at work (Grant 2006; Hough 2009)

The first and second categories and the data on companies are more representative of directors and organizations of medium and large NGOs, and thus the data reported in this chapter are systematically biased towards larger NGOs. Data on governance practices, such as they exist, will be reported where relevant in each section. It should be noted that while averages and frequencies are reported, this sometimes masks considerable diversity in the underlying data.

LEGAL REQUIREMENTS AFFECTING NGO BOARDS

As noted above, in both countries most NGOs do not incorporate. While the individual directors don't have the same limits on their personal liabilities as they would if the NGO was incorporated, this is legally permitted. If they incorporate, NGOs usually have a choice of their form of incorporation in both countries. In Australia, larger organizations tend to be "companies limited by guarantee" under the federal law, and the more numerous, smaller organizations—if incorporated—tend to be "incorporated associations" under the law of the relevant state or territory. However, there are many other legal forms, including companies formed by royal charter (reflecting Australia's history as a colony), companies with shares, trusts (which are, strictly speaking, not a form of incorporation in Australia), organizations operating under their own legislation (often religious denominations), cooperatives, and indigenous corporations. In Aotearoa New Zealand, the most popular choice is also the membership-based, incorporated society—which has been available since 1908, and on which much of the Australian states' more recent legislation is based. Thus the vast majority of NGO boards in both countries remain elected by, and accountable to, a formal membership structure. The next most popular option in Aotearoa New Zealand is incorporation of a board or society under the Charitable Trusts Act—which has no real equivalent in Australia. These entities were designed to be accountable to their trust deeds and do not require any members, though some trust deeds create members to appoint the trustees. As a result of these two relatively simple longstanding national legal frameworks, few Aotearoa New Zealand NGOs have chosen to incorporate as a company. Some of the other forms of incorporation available are as cooperatives, as school boards, under *Te Tura Whenua*/Maori Lands Act, or under their own legislation.

The legal responsibilities of directors have their origin in British law, subsequently transferred by statute or common-law rulings in each country. Common-law duties of directors include broadly stated duties to act in good faith, to exercise care and diligence, and to avoid conflicts of interest (Ramsay and Webster 2017). The leading judgment in Australian case law on the responsibilities of directors—whether for-profit or not-for-profit—is the National Safety Council of Victoria case, the Council being an NGO company limited by guarantee.[2] The Council collapsed in 1989 following a quite extraordinary series of frauds against banks by its then CEO John Friedrich, which totaled US$202.1 million (McGregor-Lowndes 1995). The directors were sued by one of the lending banks, with the board's chair being found personally liable by the court for US$76.58 million, as he allowed the company to trade and take out loans while insolvent. Likewise in Aotearoa New Zealand, NGO-specific legislation has offered little beyond broad statements on directors' duties. The Law Commission (2006 and 2013) undertook separate inquiries into the Incorporated Societies Act and legal frameworks for Māori groups managing communally owned assets and has recommended new legislation, and in both cases it is proposed to include more closely specified requirements, including for the first time statutory good governance standards, explicit duties for officers, and model constitutions.

There are special governance arrangements for those NGOs classified as charities. In both countries the definition of what constitutes a charitable organization has its origins in historic British law, namely the Statute of Elizabeth of 1601. This definition was only expanded by specific legislation in Aotearoa New Zealand in 2005, and in Australia in 2013. By decision of the High Court of Australia, even an organization with substantial business operations is charitable if the business is for a charitable purpose.[3] In the Greenpeace case, New Zealand's Supreme Court in 2014 held that neither campaigning activities nor a political purpose is an automatic barrier to being considered to have a charitable purpose.

Australian charities that wish to access federal tax concessions must register with the Australian Charities and Not-for-Profit Commission (ACNC), which has a misleading name as it regulates charities only, not not-for-profit organizations more generally. The ACNC regulations specify five minimum governance standards that must be met by most charities. Many charities consider meeting the standards not to be unduly onerous. Standard 1 relates to the not-for-profit nature of the charity and includes a requirement to make information about the charity available to the public. Standard 2 requires accountability to members, although it does not require that organizations have a wide membership. Standard 3 requires that the charity comply with Australian law, such as laws to prevent the funding of terrorism. Standard 4 requires charities to take reasonable steps to ensure that directors are not disqualified in law. Finally, standard 5 specifies that the charity take reasonable steps to comply with specified responsibilities of its directors—which reflect common-law duties. As a matter of law, it is not always clear whether the particular provisions of the ACNC Act or of some of the state-based association incorporation acts effectively remove or limit the personal legal liability of directors under common law or other statute law (Ramsay and Webster 2017). Most commentators believe it is prudent for directors to act as if they are liable. There are no equivalent standards under the New Zealand Charities Registration

Board (which replaced the New Zealand Charities Commission in 2012), though an annual report must be lodged and all officers of registered charities must be qualified in matters such as age and legal competence to manage their own affairs and must act in the best interests of their charity.

Directors of NGOs—like the directors of any other corporation—can be subject to director penalties if the organization they govern does not meet its obligations under tax law. The tax law effectively shifts the tax liabilities of organizations to directors. However, there is a range of provisions in the laws of both countries that benefit NGOs generally, as well as charities, donors to some charities, and the staff of charities. The most important are probably whether the NGO is itself exempt from income tax, whether donors are entitled to tax relief as a result of their donations, and whether employees are entitled to tax-effective salary packaging. When registered as a charity, an NGO is exempt from income tax in both countries. For example, Sanitarium health food companies, owned by the Seventh-day Adventist Church, are among the highest profile companies exempt from income tax because of their charitable status in both Australia and Aotearoa New Zealand. Some NGOs that are not considered charitable may be eligible for (slightly differing) partial income exemptions in both countries under the principle of mutuality, or a concessional income tax rate for certain Māori authorities in Aotearoa New Zealand. People who donate to registered charities that have the status of deductible gift recipients in Australia, or to any NGO that has donee status in Aotearoa New Zealand, are entitled to claim a tax credit or deduct their donations from their personal taxable income. Many NGOs highly prize this status, though there are significant differences—for example, in Aotearoa New Zealand, donations to churches generally are included, but in Australia they are not.

Staff members of charities that are registered as public benevolent institutions (PBIs) in Australia are entitled to have tax-advantageous salary packaging, which effectively increases their after-tax wages and salaries. PBIs are charitable institutions that have the main purpose of relieving poverty or distress. Examples of PBIs include some hospitals and hospices, and some disability-support and aged-care services.[4] Aotearoa New Zealand generally offers similar fringe-benefit tax exemptions for charities in respect of staff carrying the organization's charitable activities. Certain limits also apply.

NGO directors also have responsibilities—as do directors of their for-profit counterparts—under general laws related to, for example, consumer protection, competitive conduct, workplace health and safety (including bullying), employment, and environmental protection.

In Australia, directors of charities that fundraise can also be subject to conditions and responsibilities under state-based fundraising legislation. Regrettably for charities operating across state borders, they are subject to the fundraising laws of each state in which they operate, although duplication is reducing (ACNC 2017). Some legislation on fundraising has specific consequences for directors; for example, New South Wales's fundraising law prohibits directors of fundraising organizations from being paid without the approval of the regulating minister.

There is anecdotal evidence that the responsibility to prevent insolvent trading and responsibilities under the workplace health and safety legislation are those taken most seriously by many directors. However, directors who ignore other legal responsibilities do so at their peril. With these confusing and multilayered legal responsibilities, it is perhaps no surprise that directors in both countries surveyed by Grant Thornton (2014) should not always understand their legal responsibilities, and that this is more likely to be the case with smaller NGOs. As a precaution, many organizations purchase insurance to mitigate potential liabilities.

THE ROLES OF BOARDS

It is likely that the roles played by boards vary considerably with the size of the organization. For example, given that the vast majority of NGOs have no staff, boards of these organizations are likely to be working boards. Even in organizations with a small staff, the directors are likely to be more hands-on than in larger organizations. However, this reality is sometimes not reflected in survey results, because more large organizations complete surveys than small ones. This is an important caveat for the results reported below.

In one Australian survey, directors of NGOs saw their responsibilities as multifaceted, with no single role having more prominence than others (Chelliah, Boersma, and Klettmer 2016). Determining strategic direction (91% of respondents), guiding and monitoring the organization's financial position (90%) and acting as a general advisory body (85%)

were the perceived roles of boards of Australian companies limited by guarantee (Woodward and Marshall 2004). The most common areas of participation of directors were in honorary executive positions in their organization (for example, as an NGO president or treasurer; 53%), in strategic planning (38%) and in the organizational policy development (32%) (McDonald 1993). A recent Australian survey reported that in the next 12 months board priorities would be responding to changes in the operating environment (40%), diversifying income sources (30%), and clarifying strategic direction (28%) (AICD 2016).

In an Aotearoa New Zealand study, most directors (64%) saw their main responsibilities to be strategy and policy-making, while at the same time, from the CEO's point of view, boards were not sufficiently involved in strategy (Erakovic and McMorland 2009). Despite the centrality of the director role, only 63% of NGOs in the Grant Thornton (2010) survey believed their directors to be strategic thinkers.

Some organizations offer training to their directors, with surveys giving vastly different results, from 18% to 72% of organizations providing training (Chelliah, Boersma, and Klettner 2016; Grant Thornton 2015). Financial literacy in particular has been identified as a need in NGO boards, with only 59% reporting it as sufficient (Grant Thornton 2015). Furthermore, 41% of NGOs in one Aotearoa New Zealand survey believed their boards lacked adequate knowledge of relevant legislation (Grant Thornton 2006). Few NGOs in an Aotearoa New Zealand study put aside resources for board training or development, despite director willingness to participate in training (Erakovic and McMorland 2009). Furthermore, while some training in specific skills may be needed, "it is the more intangible dimensions of governance, the development of an imagination for the future, the willingness to let go of earlier identities when conditions change, the importance of relationship building and networking, of working with increasingly professionalized management—that are harder to acquire" (Erakovic and McMorland 2009).

The requirement that directors personally donate to the organizations they govern and/or be the driving force in the NGO's fundraising appears to be much less pronounced in Australia and Aotearoa New Zealand than in, say, the United States. Just 39% of directors reported donating to their organizations in one Australian study (AICD 2015). Most Australian and Aotearoa New Zealand NGOs (89%) surveyed by

Grant Thornton (2016) said they did not follow the so-called American model. Nevertheless, in the same survey, 19% of NGO directors gave a personal donation, 32% introduced associates for funding, and 32% were active in fundraising campaigns.

In recent years, various funders and regulators in both countries have emphasized a changing parade of important issues that demand attention, such as risk management, conflicts of interest, child protection, and health and safety. While each of these issues is important, no entity can pay increasing attention to each item of an ever-lengthening list of concerns. In practice, this "crowded curriculum" may merely have the effect of rapid and unhelpful swings of attention from the previous priority to the latest, without sufficient focus, when many directors are already complaining that expectations around their voluntary contributions as directors are excessive (Erakovic and McMorland 2009; Grant 2006).

BOARD COMPOSITION, ROTATION, AND RECRUITMENT

NGO boards in Australia and Aotearoa New Zealand tend to have fewer members than those of, say, the United States. An average board size of no more than 10 directors has been reported in numerous studies in both of the countries (Erakovic and McMorland 2009; Haigh 2008; Passey 2004; Rowe 2014; Woodward and Marshall 2004), whereas in the United States the average size is 15 (BoardSource 2017). Directors are overwhelmingly volunteers (80 to 92%, although they may be reimbursed for expenses) (AICD 2014; Grant Thornton 2016; Woodward and Marshall 2004. Paid directorships, however, are increasingly common for not-for-profit hospitals and some other large institutions.

Information on the demographic composition of boards is generally not robust, so the following data should also be treated with caution. For gender, the figures vary markedly, ranging from just 26% of directors being women to 70% (AICD 2016; McDonald 1993; Wiseman 2002; Woodward and Marshall 2004). It is possible that there is considerable skewing in relation to gender, with women more likely to serve on the boards of smaller or less prestigious organizations (see the discussion of differences in rates for paid directors for men and women reported in AICD 2016). Averages can also hide considerable variety. In one small study of 12 Aotearoa New Zealand NGOs (Haigh 2008), while overall 40% of directors were women, half of the NGOs had a gender-balanced board, one was female dominated, and just under half were male dominated.

In relation to age, Australian studies show that directors, on average, are around 56 years old (AICD 2016; McDonald 1993). In Aotearoa New Zealand NGOs, 80% of directors were 40 to 69 years old, and a further 12% were 70 to 79 years old (Erakovic and McMorland 2009); Haigh (2008) also found directors to be mostly over 50 years of age.

Generally, directors were found to be tertiary educated, ranging from 50 to 72% (Erakovic and McMorland 2009; McDonald 1993; Wiseman 2002) and disproportionately from a business or professional background (Haigh 2008; McDonald 1993; Wiseman 2002). There are exceptions, with Haigh (2008) finding that some organizations in his small sample (often NGOs smaller in size and more local in focus) had more directors with community development experience and fewer with business and professional backgrounds.

Directors can be elected by the membership, appointed by the board itself, be nominees of an external entity (for example, of a senior cleric in a faith-based organization), or a combination of these. Most directors are elected by the members themselves: In 63% of Australian companies limited by guarantee, 80% or more of directors are elected by the members (Woodward and Marshall 2004). However, elections are rarely contested (64%) or only sometimes contested (20%) (Woodward and Marshall 2004).

Indeed, consistent with a range of evidence from overseas, 29% of organizations reported they had experienced difficulty recruiting directors (Woodward and Marshall 2004) (this is also consistent with the in-depth case studies reported in Hough 2009). Even in charitable trusts in Aotearoa New Zealand, in which positions are commonly appointed by the remaining directors rather than elected by any membership or constituency, three out of four reported they had vacancies in one small survey (Haigh 2008).

In relation to length of service, 44% of directors in one Australian study had been on their board for more than five years (McDonald 1993); in an Aotearoa New Zealand sample, 60% of directors had been on their board more than seven years (Erakovic and McMorland 2009).

Such length of service is not surprising given difficulties filling vacancies. In less prestigious boards, the criteria for appointment to a directorship are sometimes simply possessing a pulse and being willing to serve, rather than anything more rigorous. However, other organizations invest considerable time and energy into attracting directors who are skilled, and sometimes additionally seek to reflect the diversity of the community served. Some Australian organizations seek Aboriginal or Torres Strait Islander people to serve on their boards, and some Aotearoa New Zealand organizations seek Māori and Pacific Islander directors (Haigh 2008). In some sectors, especially mental health, HIV/AIDS, and disability organizations, inclusion of people with lived experience of the health condition or disability is highly valued. Increasingly, there is also an interest in recruiting the next generation of younger directors.

Rotation requirements associated with term limits are probably not common for Australia and Aotearoa New Zealand NGO boards. However, there are exceptions, such as in our casestudy organization, discussed later in the chapter.

BOARD'S RELATIONSHIP WITH THE CEO AND OTHER STAFF

As noted earlier, most NGOs do not have a CEO, nor any paid staff. The boards of these organizations are likely to be working boards, and suggestions that boards should focus on governing and not on managing are unhelpful to these organizations. The discussion that follows in this section is focused on those organizations with a CEO. While the term CEO is used, in small organizations the most senior staff role is often titled manager or coordinator.

Overwhelmingly, directors in Australian and Aotearoa New Zealand are nonexecutive (that is, they are not also paid managers): One Australian study reported that 77% of NGO boards had no executive directors (Woodward and Marshall 2004). The same study identified that a further 18% of NGOs had a majority of nonexecutive directors, and it is likely that for many organizations it was just the CEO who was an executive member of the board and in many cases did not have voting rights. Overwhelmingly, the boards were not chaired by the CEO; this was true for 91% of the organizations. Where the board chair was an executive, this was most commonly in religious organizations.

Given that boards in the two countries are overwhelmingly independent of the CEO and other management, the relationship between the CEO and the board—and especially the board chair—is often considered one of the most critical relationships in an organization. Some 92% of directors and 95% of CEOs in an Aotearoa New Zealand survey agreed or strongly agreed that the chair of his or her board had a good working relationship with the CEO (Erakovic and McMorland 2009). Less flatteringly, among health and disability NGOs Rowe (2014) found the area of least satisfaction in interpersonal effectiveness was the balance of power between the CEO, the chair, the other directors, and the organization: Only 77% tended to agree or strongly agreed that there was an adequate balance. Most respondents (80%) in one Australian survey also reported there was good role clarity between the board and CEO (AICD 2014). However, around 20% of respondents in that survey reported that role clarity was "poor" or "fair." Anecdotal evidence is that achieving role clarity and a good working relationship continues to challenge some boards and some CEOs, with clashes sometimes receiving extensive media coverage or resulting in cases before courts, workers' compensation tribunals, or industrial tribunals (the latter having jurisdiction for hearing alleged cases of bullying of CEOs by directors). Of course, a relationship based on misplaced trust can also foster allegations of corruption and malfeasance against the CEO (Independent Commission against Corruption 2017).

ORGANIZATION OF MEETINGS AND CULTURE OF INQUIRY

Anecdotal evidence is that most organizations have a single layer of governance, although dual-layer systems can be found in some religious organizations and political parties. Boards only have authority collectively, so they generally work by meeting. Monthly meetings were the most common choice made by boards in the two countries (Erakovic and McMorland 2009; Passey 2004; Woodward and Marshall 2004). The next most common choice was quarterly meetings (Passey 2004; Woodward and Marshall 2004). Increasingly, the authors have observed that the boards of large and medium-sized NGOs meet face-to-face less often and make increasing use of information and communication technologies, sometimes with significant improvements in the transparency of processes and the quality of decision-making.

In one Australian survey, 46% of organizations reported that they had a subgroup, such as an executive committee, and 50% reported the use of board committees (Woodward and Marshall 2004). It is likely that the use of board committees increases with an organization's financial size, with committees often used for finance and audit, risk, governance, and executive remuneration (AICD 2013; Erakovic and McMorland 2009; Governance Institute of Australia 2016).

Consistent with the sequential cultural attribute identified earlier, most boards use agendas, take minutes, and use routines of decision-making by formal motion. In reality, few but the largest and/or most conflicted boards and organizations rigorously apply formal meeting procedure, and discussions tend to be oriented to building consensus. The available evidence is that 91% use some form of consensus decision-making (Woodward and Marshall 2004), despite the dominant cultural attributes of individualism and achievement identified earlier. Consensus decision-making can work to improve deliberation and decisions by drawing on the diversity of directors' insights, or it can generate poorer decisions if misapplied as a form of so-called group think, especially where there are dominant chairs or directors (Davis 1992; Janis 1972).

Only one survey (Rowe 2014) asked directors about the performance of chairs, with most tending to agree or strongly agree their chair "really knows how to run a meeting" (84%) and "has a good handle in carrying out the role of the chair" (89%). This is perhaps a surprising result, given that few boards deliberately invest time, skills, or resources in their own facilitation skills (Kaner et al. 2014). Instead, chairs are largely expected to pick up the necessary skills by osmosis, while having a conflicting array of other responsibilities.

While there is no equivalent to the United States' authoritative *Robert's Rules of Order*, it appears that most boards in Australia and Aotearoa New Zealand voluntarily adopt a watered-down version of Westminster parliamentary procedures (as documented by Renton 2005). Some organizations embrace more participatory styles of deliberation and decision-making, which are sometimes influenced by feminist values or by Indigenous culture and aims to operate more collectively and reduce distinctions between the governing and other parts of the organization. The prevalence of this approach appears to have decreased in recent years, with a number of feminist and other collectives converting to more conventional hierarchical or hybrid structures (Campbell 2011).

Board culture is challenging to define and assess, and it is thus not surprising that there is little published data on the topic. Rowe (2014) found almost all trustees report that when they or fellow trustees "feel uncomfortable about a decision, they are confident about speaking up" (92%). The limited survey evidence is that the quality of governance is improving, with 37% of directors reporting that it is "somewhat" better and 43% reporting that it is "much" better than three years ago (AICD 2016). Governance issues are only highlighted as an issue of significant concern in the sector by a minority of Australian and Aotearoa New Zealand NGOs (Grant Thornton 2014). Interestingly, in the 2014 Grant Thornton survey the smaller the organization is in revenue, the less governance was deemed a concern. Anecdotal evidence is consistent with the survey results of satisfactory governance, although there remain complaints about some boards or individual directors, ranging from that they are disengaged and ineffectual, through to that they are engaged but misdirected or even hostile.

Anecdotal evidence is that boards of medium and large organizations increasingly use consent agendas, whereby recommendations in board papers that are noncontroversial are adopted without further discussion. There is also anecdotal evidence that such boards are increasingly using so-called annual agendas to structure and prioritize the work of the board across the year (Lorsch and MacIver 1989).

EVALUATION AND MONITORING

As part of the rise in specialist consulting firms, professional institutes, and academic centers with an interest in NGO governance, the use of board evaluation instruments has increased, with some locally developed instruments (Nicholson, Newton, and McGregor-Lowndes 2012) and some adapted from overseas. Only two surveys inquired about board evaluation. In one survey, 56% of respondents reported that they "review their effectiveness as a board at least once a year," although only 23% reported that they conducted exit interviews with departing trustees (Rowe 2014). In another survey, 44% of NGOs reported that they evaluated their own performance (Grant Thornton 2006). However, it is likely that much evaluation and monitoring remains informal.

ETHICAL CHALLENGES

Five issues will be considered next for NGO boards in the two countries: Preventing the abuse and neglect of children and other vulnerable people, membership and representation, inclusive practices for women and minorities, balancing mission and financial sustainability, and what might increasingly be described as existential dilemmas going to the core reasons why organizations exist.

The need to prevent and respond to abuse and neglect of children and other vulnerable people is not controversial; however, recent formal inquiries have identified that some boards and CEOs have been deficient in their response (Royal Commission into Institutional Responses to Child Sexual Abuse 2014; The Senate Community Affairs References Committee, 2015). The Australian Royal Commission on child sex abuse notes that "child safe institutions begin with leadership, governance and culture" and that "rigid and overly hierarchical governance disconnects those governing from regular contact with staff, parents and children" (Royal Commission into Institutional Responses to Child Sexual Abuse 2014, 141). An Australian Senate inquiry into the abuse of people with disability in care, including in NGO settings, has recommended that boards be legally obliged to maintain appropriate standards to help prevent abuse and to respond to it when it is reported. This recommendation is reflected in legislation currently before the Australian Parliament.

A second area of ethical dilemma for NGOs is the role given to membership. Conflicts within the memberships of NGOs have been a source of weakness for some organizations, wasting scarce resources and distracting from fulfilling the mission. However, in other organizations an open membership has had preventative and corrective effects on self-serving and even corrupt actions by CEOs and boards. Interestingly, in an Aotearoa New Zealand survey, more than a third of managers "strongly agreed that their board was not accountable to any other body than itself" (raising the question of relationships with members, beneficiaries, staff, or other stakeholders) (Erakovic and McMorland 2009, 12). More generally, one societal role that many NGOs in both countries have historically played is related to allowing ordinary citizens to join as members, to voice issues and concerns, to act on issues of importance to them, and to vote in board elections. NGO membership potentially provides an education in democracy, allowing members to build skills and gain influence, potentially strengthening social cohesion and social capital (Guo, Metelsky, and Bradshaw, 2014; Skocpol 2003). This opportunity can be especially important for the socially and economically disadvantaged, for women, and for minorities. To the extent that NGO governance involves closed memberships and self-perpetuating boards, these opportunities are sometimes lost. Each NGO needs to decide what the appropriate solution to this dilemma is for its organization in the context of its mission (Maier and Meyer 2011).

A third dilemma—one related to the second one—concerns including women and minorities on governing boards. In Australia, this includes ensuring that Aboriginal and Torres Strait Islander people are included in the work of organizations; in Aotearoa New Zealand, inclusion of Māori and Pacific Islanders is a concern for many NGOs (Haigh 2008). However, a single person usually does not speak for a community, and genuine inclusion of women and minorities involves more than tokenism. There have been efforts to develop culturally appropriate governance practices, especially for Māori in Aotearoa New Zealand, by the adoption of a so-called two-house model (sometimes called a three-house model, referencing the joint place where both parties come back together to make decisions): Māori can meet using Māori culture, custom, protocols, and likewise non-Māori can meet using their cultures (Community Sector Taskforce 2006; Margaret 2016). Some of the better-known examples include the Methodist Church of New Zealand/*Te Haahi Weteriana o Aotearoa*, the Anglican Church in Aotearoa New Zealand and Polynesia/*Te Haahi Mihinare ki Aotearoa ki Nui Tireni, ki Ngā Moutere o te Moana Nui a Kiwa*, the Tangata Whenua, Community & Voluntary Sector Research Centre, the National Collective of Women's Refuges/*Ngā Whare Wakaruruhau o Aotearoa*, and the Adult and Community Education Aotearoa. There has also been work to develop and promote Māori governance frameworks for Māori-run organizations. For example, Penehira, Cram, and Pipi (2003) developed a three-part model that combines Māori principles and critical-practice issues. The first principle, *Hinengaro*, is about understanding Māori and Western paradigms in a Māori context, including ensuring that the voice of kaumatua (the elder) is heard. The second principle, *Ngākau*, involves demonstrating clarity of purpose and passion, and responding to challenges of power and accountability with clear analysis of external relations to government. Finally, the principle of *Tinana* involves aligning operations with organizational values and philosophies, including appreciating the potential overlap and reciprocity between governance and management.

Another consideration for community service organizations is that boards increasingly have to balance the organization's mission with commercial considerations. There are divergent factors creating this challenge. Through contracting processes or public criticism, some governments have sought to influence the conduct of NGOs and their willingness to advocate (Elliott and Haigh 2013; Grey and Sedgwick 2013; Onyx et al. 2010). Also, governments are increasingly using personalization approaches to service delivery and its funding, withdrawing direct funding from NGOs and instead allocating funds to consumers to allow them to purchase from the providers of their choice. Thus, community service NGOs subject to personalized funding regimes might now be regarded as social enterprises. Boards will find maintaining commitment to mission easier if the organization starts with a strong asset base; however, some boards have to prioritize financial considerations over mission for survival of their organization.

Finally, another area of ethical challenge is starting to emerge, which might be described as an existential challenge, as it goes to the very reasons that an NGO might exist. This is most obvious for community service NGOs operating in personalized funding regimes, such as in disability services or community aged care, but can also apply in other areas such as international aid (Werker and Ahmed 2008). The dilemma is best illustrated by example. Historically, disability service NGOs used funding—primarily from governments—to employ workers to provide support to people with disability. Now government funds people with disability to employ workers to provide the support that they need, meaning that workers might—or might not—be employed by an NGO. For savvy and capable consumers, is there a need for the NGO at all, given that technology platforms allow the person with disability and the worker to engage with each other directly? Of course, not all people are savvy and capable, but many are. NGOs need to genuinely add value for the person with disability and for the worker; otherwise, arguably, they should get out the way.

GOVERNANCE TRENDS

This chapter concludes by examining governance trends. Given the absence of robust data drawn from randomized samples and repeated across time, the discussion of governance trends that follows is more speculative than authoritative. However, there can be reasonable confidence that the last 30 years has seen significant improvements in awareness of governance issues in NGOs in the two countries. As identified earlier, those years have seen the rise of a mini-industry devoted to improving governance practice.

There can also be confidence that NGOs—especially, but not only, the more economically significant—have sought to improve the commercial acumen of their boards. For NGOs with government funding, there have been increases in that funding as a result of governments divesting services, although the latest trend towards personalization has sometimes resulted in funding going to the consumer first. As identified earlier, trends towards contracting and personalization can raise ethical dilemmas for NGO boards about the balancing of mission and commercial considerations.

We can speculate that boards of the more economically significant NGOs have probably increased their sophistication and focus. This focus has sometimes resulted from using simple strategies such as consent agendas, annual agendas, and performance dashboards, but it has also benefited from investment in board portals and apps.

There appears to be several structural changes occurring in NGO governance in both countries, most notably among the more economically significant NGOs, including the move away from local branches to more unified national structures, from larger to smaller boards, and from democratically elected boards to self-perpetuating, skills-based boards. When allied with the trend towards commercialization, these changes can sometimes result in degenerating social capital, including losses in local community engagement and in civic skills development (Nowland-Foreman 1998).

A final trend might be a paradoxical change in the respect accorded to NGO boards by government, media, and the community. On the one hand, there is evidence that governments and funders consider NGOs to be key stakeholders in society and recognize the important work that boards undertake. On the other hand, boards are increasingly subject to scrutiny by government, media, and the community and merely seeking to do good is no longer good enough. Nowhere is this more evident, and arguably more deserved, than in relation to historical responses by some NGOs to the sexual abuse of children when in their care.

The case study of Oxfam Australia will allow exploration of how one organization's understanding of what constituted good or best practice changed across time. It moved from a belief that a state and membership-based system of electing directors was best practice to believing a nominated board with a blend of skills and experience was best. It adopted Policy Governance® (a specific model for governing organizations) in the late 1990s, believing it was superior to previous practice. However, more than a decade later, it "happily" moved away from Policy Governance® to an approach to governance not based on a model but still rigorous. This is consistent with the view that organizations find it difficult to sustain Carver's Policy Governance® in the long term (see the views canvased in Hough 2002) and is also consistent with the suggestion that what makes a difference to board effectiveness is the use of *any* thoughtful approach to improved governance rather than one particular approach (Nobbie and Brudney 2003).

While so-called prescriptive board literature may be promoting a particular convergence of ideas on what constitutes best practice, there remains a remarkable divergence in actual practice (Steane 2001). When someone asserts that a particular approach represents best practice, directors might ask on what basis is it best; that is, what criteria are being used? There are numerous criteria on which board effectiveness could be assessed, including the use of recommended practices, director opinion, stakeholder opinion, or the board's impact on organizational performance. Further, what is the evidence that a particular practice is indeed best? Is this mere opinion, based on limited experience? It is also important to consider for whom this is best—communities and ultimate beneficiaries, members, funders and donors, managers, or other stakeholders? Is there is a vested interest in promoting a particular conception of best practice, sometimes by consultants and sometimes by key individuals in organizations (Paton 2003)? Even where evidence exists, how transferable is that evidence from one context to another? Finally, are there trade-offs to be made between the different understandings of best practice? For example, as flagged earlier, is democratic election of a board by members sometimes at odds with attracting a skillful board, and if so, which is the preferred approach?

Perceived best practices might result from the noted tendency of organizations operating in the same field to resemble each other over time, what is known in the academic literature by the rather grand title of *institutional isomorphism* (DiMaggio and Powell 1983). This tendency *might* result from the copied practices and structures that truly represent some elements of best practice, for example, because they are economically efficient. However, this tendency can also be the result of myths that maintain appearances and validate individuals and organizations. The academic literature identifies three forces that encourage organizations to copy what other organizations do. First, there are coercive requirements, such as those imposed by the law or by funders. Second, there can be forces of mimicry, for example, the calls for NGOs to be more businesslike, with the assumption that businesslike practices are good in themselves. Finally, professional forces can operate, including the professionalization of management, the promotion of standards of practice, and directors and managers' involvement with trade and professional associations, and with consultants.

To conclude, there is considerable diversity in NGOs in Australia and Aotearoa New Zealand. Much of the research reported has focused on medium and large organizations rather than smaller ones. Despite an avalanche of advice to NGO boards, the advice on what constitutes best practice has grown faster than the research to evaluate it. What constitutes best practice is likely to vary by size of the organization governed, by the sector of its operation, and especially by the criteria used to make the assessment. Directors should be open to ideas about improving practice, but cautious about accepting universal prescriptions.

CASE STUDY: OXFAM AUSTRALIA

To illustrate how one NGO has developed its governance practices, Oxfam Australia (OAU), an international aid organization, is provided as a case study. The case study provides insights into how notions of best practice in governance change across time, and how one large NGO has adapted its governance in response to continued growth and changing expectations.

OAU's vision is to create "a just world without poverty" (OAU 2014, 6). Oxfam works "to find practical, innovative ways for people to lift themselves out of poverty and thrive. We save lives and help rebuild livelihoods when crisis strikes. And we campaign so that the voices of the poor influence the local and global decisions that affect them" (OAU 2016, 2).

OAU began in 1953 as a church-affiliated local group that sent weekly donations to a small health project in India. Eventually local groups formed across Australia to collect money and help implement programs. It adopted the name Community Aid Abroad in 1962. It merged with the organization Freedom from Hunger in 1992. As a member of Oxfam International, it subsequently adopted the name Oxfam Australia.

OAU is widely regarded as one of Australia's most progressive charities, long disavowing child-sponsorship models of fundraising and international aid, and having a significant role in advocating for fairer public policy. It now has an annual turnover of over US$86.84 million, of which over US$35.53 million comes from donations from the public. It is the second largest international aid charity in Australia (Cortis et al. 2016).

OAU and Oxfam New Zealand are members of Oxfam International (OI), a confederation of 20 Oxfam agencies that reaches more than 22 million people in 85 countries (OAU 2016). OI is increasingly influential in defining the scope and work of its affiliates. It has set six external change goals and six enabling goals that have been adopted by OAU in its strategic plan. Under OI's 2020 Initiative, OI and its affiliates—having evolved from the Global North countries[5]—will reposition itself towards Global South countries. When providing support in the South, rather than having multiple affiliates working in one country with overlapping interventions and associated inefficiencies, OI will "empower our country teams to set one strategy that reflects local needs and local change agendas" (Byanyima 2015). As part of the reorientation to the South, OI will support new Oxfam affiliates in India, South Africa, Brazil, and Mexico.

However, back to OAU and its board. OAU is governed by a board of 14 people, all of whom serve on a voluntary basis. The organization is led by Dennis Goldner as board chair, a former partner of an international management consulting firm and now semiretired, and by CEO

Dr. Helen Szoke, who first achieved public prominence in her former role of Australia's race discrimination commissioner.

OAU's governance arrangements are influenced by its accreditation body, the Australian Council for International Development (ACFID). OAU observes the ACFID code of conduct and the associated quality system (ACFID 2016, 2017). The quality system includes 11 detailed obligations in relation to governance.

Governance Trends

There have been two major changes in OAU's governance over the years. First, there has been a move to a skills-based board. Consistent with its foundation in grassroots, citizen-based action, in the past OAU's governance was structured around state-level membership-based committees, which elected directors to the national board. The state committees were once bastions of community and organizational engagement, but sometimes controversial, as appears common in federal structures (Widmer and Houchin 1999). In 2012, under a previous board, OAU's board composition moved to a modified form of a nominated board, with new directors being selected by existing directors for their skills and experience, on the advice of a nominations committee. Members are no longer involved in electing the board but have the right to attend the annual general meeting. Members and other supporters remain involved in support and advocacy through the organization's community engagement activities.

Second, in the late 1990s the organization adopted the Policy Governance® model (Carver 2006; Carver and Carver 2006) to focus the work of the board more on governance of the organization than management.[6] Carver's model posits that the work of the board is to state the "ends," or outcomes, the organization is to achieve, to delegate by using an "executive limitations" or "thou shalt not" approach rather by than telling management the means that must be used, to link with the organization's legal and moral owners, and to assure that the organization performs as wanted.

In 2016, the board moved away from the Carver model. Helen states she found the Carver model "really impossible to work with" and Carver's limitation approach to delegation to be "clunky." Dennis says that the limitations approach to delegation did not "come naturally to me." The board's new governance policies include a board charter as the overarching document, a risk-appetite statement, and other supporting documents. In relation to reporting, Helen much prefers the new four-stream reporting arrangements, consisting of reports about finance, about risk management, a strategic update, and a report against the organization's business plan. She states she is very happy with the reporting framework, observing that "it gives me a much clearer line of accountability and frames the board's role very clearly."

Legal Status

OAU is a not-for-profit company limited by guarantee. It is a registered charity with the Australian Charities and Not-for-Profits Commission, and thus it must comply with the ACNC governance standards. OAU's income, and that of its wholly-owned subsidiary, Oxfam Australia Trading, is exempt from tax. All donations to Oxfam over US$1.55 are tax deductible for the donor. As a PBI, Oxfam can also offer tax-effective salary packaging to staff. As an organization that operates in all Australian states and territories, it is subject to the fundraising law of each jurisdiction.

The Role of the Board

In the board charter (OAU 2017, 1), the board states that it "bears ultimate responsibility for the Company achieving the purposes for which it exists" and that its role is to provide "leadership and strategic governance," including by determining the organization's purposes and beliefs; reviewing and approving plans, budgets, and initiatives, and monitoring organizational performance; and by recruiting and supporting the chief executive. However, as will become apparent, the directors are not passive observers.

Board Composition, Rotations, and Recruitment

Dennis observes that the move to a skills-based board resulted from the growth of the organization, with the previous state-based representative model having become "unwieldy" for an organization of Oxfam's size. Dennis also observes that a member-elected model based on just a few thousand members was "a bit otiose" given the organization's need to be responsive to hundreds of thousands of donors and other supporters.

Directors are selected for their skill sets and their links to other sectors, with an emphasis on complementing skills of existing directors, using a skills matrix framework. Diversity is also a consideration. Directors are generally appointed for staggered terms of four years and may serve a maximum of 12 consecutive years. The board elects the chair and deputy chair. Office bearers serve for two-year terms, for a maximum of six years. An elected "staff participant" and the CEO participate in board meetings, but they are not directors and hence do not vote in board decisions.

Board's Relationship with the CEO and Other Staff

When asked to describe the board's contribution to Oxfam's work, Dennis nominated as the first major contribution the employment and empowerment of Helen as CEO, stating that Helen is "a CEO in whom we have great faith and belief." Dennis suggested that the board makes a major contribution as a sounding board for the CEO, encouraging the CEO to discuss and test ideas. In addition, the board is stronger in the financial and business side of the organization's work than management. Further, the board adds to the management team's networks for resourcing, such as facilitating substantial pro bono contributions by management consultants or in investment advice, and to the organization's network of influence with government and the community.

Dennis states that he attaches "enormous importance" to the relationship with Helen; likewise Helen describes the relationship between the CEO and the board chair as "the most critical thing" for the organization's successful governance. Helen states that the relationship "needs to be robust, and needs to be one where the chief executive can be held to account ... Dennis makes it very clear what he thinks are the challenges for the organization and what my responsibilities are as chief executive and I value that enormously."

Both Dennis and Helen invest considerable time and energy in building a trusting relationship (as part of Dennis's average contribution of around two and a half days a week to his work as Oxfam's chair). At the start of each year, they meet for a couple of hours to talk about their individual and shared priorities for the year ahead. They meet in person for one-on-one discussions several times throughout the year. They talk by phone weekly, and communicate by email several times a week. Helen values Dennis's accessibility and his prompt responses.

The board has regular contact with other senior managers through the board's committee structure (discussed shortly) and the executives join sections of the board's meeting.

Organization of Meetings and Culture of Inquiry

The board generally meets in person six times a year, with teleconferences held as required. There is an annual program for meetings to focus the board's work across the year, with two sessions a year largely devoted to strategic issues, sometimes with external speakers. For example, the board has had strategic sessions to learn more about the organization's program work, to discuss immigration flows throughout the world and their implications for the organization's work, and to explore the implications of Big Data.[7]

The board meetings typically last six hours, which Dennis says allows "a good amount of time for discussion and debate." He comments that the board does not have a culture of "command and control," but has honest and open communication and respect for different views. Dennis further comments that the board includes directors who are "very frank and fearless." Much of the work is done prior to the meeting, "particularly on tough issues" says Dennis, often by committees. Directors come to the board meeting with well-formulated views about options, but not with decisions effectively having been made.

Board meetings begin in camera to discuss the meeting's proposed priorities and the time to be allocated to them, and to identify issues such as where the directors want clarification of information previously provided by management. The CEO then joins the meeting. A consent agenda is used to determine noncontroversial items, and then the main business items are discussed and decided. The concluding session again is in camera, and is used to reflect on what worked and what might be improved about the meeting.

In addition to the board meetings, directors participate in one or more of the board's subcommittees, namely those for finance, risk, and audit, public engagement, governance, nominations, and executive remuneration. These committees may also include other experts and are sometimes advised by external consultants, such as the consultant recently used by the Governance Committee. Both Dennis and Helen state that the committees play a very important role, allowing a "deeper dive" into the issues. Helen reports that she finds the Finance, Risk, and Audit Committee in particular to be "amazing" for the high quality of its input to the organization's work.

Decisions are usually made by an informal process to generate consensus. In the three years that Helen has been CEO, she does not recall the board needing to make a decision by a contested vote, despite the "frank and fearless contributions" of some directors reported by Dennis.

The organization has invested considerable time in developing performance indicators (against the strategic and business plans) and associated reporting systems. Driven by one director in particular, the organization increasingly uses dashboard and traffic light graphics for reporting (Butler 2012), with some (but less) emphasis on narrative explanation. One exception is reporting on programs, where Dennis states it is difficult to rely on metrics alone and inevitably there is more reliance on narrative reporting. Dennis believes that the board reports must also be useful to management. As part of the reporting regime, the board receives a report against the business plan each quarter. Every two years, the board examines outcome data.

For matters requiring decision, Helen states that she ensures that the board papers are "business ready and decision ready." Helen says that has taken some effort to achieve.

The business of the board is enabled by technology. Each director is issued an iPad with a specialist governance app. Through the app, directors can access resources, including current and past agenda papers.

Evaluation and Monitoring

OAU evaluates each board meeting in an in-camera session at the meeting's end. Dennis states the discussion is focused on "'How was it for you?' I take notes. I'm pretty silent then myself and I listen to the board members' views about what went well and what didn't go well, either in relation to management responses to the issues at hand or in relation to my chairing of the meeting."

Further, under the board's charter, the performance of individual directors is regularly reviewed, and a formal assessment of the board is undertaken at least every two years, with an external assessment every four years.

Ethical Dilemmas

OAU faces dilemmas about how it realizes its values about empowerment. These can be considered from two perspectives, one national and one international, and are perhaps paradoxical in nature. The organization's internal governance has moved away from an emphasis on a board composed of ordinary members involved in local groups and state committees, and elected directors, to the nominations model, which seeks a blend of skills, experience, and networks. Dennis acknowledges that some of the organization's traditional supporters feel disenfranchised, as the board is no longer legally accountable to the membership through the voting process. However, Dennis states that the new model has resulted in greater diversity in the board, especially in terms of the diversity of skills and experience, by increasing diversity in connections to communities, business, and the political arm of government, and by promoting diversity in demographic composition beyond its traditional membership base. For example, as board chair, Dennis deliberately sought to increase the organization's influence with the conservative Liberal-National federal government, by recruiting to the board a former Liberal member of parliament.[8]

From an international perspective, OAU has been instrumental in reorienting the work of OI and its affiliates from countries in the North to empowering the NGOs in the South. As Dennis states, "If you are going to do work in the South you have to give a voice [to] and empower the South as well." OAU has resolved its dilemmas about who to empower by prioritizing giving voice and power to the South over giving voting rights to its membership.

ACKNOWLEDGMENTS

The authors acknowledge the contributions of Professor Myles McGregor-Lowndes, OAM and Leonie Morgan, AM in reviewing the Australian content. They also acknowledge the assistance of Dennis Goldner and Dr. Helen Szoke of Oxfam Australia. Responsibility for any errors in the content remains with the authors.

REFERENCES

Australian Council for International Development (ACFID). 2016. *Revised Code of Conduct*. Australian Council for International Development

Australian Council for International Development (ACFID). 2017. *Code of Conduct: Quality Assurance Framework*. Australian Council for International Development.

Australian Institute of Company Directors (AICD). 2013. *Good Governance Principles and Guidance for Not-for-Profit Organisations*. Australian Institute of Company Directors.

Australian Institute of Company Directors (AICD). 2014. *NFP Governance and Performance Study 2014*. Australian Institute of Company Directors.

Australian Institute of Company Directors (AICD). 2015. *NFP Governance and Performance Study 2015*. Australian Institute of Company Directors.

Australian Institute of Company Directors (AICD). 2016. *NFP Governance and Performance Study 2016*. Australian Institute of Company Directors.

Australian Bureau of Statistics. 2015. *Non-profit Institutions Satellite Account, 2012–13* (Catalogue 5256.0). Australian National Accounts, Australian Bureau of Statistics.

Australian Bureau of Statistics QuickStats (database). 2017. 2016 Census Data Summary: Aboriginal and Torres Strait Islander population. www.abs.gov.au/websitedbs/D3310114.nsf/Home/2016%20QuickStats (accessed July 2017).

Australian Charities and Not-for-Profits Commission (ACNC). 2017. "Red tape reduction" (web page). www.acnc.gov.au/ACNC/About_ACNC/Redtape_redu/ACNC/Report/Red_tape.aspx.

Barraket, Jo, Nick Collyer, Matt O'Connor, and Heather Anderson. 2010. *Finding Australia's Social Enterprise Sector: Final Report*. Australian Centre for Philanthropy and Nonprofit Studies, Queensland University of Technology.

BoardSource. 2017. *Leading with Intent: A National Index of Nonprofit Board Practices*. BoardSource.

Butler, Lawrence M. 2012. *The Nonprofit Dashboard: Using Metrics to Drive Mission Success*, 2nd ed. BoardSource.

Byanyima, Winnie. 2015. "Transforming Oxfam." *Disrupt & Innovate (blog)*. www.disrupt-and-innovate.org/transforming-oxfam (accessed June 10, 2017).

Campbell, Brenda. 2011. *Governance in the Collective Context: A Study of Two Approaches*. Massey University.

Carver, John. 2006. *Boards That Make a Difference: A New Design for Leadership in Nonprofit and Public Organizations*, 3rd ed. Jossey-Bass.

Carver, John, and Miriam Mayhew Carver. 2006. *Reinventing Your Board: A Step-By-Step Guide to Implementing Policy Governance*, 2nd ed. Jossey-Bass.

Chelliah, John, Martijn Boersma, and Alice Klettmer. 2016. "Governance challenges for not-for-profit organisations: empirical evidence in support of a contingency approach." *Contemporary Management Research* 12, no. 2: 3–24.

Community Sector Taskforce. 2006. *A New Way of Working for the Tangata Whenua, Community and Voluntary Sector in Aotearoa/New Zealand*. Community Sector Taskforce.

Cornforth, Chris. 1996. "Governing non-profit organisations: heroic myths and human tales." Paper. Public Interest and Non-profit Management Research Unit, Open University.

Cortis, N., A. Young, A. Powell, et al. 2016. *Australian Charities Report 2015*. Centre for Social Impact and the Social Policy Research Centre, University of New South Wales.

Davis, James H. 1992. "Some compelling intuitions about group consensus decisions, theoretical and empirical research, and interpersonal aggregation phenomena: selected examples, 1950–1990." *Organizational Behavior and Human Decision Processes* 2, no. 1: 3–38.

DiMaggio, Paul J., and Walter W. Powell. 1983. "The iron cage revisited: institutional isomorphism and collective rationality in organization fields." *American Sociological Review* 48, no. 2: 147–160.

Elliott, S., and D. Haigh. 2013. "Advocacy in the New Zealand not-for-profit sector: nothing stands by itself." *Third Sector Review* 19, no. 2: 157–178.

Erakovic, Ljiljana, and Judith McMorland. 2009. "Perceptions of 'good governance' in New Zealand non-profit organisations." *Third Sector Review* 15, no. 2: 125–148.

Governance Institute of Australia. 2016. *Good Governance Guide: Board Structure: Not-for-Profit Sector*. Governance Institute of Australia.

Grant, Suzanne. 2006. "Community (not-for-profit) governance—what are some of the issues?" *Third Sector Review* 12, no. 1: 39–56.

Grant Thornton. 2006. *New Zealand Not-for-Profit Sector Survey 2005*. Grant Thornton New Zealand.

Grant Thornton. 2010. *Pressing Issues Impacting New Zealand's Not-for-Profit Sector Survey 2009/2010*. Grant Thornton New Zealand.

Grant Thornton. 2014. *Doing Good and Doing It Well? Grant Thornton Australia and New Zealand Not-for-Profit Sector Survey 2013/2014*. Grant Thornton New Zealand.

Grant Thornton. 2015. *Not-for-Profits: Are You Ready for the Future? Findings from Our Not-for-Profit Financial Literacy Survey*. Grant Thornton New Zealand.

Grant Thornton. 2016. *The Challenge of Change: Not-For-Profit Sector Survey 2015/2016*. Grant Thornton New Zealand.

Grey, S., and C. Sedgwick. 2013. "The contract state and constrained democracy: the community and voluntary sector under threat." *Policy Quarterly* 9, no. 3: 3–10.

Guo, Chao, Barbara A. Metelsky, and Patricia Bradshaw. 2014. "Out of the shadows: nonprofit governance research from a democratic and critical perspective." In *Nonprofit Governance: Innovative Perspectives and Approaches*, edited by Chris Cornforth and William A. Brown, 47–67. Routledge.

Haigh, David. 2008. Governance of Not-for-Profit Organisations in Auckland and Christchurch. Report. Social and Civic Policy Institute, and Unitec New Zealand.

Hough, Alan D. 2002. "The policy governance model: a critical examination." Working Paper No. CPNS 6. Centre for Philanthropy and Nonprofit Studies, Queensland University of Technology.

Hough, Alan D. 2009. "How nonprofit boards monitor, judge and influence organisational performance" (PhD thesis, School of Accountancy, Queensland University of Technology).

Independent Commission Against Corruption. 2017. "NSW Health and the Department of Family and Community Services—allegations concerning the former CEO of the Immigrant Women's Health Service and the Non-English Speaking Housing Women's Scheme Inc. (Operation Tarlo)" (web page). www.icac.nsw.gov.au/investigations/current-investigations/investigationdetail/221(accessed June 19, 2017).

Janis, Irving L. 1972. *Victims of Groupthink: A Psychological Study of Foreign-Policy Decisions And Fiascos*. Houghton Mifflin.

Kaner, Sam, Lenny Lind, Catherine Toldi, et al. 2014. *Facilitator's Guide to Participatory Decision-Making*. Jossey-Bass.

Law Commission. 2006. *Waka Umanga: A Proposed Law for Māori Governance Entities*. Law Commission.

Law Commission. 2013. *A New Act for Incorporated Societies*. Law Commission.

Lorsch, Jay William, and Elizabeth MacIver. 1989. *Pawns or Potentates: The Reality of America's Corporate Boards*. Harvard Business School Press.

Maier, Florentine, and Michael Meyer. 2011. "Managerial and beyond: discourses of civil society organization and their governance implications." *Voluntas* 22, no. 4: 731–756.

Margaret, Jen. 2016. *Ngā Rerenga o Te Tiriti: Community Organisations Engaging with the Treaty of Waitangi*. Guide. Treaty Resource Centre.

McDonald, Catherine. 1993. "Board members' involvement in nonprofit governance." *Working Paper 16*. Brisbane, Australia: Queensland University of Technology Program on Nonprofit Corporations.

McGregor-Lowndes, Myles. 1995. "Nonprofit corporations—reflections on Australia's largest nonprofit insolvency." *Australian Journal of Corporate Law* 5, no. 4: 417–441.

Nicholson, Gavin, Cameron Newton, and Myles McGregor-Lowndes. 2012. "The nonprofit board as a team: pilot results and initial insights." *Nonprofit Management and Leadership* 22, no. 4: 461–481.

Nobbie, Patricia Dautel, and Jeffrey L. Brudney. 2003. "Testing the implementation, board performance, and organizational effectiveness of the Policy Governance model in nonprofit boards of directors." *Nonprofit and Voluntary Sector Quarterly* 32, no. 4: 571–595.

Nowland-Foreman, Garth. 1998. "Purchase-of-Service contracting, voluntary organizations and civil society: dissecting the goose that lays the golden eggs?" *American Behavioral Scientist* 42, no. 1: 108–123.

NZ Navigator (online assessment tool). 2017. www.nznavigator.org.nz (accessed June 2017).

Onyx, J., L. Armitage, B. Dalton, et al. 2010. "Advocacy with gloves on: the "manners" of strategy used by some third sector organizations undertaking advocacy in NSW and Queensland." *Voluntas* 21, no. 1: 41–61.

Oxfam Australia (OAU). 2014. *The Power Of People Against Poverty: Strategic Plan 2014–2019*. Oxfam Australia.

Oxfam Australia (OAU). 2016. *Annual Report*. Oxfam Australia.

Oxfam Australia (OAU). 2017. "Board Charter." Oxfam Australia.

Passey, Andrew. 2004. *Linking Society & Economy Through Membership: Associations in New South Wales*. Report. Australian Centre for Co-operative Research and Development (ACCORD), University of Technology, Sydney.

Paton, Rob. 2003. *Managing and Measuring Social Enterprises*. Sage.

Penehira, Mera, Fiona Cram, and Kataraina Pipi. 2003. *Kaupapa Māori Governance: Literature Review and Key Informant Interviews*. Te Puāwai Tapu.

Productivity Commission. 2010. *Contribution of the Not-For-Profit Sector: Research Report*. Productivity Commission, Commonwealth of Australia.

Ramsay, Ian, and Miranda Webster. 2017. "Registered charities and Governance Standard 5: an evaluation." *Australian Business Law Review* 45, no. 2: 127–158.

Renton, Nicholas. 2005. *Guide for Meetings and Organisations*. Lawbook Company.

Rowe, Nicola. 2014. *NGO Health and Disability Network Governance Review*. NGO Health and Disability Network.

Royal Commission into Institutional Responses to Child Sexual Abuse. 2014. *Interim Report Volume 1*. Commonwealth of Australia.

Sanders, J., M. O'Brien, M. Tennant, et al. 2008. *The New Zealand Non-profit Sector in Comparative Perspective*. Wellington, New Zealand: Office for the Community and Voluntary Sector.

Scaife, Wendy, Myles McGregor-Lowndes, Jo Barraket, and Wayne Burns, eds. 2016. *Giving Australia 2016: Literature Review Summary Report*. Australian Centre for Philanthropy and Nonprofit Studies, Queensland University of Technology; Centre for Social Impact, Swinburne University of Technology; Centre for Corporate Public Affairs).

Skocpol, Theda. 2003. *Diminished Democracy: From Membership to Management in American Civil Life*. University of Oklahoma Press.

Standards Australia International. 2003. *AS 8000-2003: Good Governance Principles*. Standards Australia International.

Statistics New Zealand. 2007. *Non-profit Institutions Satellite Account: 2004*. Statistics New Zealand.

Statistics New Zealand. 2014. 2013 Census QuickStats about culture and identity. Statistics New Zealand.

Statistics New Zealand. 2016. *Non-profit Institutions Satellite Account: 2013*. Statistics New Zealand.

Steane, Peter. 2001. "Governance: Convergent expectations, divergent practices." *Corporate Governance* 1, no. 3: 15–19.

Te Puni Kōkiri. 2017. "Effective governance" (web page). www.tpk.govt.nz/en/whakamahia/effective-governance (accessed December 10, 2017).

The Senate Community Affairs References Committee. *Violence, abuse and neglect against people with disability in institutional and residential settings, including the gender and age related dimensions, and the particular situation of Aboriginal and Torres Strait Islander people with disability, and culturally and linguistically diverse people with disability*. Report. Commonwealth of Australia. 2015.

Werker, Eric, and Faisal Z. Ahmed. 2008. "What do nongovernmental organizations do?" *Journal of Economic Perspectives* 22, no. 2: 73–92.

Widmer, Candace, and Susan Houchin. 1999. *Governance of National Federated Organizations: Research in Action*. National Center for Nonprofit Boards.

Wiseman, Ross. 2002. "The experiences of governance in community-managed welfare associations." *Third Sector Review* 8, no. 2: 51–69.

Woodward, Susan, and Shelley Marshall. 2004. *A Better Framework: Reforming Not-for-Profit Regulations*. Centre for Corporate Law and Securities Regulations, University of Melbourne.

NOTES

1. Currency referenced in this chapter is in US dollars converted from Australian or New Zealand dollars on August 12, 2017.
2. Commonwealth Bank of Australia v. Friedrich, 9 ACLC 946 (1991).
3. Commissioner of Taxation of the Commonwealth of Australia v. Word Investments Limited HCA 55 (2008).
4. The interpretation of the PBI concept was expanded by the decision of the Federal Court of Australia in Commissioner of Taxation v. Hunger Project Australia FCAFC 69 (2014).
5. Ironically, Australia and Aotearoa New Zealand are regarded as Global North countries for the purposes of the north-south dichotomy.
6. In the interests of full disclosure, Alan Hough provided pro bono consulting at the time to introduce and implement the Policy Governance® model.
7. Lately, the term *Big Data* has tended to refer to the use of predictive analytics, user behavior analytics, or certain other advanced data analytics methods that extract value from data, and seldom to a particular size of data set. See www.en.wikipedia.org/wiki/Big_data (accessed November 3, 2017).
8. A *Liberal* in Australia denotes a member of the Liberal Party, which is Australia's largest moderate/conservative party. The director recruited to the board had and has an outstanding record of advocating for human rights, including voting against her own party on human rights issues.

CHAPTER 5

Central and Eastern Europe and Eurasia

Marilyn Wyatt

HISTORICAL CONTEXT FOR GOVERNANCE

Much of the impetus behind the development of global civil society in the past 30 years can be traced to Central and Eastern Europe (CEE).[1] Fueled by dormant community traditions from the precommunist period, a new sense of social solidarity, the desire to exercise fundamental freedoms of expression and association, and generous funding from Western donors, the region's citizens' groups and self-help efforts coalesced into CSOs during the early to mid-1990s. As part of the wholesale reform of legal frameworks, efforts were made to introduce laws that could shape and guide civil society—efforts that were sometimes criticized as too hasty or too slow, poorly conceived, incompletely implemented, or undercut by entrenched resistance or misunderstanding of democratic processes. Nevertheless, civil society in CEE flourished with astonishing speed, and its model soon spread to the new states of Eurasia, where, more slowly and with many fewer resources, CSOs managed to take root in very different political and cultural environments. Today, to varying degrees, and with a need for constant vigilance, it seems safe to say that CSOs have become an established feature of the regional landscape.

During the early development of civil society in CEE, the internal governance of organizations took a back seat to issues of immediate survival, such as the search for funding and demonstrable project results. Donors typically took only a cursory look at internal governance practices, focusing instead on nurturing talented individuals capable of leading their organizations with charisma, vision, and administrative skill. Their questions about the function and duties of governing bodies were few. CSOs themselves were even less concerned about the reasons for the existence of their governing bodies. The bulk of organizations survived on a shoestring, staffed only by volunteers, and they tended to view their governing bodies as a formality needed for registration but otherwise serving no discernable purpose. This collective silence about governance partly reflected continuing deficits in legal frameworks, which in most places offered little coherent guidance about the role and responsibilities of governing bodies. But there also seemed to be a tacit agreement that good governance could wait until CSOs were stabilized and better poised to grapple with longer term issues, such as strategic planning, diversified funding, internal procedures, and conflict of interest—all issues typically associated with the work of governing bodies, especially boards.

EVOLUTION OF THE SECTOR

Attitudes towards internal governance have evolved since civil society first re-awoke in CEE and Eurasia. The course of this evolution tracks with the growing complexity and sophistication of the CSO sector overall. The pace of improving governance practices has been slow, but as more organizations approach governance more self-consciously as a core responsibility, they often find that they are better able to fulfill their mission of "doing good by doing well" when their boards play a more active role. Today, scores of organizations are embracing governance practices that not only help improve operations, attract new resources, and ensure long-term survival, but also reinforce basic democratic values, such as checks and balances and the rule of law.[2]

This chapter will look at the development of CSO governance in CEE and Eurasia over the past 25 years. The emphasis is necessarily on CEE, since its CSO sector is older, larger, and much more thoroughly documented than its counterpart in Eurasia.

LEGAL ENVIRONMENT

The governance of CSOs in the countries in CEE and Eurasia share a basic starting point in two main forms of nonprofit organizations: Associations and foundations.[3] Most countries have other forms of nonprofits as well, such as cooperatives, institutes, funds, and training centers. But the vast majority of CSOs in the region are one of these two basic forms.

Associations

Associations are membership organizations that serve the interests of their members or allow members to pursue activities that benefit the public. A specific minimal number of members is usually required for legal establishment. For example, Latvia requires two members and Poland requires seven. The highest governing body of an association is the general assembly, which is composed of the organization's membership (or their representatives) and must usually meet at least once a year. The general assembly's primary duties include approving the annual financial statement and annual report and making any decision to change the statutes, merge with another organization, or dissolve the association. Associations sometimes also have an executive or management board, which is appointed by the general assembly and has authority delegated by the general assembly to run the day-to-day affairs of the association and represent the organization in, for example, the signing of contracts. In some countries, such as Albania, Bulgaria, and Hungary, the management board is mandatory and elsewhere, such as in Croatia, Kosovo, and the Czech Republic, the management board is optional—that is, it is established at the discretion of individual organizations. In some countries the management board may consist of only one person.

Foundations

Foundations are nonmembership organizations established to serve a socially useful (or, in some countries, private) purpose. They often require a minimal investment of start-up capital—for example, 5000 euro in Macedonia and an amount "appropriate to the purpose" in Albania, Hungary, Slovenia, and Serbia. Foundations usually do not have members and are governed by a board of directors, which is appointed by the founders. The board is usually self-perpetuating and has duties similar to those of the general assembly in an association, including appointing a managing director, administrator, or management team. In a few countries a foundation's founders retain key decision-making rights, such the ability to dissolve the foundation in Slovakia or remove board members in Hungary. Some countries (for example, Romania) require foundations also to have a supervisory board, which monitors the affairs of the foundation to ensure that laws are observed and organizational assets are properly used. In other countries this rule applies only to foundations with public benefit status (Hungary and Slovakia) or with annual income above a certain amount (Czech Republic).

The legal framework affecting CSO governance in CEE has undergone partial reform in the past two decades. Today the laws in many countries are moving towards identifying mandatory governing bodies and their responsibilities while providing wide latitude for individual organizations to set up their own governing processes (Rutzen, Moore, and Durham 2009, 57). In theory this approach has many advantages, as it allows organizations to determine their own approach to internal governance. But in practice it has not encouraged a robust approach to governance to develop in individual organizations—especially given the absence, at least until recently, of successful local models of governance that CSOs could emulate and of well-conceived mechanisms that effectively encourage and enforce good behavior. For example, in 2002 the author encountered an organization in Ukraine that had six governing bodies with no clear-cut hierarchy among them, no definition of their responsibilities in the organization's statutes, and no procedures governing their operations. This was an extreme case, but it illustrates how unfamiliar democratic principles such as checks and balances and the rule of law could be in the decade following the fall of communism. Or, more precisely, the degree to which these concepts were embraced intellectually as the inspiration for civil society, but had yet to be internalized to guide the behavior of individual organizations.

In countries long dominated by authoritarian governments, organizations have been uncertain how to design and implement collective forms of leadership. In the interests of expediency, founders and chief executives have often remained unconvinced that power sharing is such a good idea anyway. Moreover, external pressures have often been lacking.

For many years donors seemed indifferent to governance, and government institutions have lacked the capacity, know-how, or interest to enforce legal prescriptions applying to governance. In most places, few organizations were sanctioned if they failed to implement the governance structures outlined in the legal framework or in their own statutes (Rutzen, Moore, and Durham 2009, 39).

For all of these reasons, CSOs in CEE and Eurasia have been slow to embrace good governance as an ideal within their own operations. In recent years, however, this tendency appears to be shifting. Leading organizations are increasingly giving thought to their internal governance as an important standard of excellence. In so doing, they are exploring and refining models of governance that, eventually, can serve as models for other CSOs in the region and strengthen the CSO sector as a whole.

A BRIEF HISTORY OF REGIONAL APPROACHES TO CSO GOVERNANCE

The roots of indifference to CSO governance are deep in CEE and Eurasia, perhaps because of the loss or suppression of democratic processes during decades of communist rule. Surveys of governance practices in Hungary, Ukraine, and Bulgaria conducted between 2001 and 2003 document attitudes towards boards and governance some 10 years after the region's civil society sectors began to emerge. The survey reports describe what is aptly called a "minimalist" approach to governance. A major challenge in all three countries was that governance and management functions were poorly defined and often intertwined. For example, among Hungarian organizations, monitoring the organization's finances and overseeing programs was most often identified as the most important duty of the principle governing body (i.e., the management board or board). Yet in 92% of organizations, the chief executive was a voting member of the board and in almost three-quarters of organizations acted simultaneously as the board chair (Mura-Mészáros et al. 2002, 25–26). The situation in Ukraine was similar. In 94% of responding Ukrainian organizations—most of which agreed that the governing body's most important role was evaluating programs—the chief executive was a member of the board, nearly always with voting rights, and in more than 80% of organizations also served as board chair. Nearly two-thirds of respondents reported that staff members were also members of the governing body. In Bulgaria many governing bodies consisted of only three people, one of whom was the chief executive (Bulgarian Center for Not-for-Profit Law 2005, 25).

The conclusions of the survey reports present a picture of a nascent—one might say nearly nonexistent—understanding of the difference between management and governance.

> Ukrainian NGOs do not have a clear understanding of the differences between governance and management. This is reflected in the fact that, in addition to the formal oversight function assigned to governing bodies, more than 50 percent of respondents see as main responsibilities the management of day-to-day operations, management of staff, and program implementation. Indeed, day-to-day management is a responsibility more frequently ascribed to boards than to chief executives, whereas ensuring accountability is more often seen as a role of the chief executive than of the board.... These findings suggest that the ability to recognize conflict of interest needs further development among Ukrainian NGOs. (Hnat et al. 2003, 37)

The Hungarian report echoes these findings, agreeing that when it comes to governance, "nonprofit organizations do not generally recognize cases in which conflict of interest is involved, and do not consider such situations improper or ineffective" (Mura-Mészáros et al. 2002, 34). The report comments that the professionalism of governing bodies is low.

> Hungarian NGOs have ample room to improve: 75 percent of respondent organizations have no job description outlining expectations of board members, and only 24 percent of organizations offer orientations to new members of the governing body. At the same time—reinforcing the perception that their role is mainly a formal one—78 percent of respondents report spending considerable time listening to chief executive reports at board meetings. (Mura-Mészáros et al. 2002, 34)

In addition to traditions of authoritarian leadership, another reason for this pattern of intertwined executive and governance functions on boards was the CSO sector's very limited human and financial resources. As a Ukrainian respondent noted, "Our organization is a small one, which is why the role of the governing body is very formal. In everyday activities, we are the staff; if needed, we are formally the governing body, too" (Hnat et al. 2003, 33). A Hungarian respondent summed up the situation this way:

> Most NGOs...are "one-person" businesses. Whether we call that person the president, the executive manager, the secretary, or something else, he does everything alone, and the board is really just a representative decision-making body. If the organization succeeds in finding an agile person to run the business, then all goes well. If not, the organization simply survives on a day-to-day basis. (Mura-Mészáros et al. 2002, 30)

Yet as early as the time of these surveys a difference in governance was emerging at larger organizations. While the vast majority of CSOs in the region were tiny, with annual budgets of only a few thousand dollars, a handful of organizations were growing in size and complexity, usually thanks to donor largesse. As this happened, their governing bodies took on new importance, usually by serving an advisory purpose. "In larger organizations the board certainly matters," a Hungarian chief executive observes. "From financing to everyday operations, it's beneficial to have the support of an advisory team" (Mura-Mészáros et al. 2002, 30). Analyzing the survey of Hungarian governance practices, a Hungarian expert concludes that small CSOs at an early stage of development are not ready to absorb more complicated governance processes, such as board member turnover, terms limits for board members, and annual board orientations or chief executive assessment. But, he notes, larger organizations do have sufficient capacity, resources, and drive to refine their governance performance, and donors should encourage this trend (Sátor 2003).

The evolution of attitudes towards governance is evident in another important resource on the development of governance practices in CEE and Eurasia, the *Civil Society Organization Sustainability Index for Central and Eastern Europe* (*CSOSI*), produced annually since 1997 by the USAID. In the series, country profiles written by local partners offer ground-level snapshots of governance trends over the last two decades. They may be summarized as follows:

- During the 1990s the development of management capacity outstripped that of boards. In most places, organizational capacity was understood mainly as the ability to manage projects or fundraise. Boards were primarily seen as a requirement for registration and after registration were largely inactive. Their roles were poorly understood and vaguely defined. Legal reform in many countries helped to better position various governing bodies, but laws and regulations usually did not prohibit basic conflicts of interest, such as staff serving as board members. Boards were slow to become independent of executive directors, as the tradition of strong leaders in CSOs (as in society at large) proved difficult to overcome.
- By the early 2000s good governance began to be more explicitly linked to effective organizational performance. And, conversely, weak governance was viewed as a major challenge for CSOs in the region. The 2000 *CSOSI* report for Kyrgyzstan notes that "governance problems continue to hinder the growth and activities of the NGO sector" (USAID 2001). The 2001 report for Hungary similarly observes that "the greatest challenge remaining for the sector is the lack of effective governance. Boards of directors and governing bodies are in the very initial stages of development" (USAID 2002). Because of the decline of traditions of volunteerism and small population pools, finding volunteer board members was a challenge in some countries. However, during this period donors began to invest in board training, and as they did so, best practices in governance emerged in some of the region's larger NGOs. The report for Latvia for 2000 says that "the largest, most sustainable NGOs have boards of directors with a clear separation between their governance function and staff and boards are beginning to take part in strategic planning." In Central Asia, family members on boards remained common.
- In 2007, governance was still seen as lagging behind other areas of CSO development. Although legal reform continued to clarify expectations for governance in countries such as Macedonia and

Poland, it was still common for boards to shirk their duties. In the Czech Republic, for example, "by law NGOs must define their management structure and the responsibilities and duties of management bodies in their foundation documents. In practice, these principles are not always followed. Those structures required by statute are often not taken seriously and do not impact or govern the day-to-day functioning of NGOs" (USAID 2008). Boards still often reported that they meet only sporadically to rubberstamp staff decisions. Organizations in Armenia, Kazakhstan, Russia, and Uzbekistan often did not even have boards.

- At the same time, interest in codes of ethics and other self-regulatory initiatives began to develop, and such mechanisms usually included a (sometimes vaguely worded) theme of good governance. Estonian CSOs, for instance, developed a code of ethics that gestures towards good governance with the statement that "a nonprofit organization as a voluntary association of the members of the society values its members, ensures democratic governance of the organization, holds the governing bodies and employees of the organization responsible and reacts to their misconduct" (Roundtable of Estonian Nonprofit Organizations 2002). In addition, competition for funding from USAID, the European Union, and other public and private sources spurred CSOs to show that their boards not only existed but also were actively engaged, as in Romania. Given donors' tendencies to invest in capacity building for larger organizations that are recipients of their funds, during this period governance was one of several areas in which the gap between smaller and larger organizations and between CSOs in CEE and Eurasia countries grew more pronounced.

- Governance structures and practices continued to develop slowly, and by 2015 pockets of good practice had emerged. Whereas in Albania, Azerbaijan, Belarus, Georgia, and Hungary, most CSOs had yet to separate governance and management, and in Bulgaria, Croatia, Macedonia, Montenegro, Moldova, and Serbia, boards were weak and ineffective, in Lithuania, "CSOs are increasingly aware of the importance of boards ... [and] making more efforts to recruit and establish active boards of directors" (USAID 2016, 141). In 2016, serving on a Lithuanian CSO board "is considered increasingly prestigious" and during recent parliamentary elections "candidates who were CSO board members openly declared their affiliations with CSOs." Illustrating the growing independence of boards from dominant chief executives, the Lithuanian report cites the case of a CSO whose board dismissed its director, and when the director publicly disputed the decision, "demonstrated that it had a clear vision for the organization and was resolute about the dismissal" (USAID 2017, 140). Latvia and Slovakia note that several larger CSOs had functioning board and management structures, and in Ukraine, "several CSOs even view establishing policies and procedures for governance as an organizational priority" (USAID 2016, 245). Interestingly, the Belarus report notes a rise in the number of CSOs with one founder, who legally can make all decisions for the organization, but "in an attempt to adhere to democratic governance standards and increase transparency, some of these organizations are [voluntarily] forming collective governance bodies similar to boards of directors" (USAID 2017, 45).

- In Poland, on the other hand, an opposite approach to governance is developing, which promotes a lack of separation between governing and management roles: "There are various models of CSO management in Poland, from one CEO making all decisions, to more democratic models in which directors and managers are involved in decision-making processes. Not all CSO experts in Poland agree that it is optimal to have a clear division of roles between the board of directors and staff, as many believe that directors need knowledge of day-to-day operations in order to govern properly." A recent law allows Polish foundation board members to be paid for their work (USAID 2016, 183–184). In Eurasia, boards continue to exist mainly to satisfy legal requirements, serving no practical purpose.

Thus today the varieties of governance and boards in CEE and Eurasia are diversifying as nonprofit sectors themselves grow more complex. As a Latvian CSO leader recently remarked: "The issue of 'good governance' is no longer as exotic as it was ten years ago. More and more organizations have clear and transparent governance structures" (Pipike 2017). Overall, organizations are taking governance more seriously, but specific challenges persist. In smaller countries, for example, the lack of human resources continues to pose an intractable obstacle. In Slovenia, a country of two million people, "the size of the country [makes] avoiding conflicts of interest in a particular field of expertise very hard," observes a veteran CSO leader (Wagner 2017). In Latvia, whose population is less than two million, "there is such a small number of active people [that] it is difficult to have strong management and strong governance at the same time" (Pipike 2017). Other challenges include boards that are not transparent (for example, in Albania, "most CSOs do not even publish the names of board members on their websites" (USAID 2017, 16), boards that are composed of serial board members (in Slovakia, it is not uncommon for individuals to "act as pro forma members in several organizations" (USAID 2017, 223), and boards that simply do not exist (in Romania, "smaller organizations do not even have boards of directors that are separate from their executive teams" (USAID 2017, 191). The 2016 *CSOSI* report on Russia, in summing up the situation in that country, could be describing CEE and Eurasia as a whole:

> There is great variety in CSOs' internal management structures.... Active and experienced organizations may have multi-layered management structures, including boards, general meetings, advisory committees, audit committees, executive directors, governing councils, and others, which are reflected in their charters or statutes. Hundreds of organizations use efficient management systems, often inspired by best practices in the business sector.... At the same time, the majority of CSOs are small and generally not experienced in issues related to internal management. Even when such CSOs formally have boards, these boards do not always play an important role in organizational governance. In the majority of CSOs, leaders assume all responsibility and make all decisions. (USAID 2017, 201)

LOOKING FORWARD TO NEW PRACTICES

CSO governance is still not a front-burner issue in CEE and Eurasia. Despite the persistence of a certain indifference to governance, however, underneath the surface are some promising trends. For one thing, *conflict of interest* is better understood and taken more seriously, both on boards and in the legal framework (Rutzen, Moore, and Durham 2009, 38). For example, in Bosnia and Herzegovina and Slovenia, members of a foundation's board of directors and supervisory board may not be employees or serve on both boards (Rutzen, Moore, and Durham 2009, 71). In the Czech Republic, employees, members of the board of directors and supervisory board, and their close associates may not receive grants from the foundation for which they work (Council on Foundations 2017). In Albania, individuals associated with conflicts must be disclosed and must recuse him- or herself from relevant decisions (Rutzen, Moore, and Durham 2009, 38). In Armenia, although associations are not required to adopt a governance structure that separates boards and staff, foundations must separate these functions, as the law prohibits board members from being paid for any work with their foundations (USAID 2016, 24).

In a second promising development, Russian, Czech, and Bulgarian CSOs are beginning to include *private-sector representation* on their boards (Panov 2017; Barta 2017). Organizations find that after international donors leave, they must diversify their funding base and target private sources of funding, such as corporations and individual donors. At this point, governance and board composition can become more important, both because local supporters look more closely at how organizations are run and because board members themselves can serve as links to a wider pool of prospective donors. In the Czech Republic, for example, the Via Foundation brought on private-sector board members who proved helpful with a successful fundraising campaign that raised US$1 million (Barta 2017). Corporate board members can also introduce a higher level of professionalism on CSO boards. In Russia, many private and corporate foundations, including Evolution and Philanthropy and the new Rybakov Foundation, are managed by former businessmen, who have implemented efficient management systems based on their business experience (Drozdova 2017). The Fund for Support of Independent Journalism in the Czech Republic also has founders with "both influence and affluence," who have introduced a policy of board giving that is helping sustain the new organization (Barta 2017), while the Bulgarian Donors' Forum and Junior Achievement Bulgaria have boards composed predominately of members from business (Panov 2017).

Another promising trend is the growing recognition that a *second generation of CSO leaders* may be needed before a significant improvement in governance practices can be realized. A Bulgarian colleague notes that organizations in which the founding chief executive has yet to leave have done the least to change their governance practices (Panov 2017). Similarly, a Serbian expert observes that boards in which founders are still members often meddle the most in operational affairs (Velat 2017). She points to the Trag Foundation, the largest local community foundation in Serbia, as having managed the generational shift especially well. Trag was initially established as the Balkan Community Initiative Fund, based in the United Kingdom, and the first board was composed and operated according to UK standards. Subsequent to the foundation's indigenizing as a local organization in 2004, the board meets regularly (three to four times a year), leads strategic processes, and deals with key strategic and governance issues rather than daily operations. Board members are actively engaged in recruiting the chief executive, leading an endowment campaign, attending foundation events, and other activities. In particular, Trag takes conflict of interest seriously. All board members work without payment and the board has introduced a conflict-of-interest policy that all board members and employees must sign (Velat 2017; Ademi 2017).[4]

A fourth area in which productive attitudes towards governance are developing is *self-regulation*. Self-regulatory initiatives complement laws, and various codes and mechanisms introduced by local, European, and international bodies have helped define good governance and ensure (or suggest ways of ensuring) that they are effectively implemented. One of the earlier regional efforts to establish standards for CSO governance was *A Handbook of NGO Governance,* developed by the Central and Eastern European Working Group on Nonprofit Governance. The working group consisted of leaders of prominent organizations from across CEE, who felt that US approaches to nonprofit governance would never work in their home countries, and that to be credible, governance principles for CSOs in CEE had to be indigenous rather than imported. The group produced the handbook to provide a "consistent, locally responsive framework for nonprofit governance" capable of uniting the region's CSOs in the common goal of improved transparency and accountability (Wyatt, M., and the Central and Eastern European Working Group on Nonprofit Governance 2004, 4a). It presents eight basic principles of governance accompanied by sidebars showing how to put the theory of good governance into practice. Since it was published in 2004, the handbook has become a staple of good governance in CEE and Eurasia and today is available in 20 of the region's languages.[5] Many editions are equipped with appendices describing country-specific legal and cultural frameworks and have usually been introduced as part of a capacity-building project that includes training workshops, information campaigns, and the establishment of working groups to help with the adaptation and dissemination of good governance practices. A similar effort is *Thinking Ethically! A Think-Tank Code of Good Governance*, which aims to improve the governance, quality, and impact of independent policy institutions in CEE and Central Asia (Pajas 2011). The publication calls on think tanks to "make themselves fully accountable to the general public" by declaring a code of ethics that, among other things, includes being governed by a responsible body.

Other self-regulatory efforts address governance as part of a larger effort to strengthen the CSO sector as a whole. They include OK2015, a new system of quality assurance for Croatian CSOs developed by the Association for Civil Society Development-SMART (Novotna 2017). A similar quality-assurance system for Serbian CSOs was launched in 2016 by the organization Civic Initiatives, and more than 100 Serbian CSOs have signed a voluntary code of ethics that offers standards and principles for organizational behavior, including avoidance of conflict of interest (Velat 2017).[6] An awards system in Moldova known as the Organizational Transparency Awards recognizes outstanding CSOs after assessing them in various areas of organizational performance, including governance (European Center for Not-for-Profit Law 2015).

Finally, *governance capacity-building initiatives* can help. A project conducted by the Ukrainian organization GURT and the US organization BoardSource from 2001 to 2003 showed that efforts to strengthen CSO governance are most effective if integrated within a larger project to develop organizational capacity. Many organizations taking part in the GURT-BoardSource project needed convincing that there was value in investing time and resources in improving their governance practices, especially if it was presented solely as a moral imperative. But their enthusiasm increased if they understand good governance as intimately tied to the concrete strategic interests of their organizations. A main lesson of the project was that capacity-building initiatives need to integrate an emphasis on boards and governance into the range of essential capacities that they target, such as fundraising, financial management, communications, and strategic planning. In addition, it was clear that capacity-building initiatives must also develop the capacity of trainers to instruct, coach, and mentor boards in a new way. Trainers in the Ukrainian project often seemed even more reluctant than chief executives to tackle the issue of governance, whether because of unfamiliarity with the topic or discomfort with a departure from their usual training approaches. But boards often need customized help, and thus the development of CSOs' governance capacity may demand a different approach to training that many of the region's capacity-building resources have yet to explore.

CONCLUSION

The evolution of governance practices in CEE and Eurasia since the early 1990s is an accurate indicator of the growing complexity and sophistication of the CSO sector as a whole. From a starting position of relative indifference, the region's CSOs have begun to evince a heightened sense of responsibility about internal governance issues—not only in the establishment of checks and balances and the avoidance of conflict interest, but also with respect to the value added by boards in areas ranging from fundraising and generational renewal to professional conduct and the effectiveness of self-regulatory initiatives. This development, albeit slow, augurs well for the establishment of secure and sustainable civil society sectors in CEE, Eurasia, and beyond. As CSOs hold governments accountable, one welcomes their efforts to hold themselves accountable as well.

REFERENCES

Ademi, Tanja Hafner. 2017. CSO Governance in Macedonia. Received by Marilyn Wyatt October 5, 2017.

Barta, Jiří. 2017. CSO Governance in the Czech Republic. Received by Marilyn Wyatt September 30, 2017.

Bulgarian Center for Not-for-Profit Law. 2005. Nonprofit Governance Practices in Bulgaria. Bulgarian Center for Not-for-Profit Law.

Council on Foundations. 2017. "Czech Republic" (web page). www.cof.org/content/czech-republic#Control_of_Organization (accessed October 8, 2017).

Drozdova, Olga. 2017. CSO Governance in Russia. Received by Marilyn Wyatt September 28, 2017.

European Center for Not-For-Profit Law. 2015. *Current Trends in Self-Regulation of Civil Society Organizations in Europe: A General Overview.* http://ecnl.org/wp-content/uploads/2016/10/Current-Trends-in-Self-Regulation-of-Civil-Society-Organizations-in-Europe.pdf (accessed October 22, 2017).

General Assembly of the Roundtable of Estonian Nonprofit Organizations in Tartu. 2002. "Code of Ethics of Estonian non-profit organizations" (web page). www.arenduskeskus.ee/code-of-ethics-of-estonian-nonprofit-organizations (accessed October 22, 2017).

Hnat, V., O. Houmenyuk, M. Wyatt, and E. Zahkarchenko. 2003. Nonprofit Governance Practices in Ukraine. BoardSource; Center for Policy Studies.

Mura-Mészáros, L., J. Saidel, B. Sátor, and M. Wyatt. 2002. Nonprofit Governance Practices in Hungary. BoardSource; Civil Society Development Foundation Hungary.

Novotna, SlaÐana. 2017. *CSO Governance in Croatia.* Received by Marilyn Wyatt October 2, 2017.

Pajas, Petr Jan. 2011. *Thinking Ethically! A Think-Tank Code of Good Governance.* Policy Association for an Open Society. Accessed October 22, 2017. http://pasos.org/wp-content/uploads/2011/12/thinkingethically2011.pdf.

Panov, Luben. 2017. *CSO Governance in Bulgaria.* Received by Marilyn Wyatt September 24 and October 16, 2017.

Pipike, Rasma. 2017. *CSO Governance in Latvia.* Received by Marilyn Wyatt October 1, 2017.

Rutzen, D., D. Moore, and M. Durham. 2009. "The legal framework for not-for-profit organizations in Central and Eastern Europe." *International Journal of Not-for-Profit Law* 11, no. 2 (February). http://www.icnl.org/research/journal/vol11iss2/art_1.htm (accessed October 26, 2017).

Sátor, B. 2003. *"Hungary: Introducing the concept of governance" (web page).* Trust for Civil Society in Central and Eastern Europe. www.ceetrust.org/article/128 (accessed October 6, 2017).

USAID. 2001. *2000 NGO Sustainability Index for Central and Eastern Europe and Eurasia.* US Agency for International Development. http://pdf.usaid.gov/pdf_docs/Pnacn876.pdf (accessed October 17, 2017).

USAID. 2002. *2001 NGO Sustainability Index for Central and Eastern Europe and Eurasia.* US Agency for International Development. http://pdf.usaid.gov/pdf_docs/Pnacp212.pdf (accessed October 17, 2017).

USAID. 2008. *2007 NGO Sustainability Index for Central and Eastern Europe and Eurasia.* US Agency for International Development. http://pdf.usaid.gov/pdf_docs/Pnadm501.pdf (accessed October 17, 2017).

USAID. 2016. *2015 CSO Sustainability Index for Central and Eastern Europe and Eurasia.* US Agency for International Development. www.usaid.gov/sites/default/files/documents/1861/Europe_Eurasia_CSOSIReport_2015_Update8-29-16.pdf (accessed October 22, 2017).

USAID. 2017. *2016 CSO Sustainability Index for Central and Eastern Europe and Eurasia.* US Agency for International Development,. www.usaid.gov/sites/default/files/documents/1866/CSOSI_Report_7-28-17.pdf (accessed October 22, 2017).

Velat, Dubravka. 2017. *CSO Governance in Serbia*. Received by Marilyn Wyatt September 30, 2017.

Wagner, Vida. 2017. *CSO Governance in Slovenia*. Received by Marilyn Wyatt October 3, 2017.

Wyatt, M., and the Central and Eastern European Working Group on Nonprofit Governance. 2004. *A Handbook of NGO Governance*. European Center for Not-For-Profit Law. http://ecnl.org/dindocuments/455_Governance_Handbook.pdf (accessed October 22, 2017).

NOTES

1. CEE countries are Albania, Belarus, Bosnia and Herzegovina, Bulgaria, Croatia, the Czech Republic, Estonia, Hungary, Kosovo, Latvia, Lithuania, Macedonia, Moldova, Montenegro, Poland, Romania, Russia, Serbia, Slovakia, Slovenia, and Ukraine. For the purposes of this report the Eurasia countries are Armenia, Azerbaijan, Georgia, Kazakhstan, Kyrgyzstan, Tajikistan, Turkmenistan, and Uzbekistan.

2. For a discussion of this point, see Marilyn Wyatt and the Central and Eastern European Working Group on Nonprofit Governance, *A Handbook of NGO Governance* (European Center for Not-For-Profit Law, 2004), 11b–12a, www.ecnl.org/dindocuments/455_Governance_Handbook.pdf (accessed October 22, 2017).

3. Most of the information that follows is drawn from the invaluable discussion of association and foundation governance in CEE in Douglas Rutzen, David Moore, and Michael Durham, "The legal framework for not-for-profit organizations in Central and Eastern Europe," *International Journal of Not-for-Profit Law* 11, no. 2 (February 2009): 25–75, www.icnl.org/research/journal/vol11iss2/art_1.htm (accessed October 22, 2017). See in particular pp. 36–39, 61–63, and 67–73. In addition, see Wyatt and the Central and Eastern European Working Group on Nonprofit Governance, *A Handbook of NGO Governance* (European Center for Not-For-Profit Law, 2004), 7a–9a.

4. See also the Trag Foundation website at www.tragfondacija.org .

5. The handbook is available in Albanian, Azerbaijani, Bulgarian, Croatian, Czech, English, Hungarian, Kazakh, Latvian, Lithuanian, Macedonian, Mongolian, Romanian, Russian, Serbian, Slovenian, Spanish, Tajik, Turkish, and Ukrainian.

6. The code of ethics was developed by Civic Initiatives in 2012. See www.gradjanske .org/wp-content/uploads/2014/11/065-Eticki-kodeks-OCD.pdf. The author was the leader of this project, and the observations that follow are from an internal written report assessing its outcomes.

CHAPTER 6

Europe

Valerio Melandri

Valerio Melandri, professor in Bologna University's Masters in Fundraising Program, focuses our attention on the board's role in fundraising. For the vast majority of NGOs, fundraising is the primary instrument for ensuring stability and sustainability, and therefore boards must understand the need for an active role in it. When fundraising fails in an organization, the most likely culprit is a board that does not fully grasp this critical role. Because of the importance of the board's role in sustaining resources, any investigation into governance should always consider this vital role. The author also engages us concerning the issues of remuneration for board members and the need to analyze the composition of the board and evaluate performance. In conclusion, he describes some interesting emergent models.

Europe is fragmented in many ways and is made up of many diverse states.[1] Each state has its own history, culture, language, and legislation. The fragmentary nature of Europe affects the overall structure of the third sector here, and consequently board structures and practices vary. They do have some characteristics in common, but these are not strengths; they are limitations, which will be described in the following paragraphs. Overcoming these organizational limitations and rethinking the board here could foster the advancement of the European third sector. Its future will depend on the innovation and renewal of the governance model over the next few years.

Predictably attempts to categorize this vast and diverse region often fall under the criteria of geography, economy, history, anthropology, or politics. For our purposes we will begin by dividing Europe into four areas, each of which share a certain degree of homogeneity in its non-profit sector.

UNITED KINGDOM

The first geographic area corresponds to the United Kingdom, which has a sector and fundraising model similar to that of the United States and Canada (Hopt and Von Hippel 2010; Powell and Steinberg 2008; Adam 2004; Estelle 1989). Most International Non-governmental Organizations (INGOs) are Europe-based, many of them headquartered in the United Kingdom. NGOs here have an experience, a structure, and an operational setup that is more international,[2] and many employ the most advanced fundraising techniques.[3] This area is helped by its own industrial fabric, which over the years has allowed for the growth of a large, well-rooted, and wealthy philanthropic class. (Lincoln and Saxton 2012). To understand how much fundraising has developed and advanced in this area, one should remember that the Institute of Fundraising is the largest such association in Europe, with over 5000 members,[4] and that there is a highly developed and active labor market in fundraising. The availability of fundraising expertise aids boards in their fundraising. Moreover, governance here also benefits from the work of the Association of Chief Executives of Voluntary Organizations (ACEVO), which today has nearly 2000 associates (ACEVO 2016), and whose goal it is to connect, develop, and represent leaders in the third sector by providing numerous opportunities for professional development and learning among peers. It also encourages networking by organizing informal events and by providing a membership directory. The ACEVO lobbies the British government on behalf of its members. ACEVO's work makes the governance of NGOs, and hence the entire third sector, more professional and effective. Because of the existence of these organizations, debates about the governance of NGOs occur on an almost daily basis.[5]

CONTINENTAL EUROPE

Another geographic area to be considered is Continental Europe, which includes those states that have developed a universal welfare state over time, but whose governments have a limited commitment to direct provision of social services. In these states NGOs are largely engaged in providing these services in an already consolidated and well-regulated environment (European Commission 2015). In these countries the welfare system has been built by incorporating NGOs into public-welfare policies (without NGOs becoming public entities), and more generally into the provision of important public services (i.e., the school system in Belgium and mutual associations in Germany) (Borzaga 2003). Here there are some relatively large NGOs (large in relation to the volume of fundraising revenue) that practice fundraising successfully (Anheier and Seibel 2001). Fundraising here has found fertile ground for its development, as Continental Europe benefits from a significant presence of big companies, some with a sophisticated approach to philanthropy,[6] as well as organizations that foster the support and development of the sector.

MEDITERRANEAN REGION

A third geographical area of interest comprises those Mediterranean countries with two well-defined features: A strong Catholic culture and ethos in the population (even if it is not the religion of the state) (Knippenberg 2005) and past experience of a massive state presence in the welfare sector. In this system (which we might call the two legs of State and Church), the state covered most of the needs of the population, while the Catholic Church covered the rest. This system started to waver about 20 years ago, and today state welfare is being dismantled (Jones 1993). This has led to the creation of conditions and space for the development of the nonprofit and fundraising sectors.

This important, but recent, phenomenon has meant that fundraising has had a later start in this area than, for example, in the United Kingdom. At first glance it may appear as if the region is more backward, both from the point of view of philanthropic culture and the use of techniques and tools, but it has quickly closed the gap by advancing in some areas more rapidly than in other parts of Europe (European Fundraising Association 2015).

An obstacle to the development of the third sector in the Mediterranean Region is the absence of big industry. To illustrate: In Italy, about 95% of businesses have fewer than five employees and just over 600 companies have more than 500 employees.[7] This means that not only does big industry not exist, but that there are also very few big industrial entrepreneurs. As a result, the model of the great corporate philanthropist (along the lines of Bill Gates of Microsoft) is missing, making finding major donors more difficult. All this too has an impact on the characteristics of Italian boards, which lack an operational mentality. Too often those who sit on the board of a NGO ignore and avoid fundraising (Melandri 2017).

NORTHERN EUROPE

The last geographic area to be considered is Northern Europe, which includes the Scandinavian countries. Here, the high level of taxation empowers the state to provide wide-reaching and high-quality services. This social structure has lessened the need for NGOs, and therefore there is almost no need for fundraising. This is why there has been minimal discussion here about the practices employed in fundraising and governance. Obviously, even in these states NGOs and fundraising exist, but to date little has been done to encourage their development there (Wijkström 2004; Lundström and Svedberg 2003; Evers and Laville 2004; Harju 2006; Hilger 2008).

PROMOTING BOARD PERFORMANCE THROUGH REMUNERATION AND INCENTIVES

Many studies have been carried out on the role and functioning of the boards of for-profit companies, and a large amount of literature exists on best practices. The story is different in the nonprofit world, however, where there are still very few specific studies in which governance, leadership, and accountability (key concepts in NGO governance) are analyzed and explored (International Finance Corporation 2015; Carver and Carver 2001; Schöning et al. 2012; Hudson 2011.). This shows just how much the third sector still lacks the attention it deserves in Europe (outside of the United Kingdom and Continental Europe).

The most important difference between the governance of for-profits and NGOs is the remuneration of board members. NGO board members are all too often dismissed as mere volunteers. This view, common to all the European areas mentioned above, affects the functionality of the board right from the very beginning because it is on this basis that its members are selected. From this perspective, anyone can join the board—even lacking the requisite experience. Passion for the mission is not enough.

Qualified people are needed and we will see further on in this chapter who is best suited to be on these boards. Perhaps the moment has arrived to include paid professionals on boards (Addarii et al. 2009), because often volunteer board members see their nonprofit roles as secondary to their paid jobs. There are two ways to attract the best prospective candidates: One is economic remuneration for their work, the other involves incentives, premiums, and benefits that should be linked directly to a member's performance on the board and not just constitute a reimbursement of expenses (Williams 2014; Lampkin and Chasteen 2014; Brody 2007; Jobome 2006).

The debate is still open on whether or not we need to pay board members, but with the challenges ahead for the nonprofit world are we willing to accept substandard governance because of this situation? Perhaps this arrangement is due to some vague Victorian sense that a director is a noble volunteer and therefore unpaid?

The only debatable exception in this is the executive director, who is not legally responsible for the survival of the NGO (who, if included on the board, may or may not vote), but who is highest paid among the staff. Consequently, his or her remuneration is not part of the governance debate. Also, a board consisting primarily of volunteer directors is still common in most NGOs in Europe (Hopt and Von Hippel 2010). Because most NGOs are small, board members often act as directors, executive directors, or program supervisors. Only in large NGOs are they assisted by an executive director and/or other staff.

The presence of volunteers on boards also has important repercussions for the dynamics of governance. This is because it is often the case that those who have the free time to give to an NGO are at the very beginning or end of their careers—the young or the old. The young may yet lack experience and older persons may have lost the useful connections they enjoyed through their active involvement in the workforce. Moreover, unpaid work is sometimes seen as having less value and conferring less status than paid employment. It could be argued that the presence of voluntary and unpaid directors is, in a way, one of the biggest limitations on the development of the nonprofit sector in Europe (Carver 2006).

This is not a necessarily a challenge in large NGOs. For example, some UK NGOs (as we have already seen, some of the most advanced in Europe) pay some of their board members. Large hospitals and universities in the United Kingdom, for example, have paid professionals on their boards. Remuneration does not, however, depend on the NGO's ability to pay. The director is paid because the board recognizes that this is the only way that it can attract qualified candidates.

We must not forget that the directors who sit on these boards have big responsibilities.[8] A few years ago in the United Kingdom there was a heated debate about whether or not to pay board members (Ramrayka 2012). Those opposed to the remuneration of board members objected that:

- Board members are considered to be volunteers.
- Donors and members of the organization expect their money to be spent on services and projects.
- These organization have no shareholders.
- Boards who pay their members discourage volunteering.
- Boards who pay their members may discourage donations.
- Boards who pay their members can consider directors as part of the paid staff.
- Boards have a trustee responsibility to manage the funds of the organization.

Those in favor of the remuneration of board members claimed that:

- Remuneration attracts professional figures rather than amateurs.
- Remuneration encourages directors to be more enterprising.
- Remuneration encourages better attendance at board meetings.
- Remuneration encourages board members to become more accountable for the performance of the NGO.

To make NGOs vital components of civil society, especially in the field of welfare, professionals are required. And for the nonprofit sector to be attractive to qualified candidates, it must appropriately compensate them.

Another factor to consider is that board members of a NGO should be prepared to accept responsibility for their actions. Often they are not prepared to do so because recruitment takes place between friends, relatives, and associates who believe that they share the same vision and support the same views, and because they believe choosing members from within their circles will make for pleasant meetings, or because sometimes simply no one else can be found. Sometimes influential and wealthy individuals are chosen because it is very likely over time that they will contribute by making large donations to the organization and open doors to their network of monied acquaintances. All this could be good practice, of course, but only if it guarantees motivated, involved, and prepared people (Hudson 2011).

The sad truth is that, for the most part, directors do not exactly understand their own roles, and often, unfortunately, will not be held responsible for their own inactivity.

INNOVATIVE MODELS FOR BOARDS IN EUROPE

In the past 20 years some initiatives have appeared to improve governance in NGOs. This has led to the publishing of a variety of guidelines, codes of conduct, and professional practices, many of which, unfortunately, only have validity at a national level.

Despite efforts and various initiatives at a national level to define and codify best practice, at a European (transnational) level, few attempts have been made in this direction, and of these only a very few have been successful. To date, there is no shared governance model. There are few organizations that use a model that we might term traditional or corporate, in which the board governs and supervises functions (finance, human resources, programs, etc.) through appropriate committees and delegates those functions to management.

But a wind of change is blowing through the sector, which will enable NGOs to better deal with emergent challenges. As Europe progressively withdraws from its commitment to provide welfare services (Jones 1993), new possibilities are emerging for NGOs. But these can be realized only if a concrete debate about governance begins.

There are currently two innovative models on which the debate is focused.

The first model is the governance model being implemented by new US family foundations, such as the Bill & Melinda Gates Foundation.[9] These are NGOs invigorated by the charismatic authority of a founder who maintains a strong influence and close control. In some ways, this model already exists in Europe, for example, in Italian NGOs such as Ant,[10] Intersos,[11] and Emergency,[12] to name but a few. The model, however, has developed differently than it has in the United States. A generous founding leader exhibiting strong and charismatic leadership can adapt an NGO to societal changes. After the founder is gone, however, these organizations may no longer be able to renew themselves effectively, and thus eventually sink into irrelevance (Addarii et al. 2009).

The second innovative model is linked to the phenomenon of social enterprises, which in the broadest sense encompass the value set of the nonprofit world (Schöning et al. 2012). Their goal is to integrate the private interests of founders, members, and workers with the public interest. The major difference in comparison to traditional NGOs is that the boards of these new organizations are peopled by the professionals who created the social enterprise and will carry it forward.

This is the hope for the future. In Europe there is a strong growth in social enterprises, driven mainly by the young, who, even under challenging national economic circumstances, choose to become social entrepreneurs. Success with this model lies with the new generation (Addarii et al. 2009; European Commission 2015; Borzag 2003; Mason and Royce 2007).

GOVERNANCE STRUCTURES AND NONPROFIT REALITY

In this chapter we do not attempt to determine the most appropriate governance structure to be applied to NGOs. Rather we hope to underline the value of a constructive debate on the subject. In such a debate, it should be noted that apart from some general principles, it is the context in which NGOs operate that most defines the appropriate governance structure. The relationship between the NGO and its environment defines the ideal composition of its board (Melandri 2017). For example, if you look at an NGO in the United Kingdom, where the nonprofit has a structural role in the welfare system, it will have a different governance model structure than one in a Scandinavian country, where there is a very strong state-controlled welfare system.

Some models resemble those found in the corporate sector. The simplest for-profit governance structures that can be found in NGOs are called *one-tier* and *two-tier*. In Anglo-Saxon countries, such as the United Kingdom, the one-tier structure, in which there is a board of directors but no supervisory board, prevails. In the two-tier model, however, the board operates in parallel with the supervisory board; this is a common structure, especially in Continental European countries (i.e., Germany and Holland) (Schöning et al. 2012).

Different models may be applied to NGOs operating simultaneously in several states. Each can have a different board, which follows the pertinent state regulations. In this case there may be two types of structure. One is a continental, horizontal structure that could be defined as democratic (all boards have the same decision-making powers but may vary in operational strategies and practices). The other is a vertical structure that aims at aligning the different structures, with a tendency to limit independence and departures from common operating practices. This, of course, can hinder innovation (Schöning et al. 2012).

Finally, there may be NGOs in which the board creates commissions and delegates various functions to them. While this approach has its uses, commissions tend to lead to increased workloads, and so they should only be created for specific tasks (Schöning et al. 2012).

STRIVING FOR AN INVOLVED BOARD

With a debate on governance begun (with the goal of defining best practices that can be implemented across European NGOs), the current governance model that offers the best all-around results is a board that is actively involved in all its appropriate functions, including fundraising. This board is cognizant of its centrality within the organization and gives a 360-degree attention to internal management processes. In a model of constituents based on concentric circles, this board lies at the center. It is the beating heart of an NGO.

The best fundraising boards are ones in which all of the directors are actively engaged in fundraising (Melandri 2017). Unfortunately, it is not common and widespread for boards to understand this role. When directors say the equivalent of, "I have already given my time (don't ask me for more, including money)," it is a warning sign that they are not engaged. It is a call to action to change the board's perception of its role in the full and complete long-term economic sustainability of the NGO it administers. First and foremost, members must themselves give. Secondly, members should be actively seeking donations and trying to bring other donors closer to the NGO through their contacts. Recruitment considerations include: Are the directors visible in the community? Who are their friends? These are important questions because the ability to raise funds depends on public trust.

Several NGOs have begun to develop best practices to build an involved board, which entails first analyzing the current board. I can verify that large UK NGOs, such as Save the Children UK, Cancer Research UK, and Oxfam UK, to name but a few, use tools to evaluate their own boards. These have been summarized in Table 6.1 and Table 6.2. These are tools that I, in my consultative role, have used in board evaluations.

Usually, it is the fundraiser who analyzes the board by personally meeting with every director and asking them these questions. For each question there is an evaluation, a mark from 1 to 5, where 1 indicates serious problems and 5 indicates the highest form of preparation. Through this table, an NGO discovers if its board is, if not already engaged, ready to be involved in fundraising and needs only to develop the appropriate means to the end.

If the board refuses to answer these questions, or directors respond in the following manner: "Do you think I don't know my own organization's mission?" "Do you think I don't believe in the cause?" "Do you think I don't receive reports on fundraising activities? Of course I do." "Do you think I don't read them carefully?" "What are you getting at when you ask me to donate?" "I donate my time, isn't that enough?" The above are all real objections that I have collected over my years as a fundraising consultant (Melandri 2017).

These defensive responses point to a real problem at the heart of things. If it is not possible to constructively talk about governance structures or models of governance, if the governance itself is unable to understand its own role, how can the board improve itself? Any debate about European governance must begin with composition and profile of the current and desired board, the selection and orientation process, ongoing education of the board and encouraging a culture of inquiry and an openness to discussion of the board's own performance.

Not everyone should join the board of a NGO. The time has passed for volunteer directors animated solely by goodwill; they must be actively involved. Passion for mission might serve as an initial impetus, but for the organization to survive, develop, and prosper, the board must be an engaged and competent participant.

TABLE 6.1 How to Evaluate the Board in Fundraising

1. Awareness. Your board of directors:					
(a) Understands the mission	1	2	3	4	5
(b) Is dedicated to the mission	1	2	3	4	5
(c) Believes in the validity of the cause	1	2	3	4	5
(d) Has a sense of belonging, pride, and enthusiasm for the cause	1	2	3	4	5
(e) Recognizes the importance of fundraising to support the cause	1	2	3	4	5
(f) Has received adequate information on the fundraising activities of the board	1	2	3	4	5
2. Involvement. Your board of directors:					
(a) Asks questions about fundraising	1	2	3	4	5
(b) Looks for more information on fundraising activities	1	2	3	4	5
(c) Is made up of directors who are active in public for the good cause	1	2	3	4	5
(d) Understands that fundraising is 90% preparation and 10% asking	1	2	3	4	5
(e) Realizes that there are many important roles in fundraising (not just asking for donations)	1	2	3	4	5
(f) Participates in activities such as the identification of potential donors, and is willing to introduce the nonprofit organization	1	2	3	4	5
3. Evaluation. Your board of directors:					
(a) Interacts positively with colleagues and staff in fundraising activities	1	2	3	4	5
(b) Has the will to take on specific tasks	1	2	3	4	5
(c) Regularly receives reports on the fundraising situation and reads them carefully	1	2	3	4	5
(d) Is thanked for its efforts in fundraising	1	2	3	4	5
(e) Participates in planning for fundraising	1	2	3	4	5

(Continued)

TABLE 6.1 *(continued)*

4. Collaboration. Your board of directors:					
(a) Includes members who are willing to make personal visits if duly accompanied by a volunteer or staff member	1	2	3	4	5
(b) Talks about fundraising with their board colleagues	1	2	3	4	5
(c) Recruits other volunteers for fundraising	1	2	3	4	5
(d) Comprises members who bring their enthusiasm and their successes to board meetings	1	2	3	4	5
5. Adoption. Your board:					
(a) Believes in fundraising, and actively participates	1	2	3	4	5
(b) Is on an active fundraising committee	1	2	3	4	5
(c) Assumes responsibility for specific tasks in fundraising	1	2	3	4	5
(d) Ensures the economic stability of the nonprofit organization	1	2	3	4	5

Source: Valerio Melandri. *Melandri Fundraising: Creating Stronger Donor Relationships to Sustain Your Nonprofit for the Really Long Haul* (Toronto, Canada: Civil Sector Press, 2017).

Once the board has been analyzed regarding its real willingness to carry out fundraising, the organization moves on to analyze the board's relation to itself and its cause. It begins by defining the type of directors it requires, and then works to build an ideal board to serve its needs (see Table 6.1). It then evaluates how the professional skills and experience of individual board members can best contribute to the board's work. Does the board need two politicians (from different parties)? A journalist? A financial expert?

Demographics should also be considered. The appropriate diversity for a board may be religious or cultural in nature. For instance: Is representation from both Christian and Muslim communities necessary to ensure a balanced perspective? Will the board benefit from the outside point of view of a foreigner, or an immigrant? The inclusion of the NGO's constituents on the board can be valuable. Is the input of a person with some form of disability needed on the board? A former patient? A respected (nonboard) volunteer? Other demographics, like age, may factor in, too.

TABLE 6.2 Evaluating Board Composition

Social Relations	Real Situation					Ideal Situation					Gap				
	1	2	3	4	5	1	2	3	4	5	1	2	3	4	5
Religious organizations															
Large companies															
Education															
Media															
Politics															
Foundations															
Small companies															
Social services															
Reputation/ experience in field with NGO boards															
Leadership skills															
Drive															
Personal bond with the organization's mission															
Other															

(*Continued*)

TABLE 6.2 (*continued*)

Personal skills and competencies	Real Situation					Ideal Situation					Gap				
	1	2	3	4	5	1	2	3	4	5	1	2	3	4	5
Ability to achieve consensus															
Ability to communicate															
Ability to implement a strategy															
Ability to have vision															
Other															
Area of experience	**1**	**2**	**3**	**4**	**5**	**1**	**2**	**3**	**4**	**5**	**1**	**2**	**3**	**4**	**5**
Administration/ management															
Entrepreneurship															
Financial management															
Accounting															
Banking															
Investments															
Fundraising															
International business															

	1	2	3	4	5	1	2	3	4	5	1	2	3	4	5
Law															
Marketing/public relations															
Human resources															
Strategic planning															
Engineering/architecture															
Technology															
Real estate															
Customer service representative															
Experience with special programs (education, health, public, policy, social services)															
Other															
Age	1	2	3	4	5	1	2	3	4	5	1	2	3	4	5
19–34															
35–50															
51–65															
Over 65															
Other															

(Continued)

TABLE 6.2 (continued)

	1	2	3	4	5	1	2	3	4	5	1	2	3	4	5
Sex	1	2	3	4	5	1	2	3	4	5	1	2	3	4	5
Man															
Woman															
Other															
Ethnicity	1	2	3	4	5	1	2	3	4	5	1	2	3	4	5
EU															
Immigrant															
Other															
Resources	1	2	3	4	5	1	2	3	4	5	1	2	3	4	5
Capacity to donate															
Access to wealthy individuals															
Access to other resources (support from businesses and foundations)															
Willingness to actively participate (in cultivation or solicitation visits)															
Other															
Number of years (or terms) on board	1	2	3	4	5	1	2	3	4	5	1	2	3	4	5

Source: Valerio Melandri. Melandri Fundraising: Creating Stronger Donor Relationships to Sustain Your Nonprofit for the Really Long Haul (Toronto, Canada: Civil Sector Press, 2017).

CONCLUSION

Europe is a large and fragmented entity from a cultural, historical, legislative, and political point of view. While there are marked differences from region to region, and even country to country, geographical areas unfortunately share some limitations in common.

There are two such limitations we have discussed at length in this chapter. The first limitation is that many European boards do not understand their role in providing the necessary resources to make an organization stable and long-lasting. The second is that, while the debate on the remuneration of board members is spreading throughout Europe, there is a lack of respect for the unpaid work of voluntary boards, and consequently it can be difficult to attract top-level board members. All-volunteer boards can hamper the ability of an organization to evolve and to sustain itself.

Happily, there are boards that have overcome these limitations. There are organizations in which, appropriately, board members are paid. There are also NGOs whose boards engage in profitable fundraising activities. Happy exceptions will become the norm when all boards conduct analyses of board composition and evaluation of performance.

Another optimistic note is that two new possibilities have emerged for the renewal of governance structures. The first draws inspiration from the governance models of large US family foundations, and the second is based on the concept of social enterprise.

European fragmentation is still an obstacle to establishing constructive dialogue on best practices for boards and in determining which governance models are best suited to the nonprofit world. Good governance is the ground on which to build a healthy third sector. If Europe continues to go in the direction of delegating welfare services to the third sector, this dialogue must advance.

REFERENCES

ACEVO. 2016. *Annual Report and Consolidated Financial Statement*. Association of Chief Executives of Voluntary Organizations. www.acevo.org.uk (accessed November 7, 2017).

Adam, T. 2004. *Philanthropy, Patronage, and Civil Society: Experiences from Germany, Great Britain, and North America*. Indiana University Press.

Addarii, F., J. Baker, H. de Bode, et al. 2009. *Being Responsible: Third Sector Governance: Transparency and the Obligation of Leadership from the European and North American Perspectives.* Aperio.

Anheier, H., and W. Seibel. 2001. *The Nonprofit Sector in Germany: Between State, Economy, and Society.* Manchester University Press.

Borzaga, C. 2003. *New Trends in the Non-profit Sector in Europe: The Emergence of Social Entrepreneurship in the Non-profit Sector in a Changing Economy.* OECD.

Brody, E. 2007. "The board of nonprofit organizations: Puzzling through the gaps between law and practice." *Fordham Law Review* 76, no. 2: 521–566.

Carver, John. 2006. *Boards That Make a Difference: A New Design for Leadership in Nonprofit and Public Organizations*, 3rd ed. Jossey-Bass.

Carver, John, and Miriam Mayhew Carver. 2001. "Le modèle policy governance et les organismes sans but lucrative." [In French]. *Gouvernance* 2 (Winter), no. 1: 30–48.

Estelle J. 1989. *The Nonprofit Sector in International Perspective: Studies in Comparative Culture and Policy.* Yale Studies on Non-Profit Organizations.

European Fundraising Association. 2015. *Fundraising in Europe 2015.* European Fundraising Association.

Evers, A., and J.-L. Laville. 2004. *The Third Sector in Europe.* Edward Elgar.

European Commission. 2015. *A Map of Social Enterprises and Their Eco-Systems in Europe.* Directorate-General for Employment, Social Affairs and Inclusion.

Harju, A. 2006. *Finnish Civil Society.* KVS Foundation.

Hilger, P. 2008. "A case of human service dominance: Volunteer centres in Finland." Paper. Volunteering Infrastructure and Civil Society Conference, Aalsmeer, the Netherlands (April 24–25).

Hopt, K., and T. Von Hippel, eds. 2010. *Comparative Corporate Governance of Non-Profit Organizations.* Cambridge University Press.

Hudson, M. 2011. *Managing Without Profit: Leadership, Management and Governance of Third Sector Organizations.* London, UK: Directory of Social Change.

International Finance Corporation. 2015. *A Guide to Corporate Governance Practices in the European Union.* International Finance Corporation.

Jobome, G. 2006. "Management pay, governance and performance: the case of large UK nonprofits." *Financial Accountability & Management* 22, no. 4 (November): 331–358.

Jones, C., ed. 1993. *New Perspectives on the Welfare State in Europe.* Routledge.

Knippenberg, H., ed. 2005. *The Changing Religious Landscape of Europe.* Het Spinhuis.

Lampkin, L., and C. Chasteen. 2014. *What Is Reasonable for Nonprofit Board Pay?* Economic Research Institute. https://downloads.erieri.com/pdf/what_is_reasonable_nonprofit_board_pay.pdf (accessed September 27, 2017).

Lincoln, S., and J. Saxton. 2012. *Major Donor Giving Research Report.* Institute of Fundraising.

Lundström, T., and L. Svedberg. 2003. "The voluntary sector in a social democratic welfare state—The case of Sweden." *Journal of Social Policy* 32, no. 2: 217–238.

Mason, C., and M. Royce. 2007. "Fit for purpose—Board development for social enterprise." *Journal of Finance and Management in Public Services* 6, no. 3: 57–67.

Melandri, V. 2017. *Melandri Fundraising: Creating Stronger Donor Relationships to Sustain Your Nonprofit for the Really Long Haul.* Toronto, Canada: Civil Sector Press.

Powell, W., and R. Steinberg, eds. 2008. *The Nonprofit Sector: A Research Handbook.* Yale University Press.

Ramrayka, L. 2012. "Trustees: To Pay or Not to Pay." *Guardian*, October 19. www.theguardian.com/careers/trustee-to-pay-or-not-to-pay (accessed September 27, 2017).

Schöning, M., A. Noble, A. Heinecke, et al. 2012. *The Governance of Social Enterprises: Managing Your Organization for Success.* World Economic Forum.

Wijkström, F. 2004. "Changing focus or changing role? The Swedish nonprofit sector in the new millennium." In *Strategy Mix for Nonprofit Organizations: Vehicles for Social and Labour Market Integration*, edited by Annette Zimmer and Christina Stecker, 15–40. Kluwer Academic.

Williams, R. 2014. "A guide to setting salary and wage levels for charity employees." *Guardian*, May 14, 2014. www.theguardian.com/voluntary-sector-network/2014/may/14/guide-to-setting-charity-salaries-and-pay (accessed September 27, 2017).

NOTES

1. Europe and the European Union (EU) are not the same things. The EU is an international, political, and economic organization with a supranational character (comprising over 28 member states) inaugurated in November 1993. It should not be confused with the European geographical region.
2. ActionAid UK, Save the Children UK, and Oxfam UK, to name but a few.
3. Examples of fundraising campaigns include those run by Cancer Research UK, Crisis at Christmas, Alzheimer's Research UK, and War Child, among others.
4. www.institute-of-fundraising.org.uk (accessed November 7, 2017).
5. www.acevo.org.uk (accessed November 7, 2017).
6. www.ec.europa.eu/eurostat (accessed November 7, 2017).
7. www.istat.it (accessed November 7, 2017).

8. Take, for example, the University of Cambridge, Oxford University, King's College Hospital, and St. George's Hospital, to cite only a few.
9. www.gatesfoundation.org (accessed November 7, 2017).
10. www.ant.it (accessed November 7, 2017).
11. www.intersos.org/en (accessed November 7, 2017).
12. www.emergency.it/index.html (accessed November 7, 2017).

FURTHER READING

Eller, H. n.d. "Corporate governance in non-profit organizations in Europe by focusing the governance model" (PhD thesis, University of Latvia). c.ymcdn.com/sites/www.istr.org/resource/resmgr/WP2014/Eller_Corporate Governance_Co.pdf (accessed September 27, 2017).

Hope, C. 2015. "32 charity bosses paid over £200,000 last year." *Telegraph*, February 26. www.telegraph.co.uk/news/politics/11435754/32-charity-bosses-paid-over-200000-last-year.html (accessed September 27, 2017).

Hopt, K. 2009. "The board of nonprofit organizations: Some corporate governance thoughts from Europe." Working Paper Law Series No. 125/2009. European Corporate Governance Institute. www.ecgi.global/working-paper/board-nonprofit-organizations-some-corporate-governance-thoughts-europe (accessed September 27, 2017).

Joy, I., and P. Murray. 2016. *It Starts From The Top: Improving Governance, Improving Impact.* New Philanthropy Capital. www.thinknpc.org/publications/it-starts-from-the-top (accessed September 27, 2017).

Koele, I. 2014. "The Dutch *private foundation*: A *robust but flexible tool in dynastic struct*uring." *Trusts & Trustees* advance online access (April 25, 2014).

Kreutzer, K., and C. Jacobs. 2011. "Balancing control and coaching in CSO governance: A paradox perspective on board behavior." *Voluntas* 22, no. 4: 613–638.

Malone, D., and M. Okwonga. 2011. *The State of UK Charity Boards. A Quantitative Analysis.* Institute for Philanthropy.

Melandri, V. 2012a. *Manuale di fundraising: Fare raccolta fondi nelle organizzazioni nonprofit e negli enti pubblici* [in Italian]. Collana Maggioli-Philanthropy, Maggioli Editore.

Melandri, V. 2012b. Mallabone G., Balmer K. *Raggiungere l'eccellenza nel fundraising: L'audit come strumento per migliorare la raccolta fondi* [in Italian]. Collana Maggioli-Philanthropy, Maggioli Editore.

Nyssens, M., and J. Defourny. 2008. "Social enterprise in Europe: Recent trends and developments." EMES Working Papers No. 08/01. EMES International Research Network. https://emes.net/publications/working-papers/social-enterprise-in-europe-recent-trends-and-developments (accessed September 27, 2017).

Rosso, H., E. Tempel, and V. Melandri. 2012. Il libro del fund raising: Etica, strategie e strumenti della raccolta fondi [in Italian]. Rizzoli-ETAS.

CHAPTER 7

Latin America

Consuelo Castro

Latin America is a diverse region characterized by inequality, with a large proportion of people whose income is less than US$1 a day.[1] This reality represents a major challenge for the nonprofit sector, which is entrusted with improving lives and helping social development in this part of the world. Consuelo Castro, legal and regulatory expert, who has served as a consultant and trainer for good governance practices on nonprofit boards across the region, offers her perspective on the legal and regulatory environment for governance, explains some of the specific challenges boards face here, and shares some notable successes.

Each day it becomes more evident that governance of nonprofit organizations has a direct relation to their efficiency and effectiveness. For this reason, board members, or trustees, of CSOs, as rudders of the organization, play an important role. In Spanish, the name for the board of directors, or trustees, varies. In Bolivia it is referred to as *Directorio*, in Venezuela as *Junta Directiva*, in Mexico as *Consejo Directivo* or *Patronato*. It might be even referred to as *Secretaría Ejecutiva*. Whatever it is called, it is important to identify the leadership structure in the organization.

There are a great many nonprofit board topics we will analyze in this chapter, such as composition, roles, and recruitment, among others. Our main objective is to provide basic information regarding governance structure in Latin America, particularly in Mexico.

HISTORICAL AND CULTURAL CONTEXT FOR GOVERNANCE

Latin America is well known for its long philanthropic tradition that dates back to Spanish colonial times. A number of charities emerged as

161

an expression of religious values and practices fostered by the Catholic Church.

In Mexico, the Hospital de Jesus was founded in 1524 and is still active to date (Gascón Mercado 2014). Other charitable hospitals established in the region include the Perú Hospital in Lima (1538), the *Santa Misericordia de Todos los Santos Hospital* in Brazil (1543), and the *San Juan de Dios* Hospital in Santiago de Chile (1552). In Perú, the shelter *Recogimiento de Nuestra Señora de los Remedios* or *San Juan de la Penitencia* opened its doors to orphan girls in 1551. Another example is the *Nacional Monte de Piedad* in Mexico, which since 1775 has operated a pawnshop in which items can be pawned in exchange for low-interest loans. A fast-growing institution, with over 200 branches all over Mexico, it plans to open a branch in every Mexican city.

These early institutions were established, run, and supported through the generosity of a prominent person or family, who at the same time served as trustees. Although this governing style persists, today's board composition and performance reflects the emergence of new types of nonprofits. Since the 1970s, the formation of new organizations has come through the initiative of groups of individuals, community members, and corporations.

It is important to recognize the many and significant social, economic, cultural, and regulatory differences among countries in Latin America. Each country is unique in its approach to governance. How the regulation of nonprofit organizations affects boards in each country would fill an entire book. Therefore, in this chapter, only some general aspects are approached in order to offer a general idea about not-for-profit governance in this part of the world.

RELEVANT LEGAL/TAX REQUIREMENTS AFFECTING NGO BOARDS

There is no doubt that legal and tax requirements influence nonprofit organizations and their governance. For this reason, we will address some of the regulatory aspects that concern the board. The following section contains two parts: Legal requirements and tax requirements.

Legal Requirements

A common legal configuration in Latin America within the civil law system is the Civil Association[2] or AC (the acronym in Spanish for *Asociación Civil*), governed by civil codes and defined as a nongovernmental type of organization formed by two or more individuals to attain a common purpose that is not forbidden by law, and which is not intended for the purpose of economic gain and does not engage in commercial speculation. Notwithstanding that the law differs from one country to another, in an AC, the supreme governing body is the General Assembly of Associates or Meeting.

In addition to the legal construct of ACs, the legal framework governing nonprofit organizations in many Latin American countries (i.e., Panamá and Argentina) includes foundation law. A foundation is defined as a private nonprofit incorporated by one or more persons who allocate a permanent fund or endowment, either in life or by will, for a social purpose (Gecik 2012; Belalcázar and Riascos 2011). Some foundations grant monies to other nonprofit organizations.

In Mexico, a legal entity conducting nonprofit activities may be incorporated as an AC. It may also be incorporated as an Private Assistance Institution known as IAP, (the Spanish abbreviation for *Institución de Asistencia Privada)* or IBP (*Institución de Beneficencia Privada*). Each is governed by different statutes. ACs are governed by Mexico City or state civil codes. IAPs are ruled by different set of laws in force in Mexico City and the states.

Civil codes that regulate ACs, such as the Mexico City Civil Code (*Código Civil para el Distrito Federal 2015*), have minimal provisions: The General Assembly of Associates appoints or elects the board of directors and its committees in accordance with the bylaws of the organization. In some countries, such as Costa Rica, the *Reglamento de la Ley de Asociaciones* (Regulation of the Association Law) (CECACIER 2016) sets the legal requirements for the governance body.

AC governing laws do not necessarily impose many specific rules. However, it is customary to establish the board composition, term duration, and main responsibilities in the bylaws or statutes, and to have at minimum a chair, treasurer, secretary, and two or three members. It is quite common to find that board members are responsible for the legal representation of the organization and have a joint general power of attorney that permits them, among other things, to handle financial and property matters.

In contrast, IAPs have specific legal expectations regarding governance composition, functions, and limitations. The governance body (structure) of an IAP according to Mexico City law (*Ley de Instituciones de Asistencia Privada para el Distrito Federal,* or LIAPDF) (Private Assistance Institutions Law), called *Patronato* (trustee), is designed by the founders to legally represent and manage the organization, which must not be less than five members. Requirements for the trustees of an IAP are more stringent than for a AC. Public officers, legal entities, and persons who have been made to stand down from other boards do not qualify as members of the *Patronato*.

While ACs have organizational and management autonomy in Mexico, IAPs are controlled and supervised by a local government entity called the Private Assistance Board or JAP (*Junta de Asistencia Privada*). In certain circumstances, whenever the *Patronato* of an organization is not able to perform its duties for some reason, or has been excluded from the organization, the JAP has the power to designate a new trustee. Some of the main duties and responsibilities of trustees listed under the law are the following:

- To comply with the purpose (or will) established by the founder(s)
- To legally represent the organization
- To employ staff (but prohibited from hiring family members)
- Not to sell or mortgage a real estate property unless in case of extreme need, as authorized by the JAP
- To ensure that the employees who manage the institution's funds are bonded for the amount ordered by the JAP
- To report to the JAP if the organization is subject to any current lawsuit
- To submit to the JAP any realestate leasing agreements for authorization

Figure 7.1 shows the common structure of an AC and of an IAP.

The most typical board committees for ACs and IAPs are the finance committee, development committee, and the communications committee. Also, it is common for organizations that give some kind of recognition to have an award committee. For example, *Compartir*

ASOCIACIÓN CIVIL   INSTITUCIÓN DE ASISTENCIA PRIVADA

FIGURE 7.1   **Organizational structure of a civil association and a private assistance institution.**

Fundación Social (COMPARTIR, n.d.) (Compartir Social Foundation) is an IAP that gives awards annually to persons and organizations that have stood out for their service to the needy or have helped to transform society. Another example is the *Centro Mexicano para la Filantropía*, or the Mexican Center for Philanthropy, known as Cemefi, which bestows the Commitment to Others Recognition Award to recognize outstanding job performance within nonprofits (Cemefi 2016).

Tax Requirements

One of the key contributions governments can make to promote philanthropy and help nonprofits in their societies is the provision of incentives for giving. Pursuant to Mexico income tax law (United Mexican States 2016), as authorized donees, nonprofit organizations can receive tax-deductible gifts.

The law also protects the public from unlawful or negligent use of donations. As one example, a reform in Mexican income tax law establishes greater accountability. The most recent Mexico income tax law reform, published on November 30, 2016, establishes a new provision in 82(IX) regarding the governance of some of the Mexican authorized donees. In this last reform, a new obligation was imposed upon authorized donees. Those with a total annual income of more than US\$5519000[3], or with an endowment of more than \$27595000, must have the structure and processes of corporate governance to manage and control the organization. However, the specific fiscal rules to be complied with had not been published as of the date of release of the provision.

COMPOSITION AND RECRUITMENT CONSIDERATIONS

Nonprofit organizations are frequently started by a few deeply committed and enthusiastic persons. Initially led solely by volunteers, these start-ups often find it difficult to distinguish between board and staff functions. The board chair may also act as the CEO and carry out other staff activities.

In the author's experience, it is helpful for individuals at organizations to differentiate among roles that they are playing at any given time. For example, it can be useful to encourage participants to define whether the meeting they are holding is a board or a staff meeting, and to record the minutes accordingly.

When the board and the staff are the same, it can be the source of many problems within the organization. Having different persons serve as either board members or staff members (but not both) creates a healthy distance between operational and management matters and governance. The outside point of view provided by the board assures impartial supervision and evaluation. This is especially true if the organization's board works on a nonremunerated basis.

Having a board composed of those without an economic interest allows for a more transparent point of view that is free of conflict of interest. As the organization grows, it is increasingly important for the organization to separate board functions from those of the CEO and staff.

In some countries, such as Costa Rica, it is mandatory to establish the election process as well as the composition and terms of the governance body in order to be officially registered (SCIJ, n.d.). As noted above, Mexican law requires that an IAP appoint at least five trustees and sets certain standards that trustees must meet.

Some organizations employ a nominations committee to recruit new board members. This committee may include former board chairs to help identify and recruit nominees to serve as the next chair.

Community Representation

An interesting Mexican case study for its unusual structure is the corporate foundation *Fundación del Empresariado Chihuahuense* (FECHAC) (Entrepreneurial Foundation of Chihuahua). Supported by 34000 corporations in the State of Chihuahua in the north, it is the most important grant-making foundation in that part of the country and has granted more than US$164 million between 1994 and 2014, mainly for human services and social development. The board aims to have a representative from each region. Therefore, the State Board of Directors has 20 representatives from the nine main cities in the State of Chihuahua. The board is led by a board chair, and the general director acts as the secretary of the board with voice but no voting privileges. FECHAC is an example of an organization that aspires to have a wide representation among the community in order to best attend the needs of the people of the State of Chihuahua. The role of the general director and CEO's presence at FECHAC board meetings raises the issue of the relationship with the board, which is addressed in the next section (FECHAC, n.d.).

The Board's Relationship to the NGO, CEO, and Other Staff

Ideally the board and the CEO of the organization have a clear understanding of their separate roles and responsibilities. This promotes harmony between the board, the CEO, and other staff. The reality can be quite different if the lines are blurred.

A lack of clarity in roles can result in one of two common situations: Boards will either tend to micromanage or go to the other extreme and leave all the responsibility to the CEO, meeting randomly and participating little in actually governing the organization.

As mentioned earlier, it is quite usual, especially in small or new organizations, for the founding group to not differentiate among roles. The same person may be the president and the CEO, and may also manage programs. As the organization develops, the need to have the different positions occupied by different persons and clearly defined role separation between board and employees might eventually happen. (This is, by the way, a major step for an organization, which is sometimes fraught with tension. The help of an external consultant can help smooth the transition.) If the organization accomplishes the transition, good board and staff team work is much more likely to happen.

Another important step towards a productive board-CEO relationship is a good CEO selection process. The election of the CEO by the board is one of its main responsibilities.

Some boards take this very seriously. This author was pleasantly surprised to find that an organization called *Gestión Social y Cooperación Social* (GESOC) (Social Management and Social Cooperation), in its search for a new CEO, launched an open job call that not only outlined the candidate profile, skills, and competencies sought, but also provided a detailed description of the evaluation and selection process, in which, of course, the board of directors would play a decisive part (GESOC, n.d.).

Close collaboration between the board and the CEO is expected, especially between the board chair and the CEO. Sometimes the chair[4] of the organization crosses the line and intrudes into duties that should be entrusted to the CEO. A micromanaging chair or board is likely to be a source of tension, discomfort, and disagreements. The author has frequently found that a board committed to drafting policies on various issues will provide a clear point of reference for the CEO's performance. The CEO will know the limits of staff administration. The main goal is to build a relation based on trust and respect.

ORGANIZATION OF MEETING, CULTURE OF INQUIRY

Board meetings are a space to reflect on how the organization's mission and vision are translated into its everyday work. It is a significant opportunity, not just to hear routine reports, but also to explore strategies to advance the organization. Questions should be put on the table on the present and future of the organization, such as the feasibility of new projects, the sustainability of the organization, and the evaluation of the CEO, among many others.

Each day it is more common to find governance practices that encourage openness and inquiry in a harmonious and fruitful manner—practices in which dissenting opinions are welcome. Although not always achieved because, as the Spanish proverb says, "every head is a world," some succeed in this and prove that it is worthwhile to welcome different perspectives in a deliberative process.

A culture of inquiry not only allows boards to tackle the concerns of the day, but also helps their organizations remain relevant and effective into the future.

The hospital *Nuestra Señora de la Luz* (*Nuestra Señora de la Luz Hospital*), founded in 1894, is one such farsighted organization. Its mission is to help the poor with vision problems. It is distinguished by the excellence of its services and its commitment to utilizing the latest technology in the field (*Fundación Hospital Nuestra Señora de la Luz*, n.d.).

This hospital has managed to be at the forefront of visual health care for more than 140 years. It relies on a solid board, which anticipates the needs of tomorrow. The quality of the decision-making process of the nine members of the board is evident in annual reports. The hospital not only provides approximately 200000 services annually, it has a top-notch biomedical research center, provides specialized postgraduate studies in medicine, and has an outreach service program serving four states in Mexico. In 2016, for instance, after a deep analysis of the population needs, the board decided to acquire a piece of land in Mexico City in order to build a new clinic and committed itself to raising funds for this great project through a capital campaign (Lechuga de la Peña 2016).

ROLES AND RESPONSIBILITIES

The role of the board has expanded over the past two or three decades. Following are some of the key ways in which boards engage.

Compliance

From the moment of the legal incorporation of an organization, the board generally assumes the legal representation of the organization according to its statutes or bylaws. This is a fundamental responsibility. The board is obliged to be acquainted with general as well as specific compliance requirements within the organization's particular field, such as the health laws and income tax laws, for example, to ensure that the organization not only maintains its tax-exempt status, but also standards of health care.

Mission, Vision, Strategic Planning

At the core of an organization is its mission and vision. From the mission derives the *raison d'être* of the organization, and the board is its main guardian. The board must also monitor the pulse of changing times and know when it is time to consider a new mission. The mission and vision are the foundation for strategic planning, another board responsibility, which leads not only to excellence in mission delivery but also to organizational evolution.

Administration and Representation

The board has the legal power to represent, and enter into binding obligations on behalf of, the organization in accordance with the statutes and the law. The board is usually granted powers of attorney to be exercised severally, such as:

- *General power of attorney for acts of administration.* This power confers the board with the broadest authority to manage the property and business of the organization.
- *General power of attorney for lawsuits and collections and acts of labor management.* This power is granted so that the board may represent the organization before all kinds of persons and before judicial, administrative, civil, criminal, and labor authorities, whether federal, state, or municipal. It also grants the power to act in all kinds of labor matters.

The board is the organization's legal face to the public. This sobering responsibility encourages close oversight. The board can be charged for dishonest, fraudulent, or criminal offenses. However, nonprofit boards in Latin America rarely have liability insurance that will protect them in these situations.

Sustainability

Ensuring sustainability is a critical board function. This often means the board must play a prominent role in fundraising. Every day in Latin America, more and more board members are actively raising funds. Boards wield their influence and tap into their networks to identify potential partners, donors, and other kinds of support. Prominent board members are recruited to help attract resources to the organization. Because the CEO may not have access to those with resources, the board can provide the necessary linkage. Savvy board members know that approaching their contacts directly on a one-on-one basis is the best way to raise money.

Some board members like to remain anonymous, while celebrities agree to promote their affiliation with a nonprofit in order to generate public support. For example, *Fundación Carlos Slim* (Carlos Slim Foundation) bears the name of one of the richest men in the world (Fundación Carlos Slim, n.d.); and the organization *Solo por Ayudar* (Only to Help) is supported by the philanthropist and well-known journalist Lolita Ayala (*Solo por Ayudar, n.d.*).

Another responsibility of the board includes the joint election of the CEO. An example was already given in the section "The Board's Relationship to the NGO, CEO, and Other Staff" in this chapter.

Successful Latin American Boards

Organizational achievement is the evidence of a successful board in Latin America. One outstanding example is the medical specialty care center for children called the *Hospital Infantil de las Californias* (Children's Hospital of the Californias) (*Hospital Infantil de las Californias* 2017). This hospital was founded in 1994 as a result of a trinational initiative involving Mexico, the United States, and Canada. The hospital is the proof of what can be accomplished, beyond national borders, with the will of committed persons united in a common purpose.

The hospital's mission is "to improve the health and nutrition for children," and its vision is "to be the children's health care organization that covers the largest possible area of the region, based in the strengthening and development of high specialty pediatric medical care, top level education and research, as well as the timely prevention of diseases and the promotion of health in an environment of high quality and self-sustainability."

This vision has translated into several ambitious projects. In 2000, the board of directors and staff raised US$2400000 to build the Diagnosis Assessment Referral Treatment and Education Center.[5]

The hospital has continued to expand, and in 2012 inaugurated the Harland Sanders Ambulatory Surgery Center. There are two organizations that support this effort: The Foundation for the Children of the Californias, based in the United States, and the Canadian Friends Foundation for the Children of the Californias in Canada (Foundation for the Children of the Californias 2017). The hospital treats 3500 patients who come from both sides of the border each month.

Another shining example is the *Fundación Pro Niños de la Calle* *(Fundación Pro Niños de la Calle, n.d.)* (Pro Children on the Street Foundation). This organization will soon celebrate its 25th anniversary of helping children living in the streets or at risk of homelessness. The children range from 8 to 21 years old, and many of them are afflicted with drug addiction or other health problems. The comprehensive services include not only providing for basic needs, such as clothing, shelter, and nutrition, but also psychological counseling and working with families towards the goal of reintegrating children into the family unit.

The organization has been lauded with national and international awards, including the *Premio Reina Sofía contra las drogas* (Queen Sofía Award Against Drugs), which is an Ibero-American award that has been bestowed by the Red Cross in Spain eight times. The Mexico City Private Assistance Board (a government entity equivalent to the Charity Commission in Mexico City) also recognized the organization's trustees in 2012. This last award points directly to the impact of the board.

Transparency is a key responsibility for boards. The financial statements of the *Fundación Pro Niños de la Calle* (Pro Children on the Street Foundation), which are audited by an outside specialized firm, are reported in its annual report. The report also counts more than 30 partners of the organization from both the private and public sector; some are donors, others belong to networks with whom they collaborate.

Fulfilling roles and carrying out responsibilities are a key factor in the success of the organization. Successfully meeting ethical challenges is another critical component of governance.

Ethical Challenges

Important ethical challenges often arise around conflicts of interest. Unfortunately, however, this may be a foreign concept to the boards of some organizations.

Some boards may see no wrong in hiring a board member's relatives without following the usual hiring procedure or purchasing goods or services from a board member without securing bids from other suppliers (and recusing that board member from voting on vendor selection). The abuse of privilege, such as having staff members run personal errands for a board member, is another ethical concern.

Even if these kinds of dilemmas seem to be remote concerns, it is important to continue making the board aware of the possibility of ethical transgressions. There must be a means to raise this issue within the board. Conflict of interest policies or rules must be in place.

Another ethical challenge that sometimes arises in the boardroom has to do with the origin of the donations to be accepted, as boards make policy about what kinds of donations are acceptable. Of course, illicit funds would automatically be out of the question. Sixteen countries in Latin America (Argentina, Bolivia, Brazil, Chile, Colombia, Costa Rica, Cuba, Ecuador, Guatemala, Honduras, Mexico, Nicaragua, Panama, Paraguay, Peru, the Dominican Republic, and Uruguay) have enacted anti–money laundering regulations (GAFILAT, n.d.). They are members of the FATF. In Mexico, for instance, recipient organizations are subject to strict reporting requirements by the Mexican Financial Intelligence Unit. For this reason, Latin American organizations carefully consider the source of donated funds to avoid the risk of getting involved in money-laundering activities (GOB.mx, n.d.).

The most common ethical concern concerning donations is whether or not they align with the purpose of the organization. For example, some children's associations do not accept donations coming from corporations that produce alcoholic beverages. For other kinds of organizations this would not be a concern at all.

Board meetings should allow room for discussing the ethical issues that may lie behind decisions.

EVALUATION AND MONITORING

The subject of a board's performance and evaluation might trigger discomfort among its members. Board members are rarely compensated for their services. As they freely offer their time and resources, some might be affronted by the very thought of being judged on performance as a volunteer.

Some think that if the organization is doing fine, the board must also be doing well. This is not always the case. Regular evaluation can circumvent certain situations that might otherwise suddenly overwhelm the organization. If the board can preemptively identify and act to address the behavior of passive or negative board members, it can proactively move to the next level of performance.

If a board never gives careful consideration to its own makeup, it can also cause problems. For example, if a vacancy must be filled, it will be a challenge to identify desirable candidates without an analysis of the existing composition of the board.

Generally speaking, there is a lack of knowledge on the benefits, methodologies, and available tools for board evaluation in Latin America, where self-assessment is rare. Although many boards are engaged in the strategic planning process and evaluation of the organization as a whole, very few look inward at the board itself.

If one practice is missing in governance in Latin America, it is the evaluation and monitoring of board performance.

TRENDS AND CASE STUDIES OF BEST PRACTICES

Governance in Latin America has its challenges. We have previously described some of the common ones boards face, such as the lack of a clear distinction between governance and operations.

On the other hand, it is possible to find strong and sophisticated governance. Such is the case with the *Fundación Gonzalo Río Arronte* (Gonzalo Río Arronte Foundation) (Fundación Gonzalo Río Arronte, n.d.a). One of the most important health care foundations in Latin America, it was established with a significant endowment bequest from Gonzalo Río Arronte in 1993. One of its triumphs is its success in involving the community in its governance.

The foundation was created in 2000 in Mexico as an IAP. Between the years 2000 and 2015, the foundation has granted US$6870547953 to support 825 projects related to health care, water sanitation, and addiction recovery.

It has a twelve-member board of trustees and six active committees: The Executive Committee, the Health Committee, the Addictions Committee, the Water Committee, the Investment Committee, the

Management and Institutional Development Committee, and the Communications Committee. Each of the committees includes experts and renowned leaders from its particular area of responsibility.

The participation in committees of persons external to the organization has several advantages. It cultivates the gradual increase of involvement and commitment. It is an opportunity for the organization and the outside members to get to know each other better. In time, these persons may be elevated to serve as board members, arriving already equipped with an understanding of the organization. Another advantage is that the organization is enriched by multidisciplinary expertise, which gives the foundation an ear to the voice of the community.

CONCLUSION

This chapter provides a panoramic view of nonprofit governance in Latin America. Advancing board capacity fosters the possibility of mobilizing resources, increasing transparency, and developing leadership. Through the leadership positions they occupy, board members are entrusted to solve the problems of society. The empowerment of boards is a must for the region.

REFERENCES

Belalcázar, Edison and Luis Hernando Riascos. 2011. *Derecho de las Personas Jurídicas Sin Ánimo de Lucro* [in Spanish]. Columbia, Librería Ediciones del Profesional LTDA: 112.

CECACIER. 2016. *Reglamento de la Ley de Asociaciones de Costa Rica* [in Spanish]. www.cecacier.org/docs/Reglamento-Ley-de-Asociaciones.pdf (accessed September 27, 2017).

Centro Mexicano para la Filantropía (Cemefi). 2016. Cemefi (website [in Spanish]). www.cemefi.org (accessed November 7, 2017).

COMPARTIR. n.d. COMPARTIR (website [in Spanish]). www.compartir.org.mx (accessed December 12, 2017).

Fletcher, Kathleen. 2004. *Políticas para Organizaciones no Lucrativas: Ejemplos Prácticos México* [in Spanish]. México: BoardSource/CEMEFI.

Foundation for the Children of the Californias. 2017. Foundation for the Children of the Californias (website). www.usfcc.org (accessed November 7, 2017).

Fundación Carlos Slim. n.d. Fundación Carlos Slim (website [in Spanish]). www.salud.carlosslim.org (accessed November 7, 2017).

Fundación del Empresariado Chihuahuense (FECHAC). n.d. FECHAC (website [in Spanish]). www.fechac.org/web/index.php (accessed November 7, 2017).

Fundación Hospital Nuestra Señora de la Luz. n.d. Hospital de la Luz (website [in Spanish]). hospitaldelaluz.org (accessed November 7, 2017).

Fundación Pro Niños de la Calle. n.d. Fundación Pro Niños de la Calle (website [in Spanish]). www.proninosdelacalle.org.mx (accessed November 7, 2017).

GAFILAT. n.d. GAFILAT (website [in Spanish]). www.gafilat.org (accessed November 7, 2017).

Gascón Mercado, Julián. 2014. *Registros Testimoniales Hospital de Jesús* [in Spanish]. *Hospital de Jesús*: 3.

Gecik, Pedro. 2012. *Manual de Asociaciones Civiles y Fundaciones* [in Spanish]. Columbia, Librería Ediciones del Profesional LTDA: 539.

GESOC. n.d. "Convocatoria para la Dirección Ejecutiva de Gesoc" (job posting [in Spanish]). www.gesoc.org.mx/site/src/convocatorias/Convocatoria%20publica%20contratacion%20Direccion%20Ejecutiva.pdf (accessed November 7, 2017).

GOB.mx (website). n.d. "Donativos" (web page [in Spanish]). https://sppld.sat.gob.mx/pld/interiores/donativos.html (accessed November 7, 2017).

Hospital Infantil de las Californias. 2017. Hospital Infantil de las Californias (website [in Spanish]). http://hospitalinfantil.org (accessed November 7, 2017).

Lechuga de la Peña, Jimena. 2016. *Fundación Hospital Nuestra Señora de la Luz, 140 Años* [in Spanish]. Fundación Hospital Nuestra Señora de la Luz.

Sistema Costarricense de Información Jurídica (SCIJ). n.d. Law database [in Spanish]. Ley 218 (article 13) de Asociaciones de Costa Rica. www.pgrweb.go.cr/SCIJ/BUSQUEDA/normativa/normas/nrm_norma.aspx?param1=NRM&nValor1=1&nValor2=32764&nValor3=83259&strTipM=FN (accessed September 27, 2017).

Solo por Ayudar. n.d. Solo por Ayudar (website [in Spanish]). www.soloporayudar.org/en (accessed November 7, 2017).

United Mexican States. 2016. *Ley del Impuesto sobre la Renta* [in Spanish]. www.diputados.gob.mx/LeyesBiblio/pdf/LISR_301116.pdf (accessed September 27, 2017).

NOTES

1. The regional poverty rate in Latin America is calculated to be 29.2%, with 175 million in poverty, out of which 75 million are indigent (Economic Commission for Latin America and the Caribbean (ECLAC). 2016. *Social Panorama of Latin America 2015*. ECLAC: 18. repositorio.cepal.org/bitstream/handle/11362/39964/5/S1600174_en.pdf (accessed September 27, 2017).

2. In some countries there are special laws for foundations, and in other countries, such as Mexico, foundations may take the form of an AC or a private assistance institution (IAP).
3. Currency referenced in this chapter is in US dollars converted from Mexican pesos on June 30, 2017.
4. In Spanish the term used for the chair of an organization is *Presidente*.
5. My first personal experience with this fine institution dates from January 2001, when I had the opportunity to facilitate a board workshop while I was working at Cemefi.

FURTHER READING

Adelman, Carol, Jesse N. Barnett, and Kimberly Russell. 2015. *Index of Philanthropic Freedom 2015*. Hudson Institute. hudson.org/research/11363-index-of-philanthropic-freedom-2015 (accessed September 27, 2017).

Asamblea Legislativa del Distrito Federal, VI Legislatura. 2015. Código Civil para el Distrito Federal [in Spanish]. www.aldf.gob.mx/archivo-c9dc6843e50163a0d2628615e069b140.pdf (accessed September 27, 2017).

Axelrod, Nancy R. 2004. *El Papel Que Juega un Director Ejecutivo en la Confirmación y Desarrollo del Consejo Directivo en las Organizaciones Sin Fines de Lucro* [in Spanish]. México: BoardSource/CEMEFI.

BoardSource. 2005. *The Source: Twelve Principles of Governance That Power Exceptional Boards*. BoardSource.

Castro, Consuelo. 2001. "Mexico country report." In *El Tercer Sector Iberoamericano: Fundaciones, asociaciones y ONGs*, edited by José Luis Piñar Mañas. McGraw Hill. 1–81.

Castro, Consuelo. 2015. "Mexico." Review of "Mexico" section in the *Index of Philanthropic Freedom 2015*. Hudson Institute. 1–9. s3.amazonaws.com/media .hudson.org/files/publications/2015.Index.of.Philanthropic.Freedom.Mexico .pdf (accessed September 27, 2017).

Castro, Consuelo, and Carlos Cordourier. 2014. *Assessment for the Enabling Environment of Civil Society Organizations in Mexico*. Centro Mexicano para la Filantropía. 148.240.65.99/altaircif/Doctoelectronico/12666.pdf. (accessed September 27, 2017).

CDMX (website). 2017. www.contraloriadf.gob.mx/prontuario/index.php/ normativas/Template/ver_mas. (accessed December 22, 2017).

Chait, Richard P. 2004. *Como Hacer Que el Consejo Directivo Gobierne Más y Administre Menos* [in Spanish]. México: BoardSource/CEMEFI.

Dietel, William M., and Linda R. Dietel. 2004. *Manual del Presidente del Consejo Directivo* [in Spanish]. México: BoardSource/CEMEFI.

Dorsey, Eugene C. 2004. *El Papel Que Desempeña el Presidente del Consejo Directivo en las Organizaciones Sin Fines de Lucro* [in Spanish]. México: BoardSource/CEMEFI, second edition.

Fundación Gonzalo Río Arronte. n.d.a. Fundación Gonzalo Río Arronte (website [in Spanish]). www.fgra.org.mx (accessed November 7, 2017).

Fundación Gonzalo Río Arronte. n.d.b. "Informe de Actividades 2014-2015" (web page [in Spanish]). www.fgra.org.mx/2014-2015.html (accessed September 27, 2017).

Fundación Pro Niños de la Calle. 2016. *Informe Anual 2015*. www.proninosdelacalle .org.mx/descargables/InformeAnual2015.pdf (accessed September 27, 2017).

Ingram, Richard T. 2015. *Ten Basic Responsibilities of Non Profit Boards*. Board-Source.

Kurtz, Daniel L. 2004. *Manejo del Conflicto de Intereses: Guía práctica para el Consejo Directivo de las Organizaciones Sin Fines de Lucro* [in Spanish]. México: BoardSource/CEMEFI.

Ley de Instituciones de Asistencia Privada para el Distrito Federal (website). www.jap.org.mx (accessed December 31, 2017).

Mathiasen, Karl, III. 2004. *El Consejo en Transición: Tres Momentos Claves en el Ciclo de la Vida del Consejo Directivo* [in Spanish]. México: Board-Source/CEMEFI.

Salamon, Lester M. 1997. *International Guide to Nonprofit Law*. John Wiley & Sons.

SEGOB (website). 2016. "Ley Federal para la Prevención e Identificación de Operaciones con Recursos de Procedencia Ilícita" [in Spanish]. www.dof.gob .mx/nota_detalle.php?codigo=5273403&fecha=17/10/2012 (accessed September 27, 2017).

Stern, Herbert. 2016. "Los Primeros Hospitales en América" [in Spanish]. *Historiadelamedicinadomincana* (blog). BoardSource/CEMEFI.

Marco Jurídico que Regula a las Organizaciones Sin Fines de Lucro en Centroamérica. www.vrijmetselaarsgilde.eu/Maconnieke%20Encyclopedie/ FMAP~1/REFORM/reform3/cap33.htm (accessed September 27, 2017).

CHAPTER **8**

Middle East and North Africa

Tariq Cheema and Naila Farouky

Wealth creation in the Middle East and North Africa (MENA) region is driving a generation of actors to commit their resources to the greater public welfare (Cheema 2013). Institutionalized philanthropy is rapidly growing, and in some countries in the region there is an amplified shift in government recognition towards the vast potential of civic participation, a deeper interest in philanthropic giving by large corporate institutions,[1] and financially well-resourced individual actors with strong ties to the community willing to commit to nonprofit organizations. In this chapter, Tariq Cheema, founder of the World Congress of Muslim Philanthropists, and Naila Farouky, CEO of the Arab Foundations Forum, discuss some of the exciting opportunities and challenges for the sector in this dynamic environment. The authors offer their thoughts on building a self-actualized board and discuss some of the issues—stewardship, accountability and transparency, culture— related to governance in the region. Because of the historic opportunity presented by the potential impact of the MENA's grant-making foundations, two case studies of foundations that have implemented good governance practices are presented.

THE PHILANTHROPIC LANDSCAPE—A HISTORIC OPPORTUNITY

The philanthropic sector in the MENA region has a historic opportunity to design and establish a more sustainable, professionalized, and formal ecosystem of giving without needing to abandon the more traditional, culturally embedded forms of philanthropy as a result. By moving more towards a world governed by the objectives of long-term value creation and sustainability, progress will occur and a new, carefully driven social contract among states, the private sector, and the philanthropic sector will begin to thrive.

The growth of the philanthropic sector in the Muslim world depends very much on how government and state institutions act and respond to it. The states have a critical role to play; they are needed to introduce incentive-based policies for donors, establish effective monitoring systems to ensure transparency in charitable operations, and regulate the collection and disbursement in *Zakat*, as well as other forms of religious giving (*Sadaqqa, Oshour,* etc.[2]). In some regions of the MENA, government does not promote philanthropy. The increasingly narrowing civil society space and prohibitive restrictions mounting against the sector across much of the region is severely limiting the potential for philanthropic impact and success.

In general, the public, private, and philanthropic sectors lack harmony, and their development strengths are not aligned. The policy-making process and/or service delivery is often influenced by private, political, or corporate interests and not necessarily driven by on-the-ground realities.

Despite these challenges there is a historic opportunity for the transformation of the MENA's philanthropic sector, which lies with the numerous grant-making foundations that operate across the Arab region and Muslim world. These were established mostly by the rich and powerful of those countries, mostly royals,[3] private-sector leaders, and government officials.[4] There is a rising class of professionally run family, corporate, and state-backed foundations whose grant making is development oriented and strategic in nature.

These foundations have potential for enormous social impact. They possess a strong drive towards philanthropic endeavors and sustainability initiatives in the MENA region, but are hampered by a lack of clarity on how to best meet the demand for giving and the supply of philanthropy. Subscale initiatives, limited investment in delivery capacity, a lack of targeted, evidence-based assessment of the needs and gaps in the sector, a general lack of strategic planning around giving and philanthropy, and a generally underdeveloped civil society are all factors that contribute to hindering the best intentions of these philanthropists. Addressing these challenges requires enhancing the institutionalization of philanthropic organizations, creating a stronger and more powerful narrative on behalf of the sector to communicate the value-added proposition of the sector (particularly to garner more government support and buy-in for the sector), and increasing the professionalism and transparency of nonprofit institutions. Improving the governance of MENA foundations, and the NGOs they support, can go a long way in achieving these improvements. In this chapter we will look at improving governance, examine some key aspects of the current context, and take a closer look at best practices for foundations.

THE ROLE OF GOOD GOVERNANCE

Good governance is key to seeking proper alignment with other sectors, in ensuring that mission takes precedence over the interests of other parties, and that pragmatically sound decisions are made to deliver maximum mission impact. But what is good governance? To illustrate, Christopher Grundner (2014) derives interesting insights from Maslow's hierarchy of needs theory (Maslow 1943) and puts it into parallel for the nonprofit board (see Figure 8.1).

Tier One: Passion and Presence

Maslow's pyramid model has at its base fundamental needs such as food, water, and rest. Adapted for the nonprofit board, at the bottom of the pyramid lies the essential element of passion for the mission. Unlike the boards of private and public corporations, nonprofit boards are not driven by financial gains, profit margins, and company stock. While passion is an absolutely essential building block for success, it is not enough to build a sustainable philanthropic venture and to steer an organization towards self-actualization of its purpose and achievement of social objectives.

The nonprofit pyramid also rests on necessary duties, such as meeting the board's fiduciary and legal responsibilities and contributing resources. Board members must regularly attend board meetings and other important organizational events and personally contribute financial resources to the organization. In Grundner's opinion, a passionate, dutiful board that just shows up is not enough to bring a nonprofit to the apex of success and establish long-term organizational sustainability. Members must also aspire to meet standards and follow best practices.

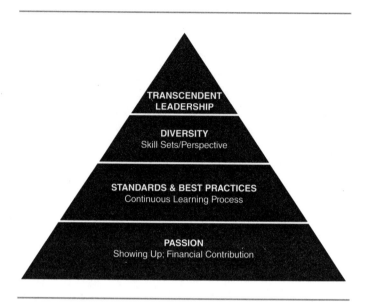

FIGURE 8.1   Nonprofit board governance.

Source: Graphic courtesy of Chris Grundner.

Tier Two: Standards and Best Practices

Implementing best practices (i.e., clearly defining job descriptions, initiating term limits, and conducting annual board performance reviews) is the next step up the pyramid. These measures create an environment of continuous learning and contribute to the board's ability to function at an optimum level. In order for these practices to work, however, it is also important that board members are held accountable.

There is oftentimes a disconnect between form and function in the MENA's NGOs, although this varies across the region. It is common practice for the form to serve mostly as a vehicle for communication with wealthy donors, and to be completely unrelated to function (the NGO's mission and objectives).

According to Grundner, form must follow function, and organizational structures and practices must transcend the agenda of any one individual, irrespective of wealth, position, influence, or personal financial contributions to the organization. It is imperative that nonprofit organizations do not accommodate the whims of board members and donors—the end result will be failure of the organization's mission.

Setting standards that are the same for everyone will help attract the best talent and plentiful resources to NGOs. Nonprofit boards should also be intentionally selected.

Tier Three: Diversity and Inclusion

Boards should select individuals who can add meaningful value to the organization, rather than simply naming persons of influence to the governing body for the sake of visibility or prestige. At the tertiary level of Grundner's pyramid are boards that include beneficiaries and representatives of the greater community. Bringing a diversity of ethnicity and perspectives, and a broad set of skills to the board, is a means of challenging the status quo, making possible critical internal discussions in pursuit of the goal of large and meaningful impact. A culture of constructive conflict should be nurtured, because purposeful disruption drives organizational evolution and growth. In addition, diversity on philanthropic boards may mean representation of a spectrum of ages, backgrounds, experiences, education, and gender. Boards that have met basic responsibilities, set standards and best practices, and conscientiously invited to the board those who can contribute to productive and creative conversation, have yet one tier to ascend.

Tier Four: Transcendent Leadership

At the top of Grundner's nonprofit board pyramid is transcendent governance, where generativity, organizational evolution, and sustainability can exist. These boards anticipate the future through succession planning, an aspect often overlooked by philanthropic organizations. New leadership invigorates mission focus and maintains forward organizational momentum. Nonprofit organizations need to be periodically infused with a bold and energetic leadership ready to meet challenges. Finally, transcendent leaders understand that their work is governing, not managing.

Organizations with strong executive leadership—whether in the form of an executive director, director general, or a CEO—do not require the board's involvement in the minutiae of day-to-day administration and the running of an organization. Instead, the board's focus is at the policy level, providing strategic oversight. Recognizing and clearly defining the board's role as separate from management can help to alleviate the burdensome dynamics of micromanaging boards.

Diverse voices in constructive discussion lead to effective decisions. Boards that just ratify the decisions of management render incompetent governance. It is the same in both the nonprofit and corporate worlds.

STEWARDSHIP

Another similarity between the two worlds is that both nonprofits and for-profits have stakeholders. Private investors have a tangible stake and vested interest in the progress and success of a company. This makes corporate shareholders vigilant. Donors, beneficiaries, and the greater community are the stakeholders in nonprofits, and they should exercise the same level of watchfulness because they, too, have much at stake.

Philanthropic board leaders often do not reap financial rewards, but they bear no less responsibility than paid corporate board directors. If anything, in increasingly complex social and regulatory environments, they shoulder ever more responsibility, accountability, and due diligence.

They are stewards of donor and community resources, and donations and grants from state institutions, private corporations, wealthy individuals, and therefore leaders must provide stringent board oversight (Farouky 2016).

There are also profound differences between corporations and nonprofits beyond the profit factor that affect nonprofit stewardship. Where corporations can make bold decisions (because they are able to financially sustain loss from such actions), nonprofits are risk averse and have a surprisingly low tolerance for failure due, in part, to fewer resources. Often operating on lean margins, they cannot afford to gamble their resources.

Furthermore, misuse of community resources can result in the deprivation of aid to beneficiaries and disservice to donors and the greater community. And of course, the legal penalties for noncompliance are severe.

CHALLENGES TO ACCOUNTABILITY AND TRANSPARENCY

Professionalizing the sector by putting in place best practices, which are necessary for creating a standard by which nonprofit organizations can be measured and held accountable, will help to lessen dependence on donors and ensure the sustainability and longevity of philanthropic organizations (Farouky 2016). This can only happen in a culturally relevant framework.

One of the challenges *vis-à-vis* the standardization of metrics of accountability and transparency in the MENA stems, in part, from the fact that (with few exceptions) there is no expectation on the part of the public for either. MENA governments, in general, have not modeled principles of transparency and accountability, and so the people do not expect—or are not conditioned to expect—transparency and accountability from public service institutions. There are other reasons why the environment may not be conducive to transparency (i.e., in countries where NGOs have been marginalized and face intense scrutiny). Nevertheless, in order for the sector to thrive and deliver long-term impact regionally—as well as to raise the visibility of the MENA's philanthropy on the global stage—the cultural context of these challenges must be reconciled with the more universally accepted models of conducting business based on the principles of accountability and transparency.

As an example of the type of challenges NGOs face in some parts of the MENA, let us turn to the situation in Jordan.[5] The government has implemented a program of regulation and relentless monitoring of NGO activity, and in this way, the State controls the philanthropic narrative of the country (Doyle 2015). Organizations that defy the status quo are quashed through stifling legalities and banking and government measures. For instance, the mandatory placement of former state/government ministers or other personnel on NGO boards keep Jordanian authorities informed of civil society ideology as it develops. They know the narrative to be controlled.

Organizations in Saudi Arabia are tightly controlled in a similar fashion. NGOs must be registered with the state and listed by the National Authority for Associations and Civil Organizations (NAA) (El Taraboulsi-McCarthy 2017). The NAA reserves the right to veto development initiatives and programs, as well as retaining the power to approve board appointments.

Jessica Leigh Doyle, in her 2015 article "Civil Society as Ideology in the Middle East: a Critical Perspective," relates this phenomenon of state restriction and interference in civil society to Antonio Gramsci's[6] argument that the dominant class produces the leaders of both civil and political realms. A study of civil society in Egypt provides further evidence that a tightly interconnected network of corporate board members and state bureaucrats wield a powerful influence in the state system. This network weighs heavily in NGO policy formulation (Abdelrahman 2004). The problem, of course, is that the political and economic interests of business enterprises are often at odds with those of the poor and disenfranchised.

Scholars of civil society and democracy in the MENA have drawn in detail the involvement of nonprofits in aiding and abetting the economic and political agenda of the ruling elite in government, society, and business. Doyle (2015) describes how Hawthorne (2004) found that NGOs often work in "partnership with states to spread the ideology of the dominant development agenda." Arguably, this may or may not be consciously intended—NGO boards need affluent state players on their boards to ensure financial sustainability.

Outside influences are not limited to local government. Others employ nonprofits to spread ideas and build consensus; supranational states and organizations and foreign states have used domestic nonprofits to advance their agendas. NGO mission and programming can also be clouded as the result of a need to network and maintain relationships with foreign donor organizations.

NEED FOR STUDY OF THE SECTOR

Nonprofit organizations are complex. They often provide "collective goods which complement or compete with those provided by the State" (Ben Nefissa 2000, 20). They differ from the State in that benefits are not provided to the individual voter, but to a community or all of society. NGOs have both apparent and underlying functions—they have organized and regulated areas where "different power plays, legitimacies, material and symbolic interests and ideologies are acted out" (Ben Nefissa 2000, 20). Because NGOs have a unique place in the overall scheme of things, and can mediate between donors and society, they deserve and need careful study, which they lack (Ben Nafissi 2000).

What study does take place is undertaken by research centers and experts whose aims are mainly short term, selective, and empirical. Additionally, much of the research and analysis of research on the topic is rarely produced from within the MENA. Instead it is produced by non-local institutions and lacks a nuanced, contextualized understanding of the region and its unique challenges and opportunities. There are limits to the applicability of studies conducted elsewhere. The NGO sector did not develop along the same lines as its counterparts in the West, and while Western-style taxonomy may be borrowed, it must be very carefully tailored for the MENA to ensure its applicability in a meaningful way. There is a true risk in the lack of data and analysis produced in MENA—when the narrative is not locally owned, it is not accurately reflective of the local reality. A region that does not own its narrative cannot, in turn, tell its story.

MENA CULTURE

Culturally appropriate avenues must be found to raise NGO standards—ones that reference how the charitable and social work of Arab organizations is closely bound up with a culture shaped by religious, social, tribal, and political elements (Ben Nefissa 2000).

Religion

The earliest historical reports of Arab philanthropy involve the charitable initiatives of wealthy Muslims, Christians, and other secular reformists. Early philanthropy possessed "both modern and traditional features" (Ben Nefissa 2000, 27). Modern because some early associations were structured to include a board of directors, elections, and annual general meetings.

Philanthropy and charitable giving are neither new nor nascent concepts in the MENA or within Islamic tradition. These are deeply embedded values within the fabric of the culture and religion, and are long-held traditions that have survived for centuries. That being said, there are aspects of this paradigm that present some impediments to the more modern, practical application of giving today. For one, the informal nature of religious giving means that much of it is unaccounted for, leaving the sector with the inability to accurately account for its impact. For another, the lack of a more diversified mechanics for channeling giving in the region leaves a gap where opportunities for nonreligious, secular giving is disincentivized.

Religion today drives giving in countries such as Saudi Arabia that are largely motivated by religious belief. "Saudi philanthropy has largely been ad hoc, informed by religious and charitable impulses rather than any long-term vision" (El Taraboulsi-McCarthy 2017). Many philanthropic organizations operating within the country rely heavily on funding derived from the religious act of almsgiving, and because of its ad hoc nature, have trouble establishing sustainability.

Another example can be seen in Lebanon, where giving is governed by 18 *waqf* laws—one *waqf* per recognized sect—but where there is no law within Lebanon's constitution that allows for giving via secular, non-religious channels. The Arab Foundations Forum, in partnership with the Arab Human Rights Fund, has drafted a nonreligious giving amendment to be introduced to the Lebanese Parliament, which outlines a means for those wishing to give outside of the *waqf* system, but that amendment has yet to be officially presented to the Lebanese Parliament, due, in, part, to the instability of the government in recent years.

Society

In Arab culture the family is a seminal unit, and it can influence organizational structure. For instance, in Lebanon,[7] social organizations that have "connections with leading Lebanese families follow an organizational pattern similar to that of traditional family" (Ben Nefissa 2000, 24).

Politics

NGOs defer to powerful politicians, administrations, and patrons. In order to function at all, MENA NGOs are virtually "forced" (Ben Nefissa 2000, 31) to build close relationships with government. This is because of the important role played by state authorities and the regulatory system (which authorizes NGOs to collect funds). Many organizations feel that they need to recruit prominent political figures to leadership positions to maintain a basic good working relationship with the government and to avoid unnecessary legal roadblocks. Government needs nonprofits too, because they can help to broaden grassroots influence, can serve as electoral or political platforms, and also can be a conduit for the feedback of the general public.

Most Egyptian members[8] of parliament hold high positions of leadership within the philanthropic sector, irrespective of their political affiliations. Reliance on transient political power, however, weakens organizations. NGO activities may change course abruptly or even cease altogether when there is a change in board leadership. This why it is vital to promote formal policies of board transition and succession. Without them, sustainability is not possible.

NGO sustainability is also at risk because of the short-term horizons of grant-giving organizations and a tendency to relate individual-to-individual instead of building holistic long-term organizational relationships. Once a favorite of a grantor leaves the NGO board, the relationship can end. Cultivating relationships between grantor and grantees over time, creating partnerships to achieve common mission goals, is the road to mutual success.

The consequences of an unaccounted sector are far reaching—if the region cannot accurately account for its giving in a formal way, it is unable to claim credibility and impact, both of which are necessary for lending gravitas to the sector. Without legitimacy, the sector is thus limited in its capacity to incentivize giving across all sectors of society and to encourage donorship and partnership building among other funders (both local and global), and is ultimately unable to measure its success in either the long term or short term.

One way to begin formalizing and professionalizing the sector in the region is to ensure that board governance of NGOs is cognizant of and conscientious towards the implementation of governance vis-à-vis these values.

Despite the challenges described above, some boards have committed themselves to raising standards. Following are case studies of two MENA foundation boards that have successfully adopted best governance practices.

CASE STUDY: EMIRATES FOUNDATION

The Emirates Foundation is headquartered in Abu Dhabi, United Arab Emirates (UAE). Its board consists of 12 members—5 women and 7 men. Among them are government representatives, including some ministers (per UAE Emiriti decree), leaders of civil society, and the private sector.

Diversity

Because the foundation receives donations from the private sector, the government, and individuals, and so is accountable to many stakeholders, the board has purposefully focused on diversifying its composition. Initially it recruited celebrated, widely recognized, and accomplished persons from the private sector and from civil society, which helped to advance the foundation's work by raising the visibility of its programs. As the Emirates Foundation's philanthropic initiatives have gained traction and visibility, recruitment has shifted away from prominent public figures and more towards those with academic knowledge and/or experience related specifically to the organization's mission and programs.

It has also sought a better ratio of men to women on its board. In 2012, only one of the board's seven members was a woman. The board of that time represented diversity in experience, but the gender ratio was imbalanced. Over the past five years the board has expanded to include several women, all of them experienced, renowned, and highly educated. The addition of Muna Al Gurg[9] and HE Shamma bint Suhail bin Faris Al Mazrui[10] are examples of the outstanding women who now sit on the board of directors of the Emirates Foundation.

Relationship to Management

The board appoints the senior management team of the foundation, comprised of many Emirati and international experts, who are compensated financially on the basis of expertise and experience (the board itself is not compensated). A board level committee oversees the foundation's investments, and the board supervises and approves foundation budget plans, but avoids petty micromanagement (for example, it established a level of autonomy for the CEO of the foundation: The CEO may approve funding requests of up to US$270000.[11] Larger expenditures are subject to board approval).

Policies

The Emirates Foundation's board members and foundation employees comply with an internal code of conduct, which includes a commitment to environmental sustainability. In 2008, the foundation joined the Abu Dhabi Sustainability Group to measure the foundation's environmental carbon footprint and to assist the foundation in integrating green practices into the code. The Emirates Foundation's code also gives priority to purchasing from local and national vendors and small business owners, thus encouraging the health of the local economy.

Programs

The Emirates Foundation looks to the future of the UAE. The foundation has recently shifted its programmatic focus to youth development. This shift has reshaped the organization's mission and strategies, and the formation of goal-specific projects and initiatives. Many board members take a personal interest in the programs, choosing to be involved with the foundation's outreach programs and serving as mentors to the young people who are benefitting from the Emirates Foundation's generosity.

CASE STUDY: AM QATTAN FOUNDATION

This family foundation is the legacy of one man—Abdel Mohsin Al Qattan, who has donated a large portion of his private wealth to philanthropic initiatives.

Diversity

The board of trustees once consisted only of Qattan family members, and they are still an actively involved majority, but today several renowned experts from the field also sit on the board. Experts such as Nadia Hijab[12] (the first addition from outside the Qattan family) and Dr. Khalil Hindi[13] provide informed opinion to foundation decisions.

The foundation also seeks to include more persons from within the family. In addition to the governing board of trustees, there is an honorary board. It is exclusive to the Qattan family—those over 30 years of age who wish to be involved with the foundation through various activities and playing different roles.

Roles and Responsibilities

Board meetings are held twice a year. Clearly defined roles have been established for the chair, deputy chair, and corporate secretary. Board committees have been established for Nomination and Governance, and one for Management.

Policies

The foundation has set clear protocols for the handling of internal audits, financial approvals, and foundation policies. Policies for accounting and procedures (such as procurement; i.e. suppliers and vendors) are in place. The foundation's funding policies limit outside contributions to a certain percentage—this is a method by which the Qattan family maintains independence in its programs and status as the primary stakeholders. The Qattan family bears all administration costs for the AM Qattan Foundation. At the same time, the foundation acknowledges its accountability to its various funding and project partners; for instance, it has clearly articulated an annual general meeting framework.

Transparency and Accountability

The foundation publishes on its website its audited annual reports, financial statements, strategic plan, and policies, making available to the public the following:

- Board governance manual
- Human resource policy
- Financial policy
- Resource development policy
- Risk management policy

Programs

Cultural connectivity, the AM Qattan Foundation's vision since its inception, transcends borders. Foundation leaders saw that, if their mission was to be fully realized, they needed to keep pace with today's rapid globalization. Their programmatic footprint in the world was enlarged, and today the AM Qattan Foundation is registered in London, Gaza, Ramallah, and Lebanon. The foundation still honors its roots. Because the family has strong ancestral ties to Palestine, it aims to create culturally inclusive and safe places for the community in places like the Occupied West Bank. At the same time, it also has created cultural spaces in London—transporting Arab culture into the Western world to counter a negative narrative through culture, art, and literature.

TAKEAWAY POINTS

From the above case studies (and the example of others), we offer eight takeaway points for readers seeking to employ best practices:

1. Define the mission, charter, and fundamental governance. Next, an organization should identify its beneficiaries and other stakeholders, clearly mapping out to whom the foundation owes accountability.
2. Understand the social compact component the foundation has with its stakeholders and the greater community. Explore such questions as What do we do to stay socially relevant? and What is our level of interaction with the State and government institutions? (Grady and Roberts 2017).
3. Evaluate the core competencies, operating capabilities, and the capacity-building of the board. Explore the interplay between the board charter, the social compact, and operating capabilities (Grady and Roberts 2017). This can open up thinking, leading to having available more options for programs and different models for operations.
4. Strive to become a strategic board. The board should be presented with a social problem relevant to its mission that has potential for maximum impact. If the board is concerned with isolated aspects of the programs, the vision of the foundation will be compromised and social impact minimized. Becoming a strategic board may require some changeup in board composition. In designing a smooth transition, a strategic performance framework will be needed.
5. Organize the board structure to meet the foundation's needs and to fit the environment. For most foundations, this will be some adaptation of a centralized structure.
6. Initiate bold programs for these times of rapid globalization—nonconventional initiatives that promote research, innovation and leadership (World Congress of Muslim Philanthropists 2010).
7. Establish endowments and other sustainable-giving vehicles. As important as emergency assistance will always be, foundations must

also engage the root causes of deprivation and conflict by making investment in longer term solutions (World Congress of Muslim Philanthropists 2010).

8. Emphasize the need to build capacity at all levels, creating best practices and encouraging informed giving.

CONCLUSION

Good governance has become a vital issue for political, economic, and social arenas. Certainly this is true for civil society, as the state delegates more and more of its responsibilities to NGOs, and the need for leadership for the sector grows. We are confident that that the philanthropic sector in the MENA will recognize the critical role of good governance in achieving the transcendent leadership it needs.

REFERENCES

Abdelrahman, Maha. M. 2004. *Civil Society Exposed: The Politics of NGO's in Egypt.* Tauris Academic Studies.

Ben Nafissi, Sara. 2000. "Management of social transformations." MOST Discussion Paper No. 46.

Cheema, T. 2013. "Our historic opportunity." *Philanthropy Age,* 16–17.

Civil Society Facility South. 2015. *Mapping Civil Society Organizations in Lebanon.* Civil Society Facility South.

Doyle, Jessica Leigh. 2015. "Civil society as ideology in the Middle East: A Critical Perspective." *British Journal of Middle Eastern Studies,* 403–422.

El Taraboulsi-McCarthy, Sherine. 2017. *A Kingdom of Humanity? Saudi Arabia's Values, Systems, and Interests in Humanitarian Action.* Humanity Policy Group.

Farouky, Naila. 2016. "The state of Arab philanthropy and the case for change." *Development in Practice* 26, no. 5: 637–645.

Grady, Heather, and Jonathan Roberts, eds. 2017. *The Theory of the Foundation: European Initiative Report 2016.* Rockefeller Philanthropy Advisors; LSE Marshall Institute.

Government of Egypt. 2002. *Law on Non-Governmental Organizations.* Part I: Associations Purposes, Rights and Obligations of Associations, Article 11. http://www.refworld.org/pdfid/5491907d4.pdf (accessed January 5, 2017).

Grundner, Chris. 2014. "Modern nonprofit board governance—passion is not enough!" TED Talk. www.youtube.com/watch?v=MIF9yJVldwQ2014 (accessed December 12, 2017).

Hawthorne, A. 2004. "Middle Eastern democracy—is civil society the answer?" Carnegie Papers.

Maslow, A. 1943. "A theory of human motivation." *Psychological Review* 50: 370.

World Congress of Muslim Philanthropists. 2010. *10 Guiding Principles for Muslim Giving.*

NOTES

1. Corporate social responsibility has become vastly important for the MENA's corporate institutions. Al-Futtaim Carillion (UAE) and Gulf Petrochemical Industries (Bahrain) were winners of the prestigious Arabia CSR Awards in 2016 for their CSR and sustainability initiatives in the Large-Scale Enterprise category.
2. Mandatory almsgiving in the Muslim world is regulated by the government through law and implemented through banking institutions. This is a major source of funds for charity used at the discretion of the government.
3. Per Emiriti decree, all foundations and organizations must have a government representative and ministers on the board.
4. The Jordanian government requires all groups and organizations to register with ministries, and they are regulated and monitored by government units.
5. Current Jordanian law criminalizes any association that is not licensed with the Ministry of Social Development under Law 33, Article 5a (1966) on Public Gatherings. The government's Draft Law on Voluntary Societies and Civil Society (2007) does not explicitly prohibit associations other than those regulated by law. It requires 25 persons to establish an association. Civil society's Draft Law on Civil Society Organizations (2006) also does not mention unregistered, informal associations, but lists different types of associations with as few as three members. In addition to the minister's current unchecked power to license NGOs, the Ministry of Social Development under the proposed law can remove temporarily an NGO's management board and shut down an NGO (1966 NGO Law, Articles 16 and 18; Proposed 2007 NGO Law, Articles 20, 21, and 22; 2006 NGO Draft Law, Article 30). Under current as well as the proposed 2007 law, the minister can appoint a temporary management board if the current management is unable to meet for lack of a quorum or if the ministry suspects violations of the NGO law or the NGO's bylaws, such as failure to convene a general assembly of members and hold elections or failure to allow new members to join. The minister can appoint temporary management provided the NGO has not rectified the suspected violation within one month of receiving of the ministry's written warning (Proposed 2007 NGO law, Article 21.a). The temporary management has 60 days remaining to continue operations of the NGO and to hold elections for a new management board (Proposed 2007 NGO law, Article 21.b., 1966 NGO law, Article 18). The proposed NGO Law of 2007, however, would allow the minister to extend the temporary management's tenure by another 60 days, or to appoint a new temporary management board. There are no apparent limits on the appointment of new temporary boards (Proposed 2007 NGO Law, Article 21). The proposed 2007

law also broadens the basis for ministerial intervention by including the submission of incorrect information to a government body and the refusal to permit a ministry official access to the NGO's premises to search any files or other items in the list of violations leading to closure (Proposed 2007 NGO Law, Articles 20.4 and 20.5).

6. Antonio Francesco Gramsci was an Italian Marxist theorist and politician. He wrote on political theory, sociology, and linguistics.

7. Management, leadership, and internal governance systems were identified as factors contributing to weakening performance of nonprofit organizations in *Mapping Civil Society Organizations in Lebanon* (Civil Society Facility South 2015, 82).

8. Egypt's relationship with nonprofits follows the history of its governmental regimes. There was a surge in NGO activity post-2011; however, the regimes after Mubarak's overthrow cracked down on the NGO sector with smear campaigns and rigorous policy regulations. Article 11 of Law 84/ 2002 expressly prohibited organizations from engaging in activities that could be deemed political or that threatened "national unity" or violated "public order or morals" (Government of Egypt 2002).

9. Muna Al Gurg is a businesswoman. She has an MBA from the London Business School in the United Kingdom and is a Fellow of the Middle East Leadership Initiative of the Aspen Institute and a member of the Aspen Global Leadership Network.

10. HE Shamma bint Suhail bin Faris Al Mazrui is UAE Minister of State for Youth Affairs in the new cabinet, making her the youngest minister in history.

11. Currency referenced in this chapter is in US dollars converted from UAE dirham as of September 21, 2017.

12. Nadia Hijab is a prominent Palestinian political analyst, author, and journalist who comments frequently on Middle East issues, human rights, and the situation of the Palestinians in particular. She is director of Al-Shabaka, The Palestinian Policy Network, a virtual think tank she cofounded in 2010, and on which she serves pro bono.

13. Khalil Hindi is currently a professor of management science at the Olayan School of Business, American University of Beirut.

FURTHER READING

Herrold, Catherine, E. 2016. "NGO policy in pre- and post-Mubarak Egypt: effects on NGOs' roles in democracy promotion." *Nonprofit Policy Forum* 7, no. 2: 189–212.

Law, R. T. 2007. www.hrw.org/reports/2007/jordan1207 (accessed December 12, 2017).

Rahman, M. 2005. *A Civil Society Exposed: The Politics of NGOs in Egypt*. Tauris Academic Studies.

UNESCO. 2000. *NGOs, Governance and Development in the Arab World*. UNESCO.

CHAPTER 9

North America

CANADA

Krishan Mehta

This section provides a summary and analysis of the frameworks and best practices that characterize NGO boards in Canada. Author Krishan Mehta, PhD, begins with an overview of the size and scope of the sector, followed by an outline of the organizing bodies and guidelines that are supporting nonprofit boards. He then briefly explores the work of DiverseCity onBoard, an organization that provides inclusion training and board-matching services for potential NGO volunteer candidates and employers from coast to coast. Finally, he outlines key policy and legislative and governance issues that are shaping the future direction of voluntary organizations at national, regional, and local levels.

NGO Volunteering in Canada

The majority of Canada's population of 36.4 million lives and works in urban settings from coast to coast. Against this backdrop, Canada boasts a large and robust NGO sector, with an estimated 170000 nonprofits and charities spanning all of the major metropolises and regions. While 54% of these organizations are run solely by volunteers, the sector employs over two million people, and together these organizations represent US$84.6 billion[1] in economic value, or 8.1% of the gross domestic product (GDP), a figure larger than the automotive and manufacturing industries. The top 1% of organizations command 60% of all revenues, which speaks to the powerful influence of larger NGOs on the entire landscape in Canada.

Given that NGO boards are volunteer based, let's take a moment to review what is known about volunteers in Canada. According to federal records, Canadians volunteered close to two billion hours in 2013, which amounts to approximately one million full-time jobs. Here the definition of *volunteering* is quite broad (and includes unpaid help to schools, religious organizations, sports teams, and community associations), yet instructive insomuch that it provides clues to the vast range of volunteer roles in the sector, which may include fundraising, coaching, advocating for issue-based causes, and, of course, serving on a board. Overall, more than 4 in 10 Canadians volunteered in 2013, further illustrating a strong volunteering ethos across the country.

Age

One of the distinguishing features of the Canadian context rests in our capacity to probe into the demographic information we have about volunteers. In fact, the statistics show that there are major intergenerational issues at play. For example, youth between the ages of 15 and 19 volunteer an impressive average of 110 hours per year, although adults 55 years old and over continue to contribute the most (39%). Youth volunteerism is likely influenced by compulsory community service programs that are embedded in Canadian secondary school systems. In Ontario, for example, students are required to complete 40 hours of volunteer service in order to graduate from high school. Across Canada, one in five volunteers aged 15 to 19 reported compulsory volunteering. This figure compares to 7% of people aged 20 years and over.

Gender

Fifty-two percent of women aged 35 to 44 performed volunteer work in 2013, compared with 44% of men in the same age range. Among parents in this cohort who were working full time, 56% of women volunteered, compared to 48% of men. When it comes to board participation, a study of 240 nonprofits revealed that women held 44% of available boardroom seats; 12 of the boards were found to be all female, while 4 of them were all male. The variances are even greater when we look at tables of women's participation on corporate boards. A 2016 report found that women held only 21.6% of board seats of the Financial Post 500 companies, and almost half of the 677 publicly traded companies listed on the

Toronto Stock Exchange had no women on their boards. These figures illustrate how gender issues are certainly divided along nonprofit and for-profit lines in Canada.

Education

A more educated corps of volunteers with post-secondary credentials is on the rise, and the type of voluntary work they are drawn to tends to be professional or administrative in nature. From 2004 to 2013, the percentage of volunteers aged 25 to 64 with a university degree rose by four percentage points to 39%. University-graduate volunteers were more likely to teach, educate, and mentor than those with lower levels of formal education (27% of those who completed a college or trade certificate or diploma, and 21% of volunteers with a high-school diploma). They were also more likely to sit as members of a committee or board (41%, compared to 30% of those without a university degree). In contrast, volunteers aged 25 to 64 with a university degree were less likely to perform volunteer work associated with the maintenance, repair, or building of facilities or grounds (13% compared to 19% of those who did not complete a university degree). In essence, NGO board members with post-secondary credentials or advanced degrees or designations tend to volunteer for professional work, such as accounting or human resources work.

Issues and Trends

There are four other distinct issues and themes facing NGO boards in Canada: The availability of different governance models, causing confusion for some; a more strategic approach to decision-making; an emphasis on advocacy; and marked success with inclusion and diversity.

Governance Models

One concern is that some organizations tend to employ more than one governance model at the same time, causing confusion for board members who are tasked with, for example, governing while also supporting fundraising activities, providing operational oversight, event planning, and so on. That said, the most common governance framework found in Canadian NGOs centers on policy and governance matters.

According to researchers from York University, there are both pros and cons for this kind of framework. On the positive side, all volunteers have clarity about their roles and responsibilities; other advantages include:

- The external focus of the board connects it with other boards and stakeholders.
- The leadership role of the board is often satisfying for board members.
- The model liberates, empowers, and supports the most senior staff person.
- The board engages in systems activities by scanning the environment, becoming familiar with big-picture issues as well as major internal trends, and entering into partnerships with other stakeholders.
- The board takes on the responsibility of ensuring adequate resources are available to accomplish the mission (fundraising) (Bradshaw et al. 2007).

While this model adheres to legislated requirements in Canada, there are perceived negative aspects as well, including:

- Board and staff relations are vulnerable and disconnected because of the emphasis on separate and distinct roles. This can interfere with developing a productive board-staff partnership. The board often feels disconnected from programs and operations—operational information is less relevant in this model.
- Staff often mistrust the board's ability to govern because of a perception that the board does not understand the organization's operations. Links between policies, operations, and outcomes are often tenuous.
- Directors of the board (or the board executive) may exercise their power in overriding the other's role. Power is concentrated in the hands of a few (Bradshaw et al. 2007).

Strategic Decision-Making
Canadian boards that are active in strategic decision-making tend to enhance the outcomes and missions of their organizations. A 2014 study of 217 for-profit and 156 NGOs in Canada found that board processes (i.e., board meetings, outside-board-meeting reviews, and information exchanges) affect the successful involvement of boards in strategic

decision-making, which in turn shapes organizational performance (Zhu, Wang, and Bart 2016).

NGO board leaders in Canada are also paying considerable attention to their evolving fiduciary and management duties. Considerable Canadian-based research on regulation and transparency, the implementation of new models of revenue generation, the use of technology in nonprofits, and tax/financial auditing practices has been undertaken (for examples, see Phillips 2013; Rathi and Given 2013; Fack and Landais 2016; and Gras and Mendoza-Abarca 2014).

Advocacy

One of the obvious roles for NGO boards is to serve as advocates for an organization. However, sometimes the lines between advocacy and political organizing can become blurry, especially for NGOs that focus on international cooperation and development, social justice and minority rights, and environmental stewardship. Over the past 10 years, these advocacy-oriented NGOs have been subject to charitable audits conducted by the Canada Revenue Agency (CRA). According to the Income Tax Act, charities are limited to using only 10% of their resources (including financial, staff, and volunteer time) on political activities. The federal government has stated that a charity may take part in these sorts of activities if they are nonpartisan in nature and subordinate to the charity's purposes. It presumes an activity to be political if an organization:

- Explicitly communicates a call to political action (that is, encourages the public to contact an elected representative or public official and urges them to retain, oppose, or change the law, policy, or decision of any level of government in Canada or a foreign country)
- Explicitly communicates to the public that the law, policy, or decision of any level of government in Canada or a foreign country should be retained (if the retention of the law, policy, or decision is being reconsidered by a government), opposed, or changed
- Explicitly indicates in its materials (whether internal or external) that the intention of the activity is to incite, or organize to put pressure on, an elected representative or public official to retain, oppose, or change the law, policy, or decision of any level of government in Canada or a foreign country (CRA, 2017).

Currently, the sector is calling for considerable legislative change, as participating in a political action may be subject to investigation by the federal government. And, in some cases, an organization's charitable status may be suspended or revoked if a NGO is found to be out of compliance.

Inclusion and Equity

Canada is often cited as a nation made up of immigrants. Accordingly, diversity and inclusion are distinguishing hallmarks of Canadian society. However, prior to European migration to North America, Canada was the indigenous home to millions of people who had a rich culture of giving and sharing. These communities were decimated by periods of colonial genocide. Recently, reconciliation efforts have taken place with Indigenous peoples, significantly influencing NGO governance. From 2008 to 2015, the Truth and Reconciliation Commission (TRC) of Canada developed a platform to address the colonial injustices and legacies that continue to impact Indigenous communities, including the establishment of the residential school system. The TRC developed a series of calls to action and, as a companion to these commitments, a Declaration of Action was developed by the philanthropic community (Circle on Philanthropy and Aboriginal Peoples in Canada 2015). To date, the boards of many NGOs and family/private foundations have signed on to this declaration, which seeks to actively work towards reconciliation and healing through education, sharing networks, public engagement, and the building of trusting relationships. As awareness of this declaration grows, it is expected that more nonprofit boards and grant-making organizations will commit to advancing these important goals.

Case Study: DiverseCity onBoard: Making Canadian Nonprofit and Public Sector Boards More Inclusive

According to a recent report, 30% of Canada's population could be made up of immigrants by 2036. In response to the already robust diverse and multicultural milieu of Canada, DiverseCity onBoard, currently based out of the G. Raymond Chang School of Continuing Education at Ryerson University in Toronto, helps accelerate inclusion in nonprofit and public-sector governance boards through director development, board-matching services, research, and capacity building. Here, Cathy

Winter, program manager of Diversity onBoard, provides an overview of the program and how it has positively impacted organizations and individuals across the country:

KM: How did DiverseCity onBoard form?

CW: DiverseCity onBoard has grown from a small, local program based in the greater Toronto area, focused on connecting visible minorities to not-for-profit and public boards, to a national program currently spanning eight cities across Canada. It has also expanded to serve Indigenous communities, LBGT+ (lesbian, bisexual, gay, transgender) communities, women, all ethnocultural communities, and persons with disabilities. In addition, it provides the only comprehensive, affordable, self-paced, Accessibility for Ontarians with Disabilities Act–compliant online governance training for not-for-profit boards in the country. To sustain the quality and currency of the program it operates under a social enterprise model.

The lack of diversity in leadership was identified as an important local issue in 2006. The call for more action on diversity was heard across conversations on issues including housing, transportation, health, and education. When we asked the reason for this disconnect, sector leaders reported that they did not know where to find qualified visible minorities to serve on their boards, and qualified visible minorities reported they were not aware of board opportunities. In response, DiverseCity onBoard was formed to connect these parties to each other.

Funding from the Ontario government in 2007 saw the creation of the Greater Toronto Leadership Project, of which DiverseCity onBoard was one of the initiatives. Our founding partners are the Maytree Foundation, TD Bank Group, and the J.W. McConnell Family Foundation.

KM: Governance training is a major pillar of your program. Why is this focus so important?

CW: DiverseCity onBoard is not about tokenism—it is about creating a culture of good governance. Therefore, any individual who is matched to a board opportunity through our program must be interviewed by a DiverseCity onBoard staff member and must complete our governance-training program. We ensure that the individuals who are referred to governance opportunities through our program have the required competencies necessary to serve and add value to governance boards. Moreover, focus groups held during our expansion planning sessions revealed that there was an absence of affordable and accessible training for not-for-profit boards. It was a void which needed to be filled. Therefore, we offer our training to everyone, regardless of background, and to all boards to strengthen board capacity.

KM: How do potential board members find NGO or public-sector opportunities?

CW: DiverseCity onBoard's online board matching system (much like a dating system) connects individuals to board opportunities and vice versa. Individuals apply through our website, input their skills, experiences, interests, and post their resumes. We then interview them to get a more personal perspective and once they "pass" the interview they must then complete our board governance training program before they are placed in the matching database, where they get access to board opportunities. Organizations apply online as well. We ask that they post their board vacancies, outline the skills/competencies required for each position, and provide any information particular to their organization. The online system then matches the individual's competencies with the competencies required for the vacancy. The individual gets a list of the board matches, and the organization gets a list of the individuals matched to the vacancy. Either side may then contact the other. The board then conducts its own selection process.

KM: Tell us about some of the noteworthy placements you have made.

CW: DiverseCity onBoard has facilitated over 900 appointments across all sectors in the not-for-profit, provincial, and municipal sectors. They range from the Toronto Board of Health, Ontario Hydro, and several hospitals to a small women's shelter, a publicly funded radio station, and environmental organizations. Organizations have told us that the diverse perspectives brought to the board leads to better decision-making as it breaks the mold of groupthink; individuals have told us that the governance training has given them the competencies and confidence to add value to board discussions, enhanced their professional development, and created new networks.

KM: Are there other similar programs in Canada or internationally?

CW: DiverseCity onBoard is really unique for Canada and the rest of the world. While there are a few programs that offer board training in Canada, they are geared primarily to the corporate sector and are quite expensive. Similar organizations internationally include Binoq Atana in the Netherlands, Diversity in Public Appointments based in the United Kingdom, and the African-American Board Leadership Institute in Los Angeles, California.

KM: What does the future of DiverseCity onBoard look like?

CW: The future looks really bright. We continue to be recognized as the leading resource for good governance through inclusion across Canada. In essence, DiverseCity onBoard is all about putting social impact in practice.

Opportunities

Over the years, there have been a number of efforts—within the federal government and the sector itself—to help clarify the roles and responsibilities of NGO boards. Some highlights from our recent past are described next.

Canada Not-for-Profit Corporations Act

In 2009, the Canada Not-for-Profit Corporations Act (NPCA) (Government of Canada 2012) received Royal Assent in Parliament, ushering in a more modernized framework for NGOs and charities in Canada. The principles underlying this legislation and policy directive were to remove government discretion over sometimes trivial bylaw matters and to mirror the operational efficiencies of for-profit share capital corporations, in which members' rights supersede those of the government. Prior to 2009 (and 2011, when the act went into force), incremental changes were made to a nonprofit statute dating back to 1917. The NPCA details the responsibilities of board directors, which are summarized in a useful backgrounder produced by the federal government. Accordingly, directors are responsible for the management of the corporation and have the duty to:

- Act honestly and in good faith with a view to the best interests of the corporation and exercise the care, diligence, and skill of a reasonably prudent person.

- Disclose any conflict of interest.
- Comply with the act, articles, bylaws, and any unanimous member agreements.

The NPCA also provides information and directives on a number of issues related to board liability and decision-making. To this end, the act provides directives on matters such as director and member meetings, quorum and attendance, the appointment/removal and remuneration of directors, and election processes/timing.

Canadian Code for Volunteer Involvement
In 2001, Volunteer Canada, a national organizing, research, and policy center focused on volunteers in the nonprofit sector, established the Canadian Code for Volunteer Involvement (Volunteer Canada 2017). This code, which was updated in 2012, has been adopted by hundreds of NGOs across all Canadian provinces and territories. While the code applies to different volunteer types, Canadian boards have found these principles useful in the development of board handbooks, guidelines, and manuals. The values and priorities outlined in the code are as follows:

Mission-based approach. The organization's board of directors and senior staff acknowledge, articulate, and support the vital role of volunteers in achieving the organization's purpose or mission. Volunteer roles are clearly linked to the organization's mission.

Human resources. Volunteers are welcomed and treated as valued and integral members of the organization's human resources team. The organization has a planned and integrated approach for volunteer involvement that includes providing appropriate resources to support volunteer involvement.

Policies and procedures. A policy framework that defines and supports the involvement of volunteers is adopted by the organization.

Volunteer administration. The organization has (a) clearly designated individual(s) with appropriate qualifications responsible for supporting volunteer involvement.

Risk management and quality assurance. Risk management procedures are in place to assess, manage, or mitigate potential risks to the volunteers, the organization and its clients, and members and participants that may result from the delivery of a volunteer-led program or service. Each volunteer role is assessed for level of risk as part of the screening process.

Volunteer roles. Volunteer roles contribute to the mission or purpose of the organization and clearly identify the abilities needed. Volunteer roles involve volunteers in meaningful ways that reflect their skills, needs, interests, and backgrounds.

Recruitment. Volunteer recruitment incorporates a broad range of internal and external strategies to reach out to diverse sources of volunteers.

Screening. A clearly communicated and transparent screening process, which is aligned with the risk management approach, is adopted and consistently applied across the organization.

Orientation and training. Volunteers receive an orientation to the organization, its policies, and its practices, appropriate to each role. Each volunteer receives training specific to the volunteer role and the needs of the individual volunteer.

Support and supervision. Volunteers receive the level of support and supervision required for the role and are provided with regular opportunities to give and receive feedback.

Records management. Standardized documentation and records management practices and procedures are followed and are in line with current relevant legislation.

Technology. Volunteers are engaged and supported within the organization through the integration and intentional use of current technology. New opportunities to strengthen volunteer engagement and capacity through the use of technology are evaluated continually.

Recognition. The contributions of volunteers are acknowledged by the organization with ongoing formal and informal methods of recognition, applicable to the volunteer role. The value and impact of volunteer contributions are understood and acknowledged within the organization and communicated to the volunteer.

Evaluation. An evaluation framework is in place to assess the performance of volunteers and gauge volunteer satisfaction. The effectiveness of the volunteer engagement strategy in meeting the organization's mandate is also evaluated.

Code of Conduct Policy for Canadian NGO Boards

Another resource for Canadian boards is Governing Good, an online resource center that houses many practical tools NGO leaders can adapt to suit their organizational needs. In 2016, Governing Good published a sample board members' code of conduct policy (Governing Good 2017), which can be used by Canadian and international charities alike. This policy framework helps organizations delineate between governance and operational matters, as described below.

The board of directors is committed to teamwork and effective decision-making. Towards this end board members will:

- Endeavor to represent the broader interests of members and/or stakeholders.
- Seek to balance their contribution as both advisors and learners.
- Be honest with others and true to themselves.
- Refrain from trying to influence other board members outside of board meetings that might have the effect of creating factions and limiting free and open discussion.
- Be willing to be dissenting voices, endeavor to build on other director's ideas, and offer alternative points of view as options to be considered and invite others to do so too.
- As an individual board member, be balanced in one's effort to understand other board members and to make oneself understood on important issues.
- As an individual board member, support the decision even if one's own view is a minority one once a board decision is made.
- Not disclose or discuss differences of opinion on the board with those who are not on the board. The board should communicate externally with one voice.
- Respect the confidentiality of information on sensitive issues, especially in personnel matters.
- Be advocates for the organization and its mission wherever and whenever the opportunity arises in their own personal and professional networks.
- Disclose their involvement with other organizations, businesses, or individuals where such relationships might be viewed as conflicts of interest.

- Refrain from giving direction, as an individual board member, to the executive director or any member of staff.
- Refrain from investigating or discussing the executive director's performance with staff members or stakeholders without board authorization.

NGO Accreditation and Performance Measurements

In 2012, Imagine Canada launched a voluntary standards program designed to award and accredit charities that demonstrate excellence in five key areas: board governance, financial accountability and transparency, fundraising, staff management, and volunteer involvement.[2] The standards program divides its assessment criteria based on organizational size and budget: Organizations with up to five full-time employees and up to US$1.6 million in annual expenses, organizations with up to 50 full-time employees and up to US$8.01 million in annual expenses, and organizations with more than 50 full-time employees or over US$8.01 million in annual expenses. In addressing the issue of board governance, the standards program considers the following factors and responsibilities, albeit to varying degrees based on the organization's level:

Mission statement. The organization has a mission statement that is approved and revisited by the board at least every five years to assess its continuing relevance.

Strategic plan. The board ensures a strategic plan is in place and is responsible for approving a strategic plan, and it has a process in place to evaluate progress in achieving the plan's priorities.

Recruitment and orientation of most senior staff person. The board is accountable for the recruitment and orientation of the most senior staff person in the organization; the recruitment process is fair and transparent, and managed in a professional manner by the board. The board is accountable to ensure that the most senior staff person receives the appropriate orientation required to assume his/her responsibilities.

Management of most senior staff person. The most senior staff person reports to the board and has a written job description or terms of reference; the board also approves annual performance objectives and conducts an annual performance review.

Compensation and expenses of most senior staff person. The total compensation package of the most senior staff person is approved by the board or a board committee and expenses are reviewed at least annually by members of the board.

Succession. The board annually discusses the succession plan for the most senior staff position in the organization.

Risk management. The organization has a process to identify its major strategic and operational risks and a plan to minimize and mitigate these risks. The plan is reviewed annually by the board.

Insurance. The organization has a process to review its insurance coverages. A summary report is reviewed annually by the board.

Legal compliance. The board or a board committee oversees the organization's compliance with its own governing documents (e.g., letters patent, bylaws) and all applicable federal, provincial, and municipal laws and regulations. Organizations conducting programs outside Canada will also abide by applicable laws, regulations, and conventions in that jurisdiction, unless these are in conflict with laws in Canada.

Communication and consultation with stakeholders. The organization identifies its stakeholders and ensures there is a strategy for regular and effective communication and consultation with them about the organization's achievements and work.

Code of ethics/conduct. The organization has codes of ethics/conduct that apply to directors, staff, and volunteers.

Conflict of interest policy. The organization has conflict of interest policies for board, staff, and volunteers that provide for disclosure, review, and decision on actual or perceived conflicts of interest.

Privacy policy. The organization has a privacy policy that is posted in a readily accessible location on its website.

Complaints policy. The organization responds promptly to complaints by external stakeholders and informs the board at least annually of the number, type, and disposition of complaints received; in addition, the organization has a complaints policy applicable to external stakeholders that is posted in a readily accessible location on its website.

Whistleblower policy. The organization has established and implemented policies and procedures that enable individuals to come forward with information on illegal practices or violations of organizational policies. This whistleblower policy must specify that the organization will not retaliate against, and will protect the confidentially of, individuals who make good-faith reports.

Number of meetings. The board holds a sufficient number of meetings annually to ensure appropriate direction and oversight of the organization's activities. At minimum, the board should hold two meetings per year at which the agenda is not restricted to a specific issue or issues (e.g., appointment of officers).

Board terms of reference. The board has written terms of reference outlining how it will review, approve, and monitor the mission/strategic direction, annual budget and key financial transactions, compensation practices and policies, and fiscal and governance policies.

Board composition. The board is composed of no less than three (but preferably five or more) directors, a majority of whom must be at arm's length to each other, to the most senior staff person, and/or to other management staff. No employee may be a director.

Board compensation. No member of the board is entitled to receive, either directly or indirectly, any salary, wages, fees, commissions, or other amount for services rendered to the organization in his/her capacity as a director.

Board orientation. A process is in place to ensure orientation of new board members. Board members must understand their legal and fiduciary responsibilities, exercise due diligence consistent with their duty of care, be familiar with the organization's activities, and be fully informed of the financial status of the organization.

Board records. Proper minutes of board meetings and record of policies are kept.

Board succession. The board has a process to annually review plans for succession to the positions of board chair and committee chairs.

Board development. The board has a process to annually consider development opportunities for potential board chairs and committee chairs.

Performance of the board. The board has a process to annually review the performance of individual directors, and, in some cases, the board as a whole.

Over 200 charities across Canada have successfully received this accreditation to date, which serves as a seal of approval regarding the ethical values and governance practices of those organizations. On the question of trust, a 2013 national opinion poll of almost 4000 people found that trust levels in nonprofits have remained relatively stable over the last decade. In reference to board oversight, when asked what type of governing body should be responsible for monitoring the activities of NGOs, Canadians overwhelmingly favor some sort of independent organization or agency that is not part of the government or the charity. Nearly two-thirds (62%) of Canadians prefer this option, while almost a quarter (23%) would support some sort of government agency, and about one in eight (12%) think the NGO's board of directors should manage this responsibility (Muttart Foundation 2013).

In 2014, the Fraser Institute, a national-policy think tank from Vancouver, British Columbia, published a report on how to meaningfully measure the performance of NGOs in Canada based on a series of metrics and key functions focused on financial and strategic management, income independence, board governance, volunteer activity, staff engagement, innovation, program costs, monitoring, and accessibility (Jackson and Clemens 2014). Unlike many of the other reports and studies on nonprofit outcomes, the report states that the financial or charitable contributions of the board should, in part, be figured into the assessment of an organization's performance. Indeed, many nonprofit and charitable boards expect their directors to make donations to support the programs and services of the organization. Together, all of these tools, studies, and reports give NGO boards in Canada clarity in direction and the means to carry out their duties in an ethical and responsible manner.

Conclusion

In summary, over the past 30 years NGO boards in Canada have grown and pivoted in light of demographic shifts, new policy prescriptions, and an overall desire to have baseline standards and better coordination across the sector. The vast range of societal concerns that nonprofits address have certainly led to a dramatic increase in the number of organizations and a corresponding uptick of board governance participation. With a critical mass of volunteers around boardroom tables, a number of issues have surfaced—and solutions developed. From the implementation of inclusive board recruitment practices and legislative frameworks to the development of accountability metrics and standardization programs, Canadian boards continue to rely on these theories, frameworks, and tools to ensure that ethical governance remains one of the hallmarks of our NGO sector.

CANADA REFERENCES

Bradshaw, P., C. Fredette, and L. Sukornyk. 2009. *A Call to Action: Diversity on Canadian Not-For-Profit Boards*. Schulich School of Business.

Bradshaw P., Hayday, B., Armstrong, R., et al. 2007. "Nonprofit governance models: problems and prospects." *Innovation Journal* 12, no. 3: 5.

Canada Revenue Agency (CRA). 2017. *Policy Statement on Political Activities of Charities* 2017. www.canada.ca/en/revenue-agency/services/charities-giving/charities/policies-guidance/policy-statement-022-political-activities.html (accessed September 27, 2017).

Circle on Philanthropy and Aboriginal Peoples in Canada. 2015. *Philanthropic Community's Declaration of Action.* www.philanthropyandaboriginalpeoples.ca/declaration (accessed September 27, 2017).

Fack, G., and C. Landais, eds. 2007. *Charitable Giving and Tax Policy: A Historical and Comparative Perspective*. Oxford University Press.

Governing Good. 2017. "Sample policy: board member's code of conduct." www.governinggood.ca/wp-content/uploads/2017/04/Board-Members-Code-of-Conduct-Sample-Policy.pdf (accessed September 27, 2017).

Government of Canada. 2012. "Canada Not-For-Profit Corporations Act." Background paper. www.strategis.gc.ca/eic/site/cd-dgc.nsf/eng/cs05170.html#part9 (accessed September 27, 2017).

Gras, D., and K.I. Mendoza-Abarca. 2014. "Risky business? The survival implications of exploiting commercial opportunities by nonprofits." *Journal of Business Venturing* 29, no. 3: 392–404.

Jackson, T., and J. Clemens. 2014. "Nonprofit performance report: an analysis of management, staff, volunteers and board effectiveness in the nonprofit sector." Donner Canadian Foundation Awards for Excellence, Fraser Institute. www.donnerawards.org/files/pdf/2014-NPPR.pdf (accessed September 27, 2017).

Muttart Foundation. 2013. *Talking about charities*.

Phillips, S.D. 2013. "Shining light on charities or looking in the wrong place? Regulation-by-transparency in Canada." *Voluntas* 24, no. 3: 881–905.

Rathi, D., and L.M. Given. 2013. "Use of technology in nonprofit organizations (NPOs) for knowledge management." In *Proceedings of the Annual Conference of CAIS* (November).

Volunteer Canada. 2017. *Canadian Code for Volunteer Involvement.* volunteer.ca/content/canadian-code-volunteer-involvement-2012-edition (accessed September 27, 2017).

Zhu, H., P. Wang, and C. Bart. 2016. "Board processes, board strategic involvement, and organizational performance in for-profit and nonprofit organizations." *Journal of Business Ethics* 136, no. 2: 311–328.

CANADA NOTES

1. Currency referenced in this chapter is in US dollars converted from Canadian dollars on August 25, 2017.
2. Imagine Canada. 2014. *Standards Program for Canada's Charities and Nonprofits.* www.imaginecanada.ca/sites/default/files/standards_program_handbook_en_2015.pdf (accessed September 27, 2017).

CANADA FURTHER READING

Canadian Board Diversity Council. 2016. *2016 Annual Report Card.* www.boarddiversity.ca/sites/default/files/CBDC-Annual-Report-Card-2016.pdf (accessed September 27, 2017).

Imagine Canada. 2017. *Key Facts About Canada's Charities.* www.imaginecanada.ca/resources-and-tools/research-and-facts/key-facts-about-canadapercentE2percent80percent99s-charities (accessed September 27, 2017).

Lasby, D., and C. Barr. 2015. "Giving in Canada: strong philanthropic traditions supporting a large nonprofit sector." In *Palgrave Handbook of Global Philanthropy*, edited by P. Wiepking and F. Handy, 25–43. Palgrave Macmillan UK.

Statistics Canada. 2017. *Immigration and Diversity: Population Projections for Canada and Its Regions, 2011 to 2016.* www.statcan.gc.ca/pub/91-551-x/91-551-x2017001-eng.htm (accessed September 27, 2017).

UNITED STATES

Paloma Raggo and Penelope Cagney

The United States has had an undeniable influence in shaping the nonprofit sector and board governance practices around the world. Books, articles, and online resources about board governance in the

United States are plentiful, which can have the unintended consequence to overwhelm practitioners with valuable information. In this section Paloma Raggo and Penelope Cagney aim to offer a concise overview of some typical board governance practices and to discuss some of the challenges the nonprofit sector faces in balancing its responsibilities, duties, and its mission with respect to all possible stakeholders within their organizations.

Historical and Cultural Context for Governance

The United States' sizeable philanthropic sector has its origins in an immigrant past and it continues to be shaped by the diverse perspectives of its citizens.

History

Much of the civil society sector as we know it today in the United States can be traced to the early British and European settlers who brought with them their own charitable traditions. The US Constitution, ratified in 1788, further shaped the sector through the First Amendment, which makes fundamental "the right of the people peaceably to assemble," and the Tenth Amendment, which states that all powers not explicitly reserved to the federal government "are reserved to the States respectively, or to the people." As Alexis de Tocqueville observed, the diversity of American civil society and its associations of people is a reflection of the strength of a democracy in which citizens form groups to promote ideas and the welfare of others. Today, Americans still rely more on the philanthropic sector to provide social infrastructure (education, health care, cultural opportunities) than some countries do.

Another historic and ongoing influence to civil society here has been the continued influx of a diverse and vibrant body of immigrants. The United States is particularly diverse when the ethnic, cultural, and racial variety of its population is considered. As of July 2016, 17.8% declared a Hispanic or Latino ethnicity and 13.3% declared solely as Black or African-American (US Census, 2016). There are, in addition, various other groups, among them a rapidly growing Asian population and a Native American population. The United States is on its way to becoming a majority nonwhite nation.

Culture By Penelope Cagney

American culture is important to understanding US philanthropy. As explained in Chapter 1, culture can be defined as the way people solve problems (Trompenaars 1997).

It is not simply that US culture is different from that of other nations. As is the case everywhere, there are cultural variations from cities to rural areas. Variations are also regional. For our purposes we will consider culture as a whole, using Trompenaars' (1997) scale of cultural characteristics outlined in Chapter 1. In general, we can consider American culture to be:

Universalist. Americans tend to value rules above relationships.

Individualist. The achievement of the individual may be prized above that of the group.

Expressive. Although the culture values rationality and objectivity, it is more casual than some.

Specific. Americans have more public than private space.

Achievement-oriented. America views itself as a meritocracy.

Sequential. To Americans, time proceeds in a linear fashion, and so punctuality and adherence to the agenda is valued.

Oriented to internal control. Americans believe that they can control their own destinies.

Legal and Tax Environment

The American civil sector contains more than 1.4 million registered tax-exempt nonprofit organizations, which contribute more than 5.4% to the GDP (McKeever 2015). There are 29 different categories of IRS 501(c) tax-exempt organizations, but the ones we are most concerned with are those bearing the 501(c)(3) designation, which covers a wide range of missions, from arts organizations to education, health care, and human service organizations. The IRS has three clear, fundamental criteria that these organizations must abide by to benefit from a tax exemption (IRS 2017). These organizations must:

- Have a charitable mission that includes but is not limited to poverty alleviation, cruelty prevention against children or animals, advancement of education, amateur sports, science, or religion.
- Not be for the benefit of private interests or any individual with private interest in the activities of the organization.
- Not support or oppose a specific candidate (or set of candidates) in political campaigns.

Registered 501(c)(3)s are not only exempt from federal tax but can accept tax-deductible contributions and enjoy other benefits (reduced postal rates, for example). With these benefits come essential responsibilities, such as an annual tax filing, adequate financial and nonfinancial record keeping, and the requirement disclosure to disclose recent tax returns if requested. Furthermore, these tax-exempt nonprofits must adopt their own bylaws, but the language of bylaws can vary greatly and depends on the varying requirements of individual states.

The IRS notes that good governance increases nonprofits' ability to comply with the law and ultimately serve their intended purpose. Indeed, research on board governance has shown that there is a self-reinforcing dynamic: The better your board is, the better off your organizational outcomes will be. Herman and Renz (2000) show that nonprofit boards utilizing sound board practices were more likely to implement appropriate measures within their organizations.

Composition and Recruitment

The IRS encourages an active and engaged board composed of informed persons who are selected with the organization's needs in mind (e.g., accounting, finance, compensation, and ethics) and who actively oversee finances. While the government doesn't specify the number of board members required (although state laws may), it does suggest that the size be sufficient to ensure that the organization obeys tax laws, stewards its resources, and strives to achieve mission. Boards should be independent. They should represent a broad public interest and care should be taken to identify any potential for insider transactions that could result in misuse of charitable assets.

At a basic level, nonprofit organizations must not only find people willing to voluntarily serve on their boards and commit their talents, time, and resources, but they must balance three important aspects of board composition: size, diversity, and capacity.

Size

There is no one size that fits all nonprofit boards. Determining what constitutes the ideal composition for any one board is complex and debatable. These considerations may help in determining the number of board members to recruit: The age of the organization, its operational size, its tenure terms, and its needed competencies. Younger organizations will face different challenges than more established organizations, including financial stability, staff recruitment and retention, and generally learning about their operational environments. By answering one fundamental question, it will be easier to determine how to best assemble a board that reflect those needs: What does this organization need to ensure its mission and develop a strategic vision for the future? It is important to remember that needs and priorities will change over time. A nonprofit's particular stage in its life cycle should be taken into consideration when recruiting new board members. Mature boards have different needs than start-ups.

Younger nonprofits must also recognize their potential limitations in developing effective boards. For instance, more recently established nonprofits do not always have access to a wide network of people willing to serve on their boards. Furthermore, younger, less-established organizations will often focus on securing financial resources to ensure their long-term survival, resulting in their boards developing tunnel vision towards their fundraising goals and ignoring other strategic imperatives. Recent research suggests that other challenges to younger organizations may include struggles with board development and appropriate delegation to executive directors, but balance can be achieved over time (Leroux and Langer 2016).

Research has long shown that the size of the organization relates to the size of board membership (Pfeffer 1973). As a nonprofit grows, the requirements for maintaining its mission, the fundamental role of the board, will be more complex and will require more resources.

As many practitioners know, too large, and a board can become slow in making decisions, as it may require extensive time for consultation and deliberation among board members; too small, and the board may not adequately represent the interests of a broad range of organizational stakeholders or have the capacity to champion the mission of the organization. There is no consensus on the optimal size of a nonprofit board. The average size of US boards has declined over the past 20 years, from 19 to an average of 15 members (BoardSource 2017). However, there is no magic number and nonprofits should consider adjusting the number of members if necessary.

Diversity

Another important consideration is diversity. As noted earlier, the United States is on its way to becoming a majority nonwhite nation, yet a recent study showed that 84% of board members and 90% of board chairs are white (BoardSource 2017, 10). Beyond racial diversity, nonprofits still struggle to have diverse boards that include a more representative makeup of their stakeholders and the general population. Research suggests that increasing board diversity can lead to better organizational performance while potentially creating conflicts and lack of consensus (Brown 2005, 324). The latter may be one reason for the homogeneous makeup of boards; a diversity of viewpoints can be inconvenient.

How to recruit board members and foster diversity? Nonprofit executives suggest the passion for the mission, community connections, and specific desired skills are the most important elements when recruiting board members (BoardSource 2017, 15). While a laudable goal, a recruitment emphasis on those with connections can also have the unintended consequences of excluding from consideration traditionally marginalized groups who do not have the desired community connections.

While US boards acknowledge a deficiency in seeking greater diversity, neither board nor staff leaders seem to be making it a priority (BoardSource 2017). Until they do, they will fall short in this important dimension of accountability and representation of the population served. To recruit a diverse board, diversity must be a deliberate and strategic consideration in approaching new board members.

Capacity

Lastly, the capacity and limitations of a nonprofit organization should be considered when recruiting new board members. What skills are needed to develop an effective board? Occupation, experience within the community, financial literacy, fundraising expertise, and strategic acumen are vital for any nonprofit board. It is important that the skills of the board align with the specific needs of the organization. Clear descriptions of these competencies during the recruitment process are vital for most effective organizations (Herman and Renz 2000). Approaching new members with descriptions of their roles and responsibilities can resolve a lot of communication issues that can lead to inefficient board engagement. Beyond recruitment, nonprofits seeking to develop their boards should consider implementing effective orientation and training for board members, as well as evaluating their overall board performance (Brown 2005).

Soft Skills

Some boards also consider soft skills, such as communication, listening, intuition, creativity, emotional intelligence, social competencies, and the ability to work on a team in recruitment. Some even look to identify the so-called style of individual board candidates in relationship to the culture of the whole board. Obviously, these things are more difficult to identify and evaluate than other factors, but they may be important in achieving the right blend of members.

In order to more effectively recruit new members, many boards have created governance committees to oversee the recruitment process. These committees also are charged with evaluation and development, and with addressing other specific board concerns.

Roles and Responsibilities

Much has been written about the roles and responsibilities of a nonprofit board (BoardSource 2015). Boards and their members have legal duties, fiduciary responsibility, and specific functions to ensure good governance (Renz 2010, 128–134). Board members have a duty of care to act in the best interest of the organization, a duty of loyalty to avoid conflicts of interest, and a duty of obedience that requires respect for the organization's mission, code of conduct, and bylaws. IRS rules may offer some policy guidance regarding the legal responsibilities of boards, but state-level legislation can vary widely across the United States. Renz

(2010, 130) describes the fiduciary duty as "the stewardship of all of the assets and resources of the organization." There are several fundamental functions of the board (see Renz 2000; Ingram 2015):

- Leadership towards the organization's mission and purpose
- Policy development to oversee the organization's operations
- Fundraising and friendraising to ensure the organization's financial stability and human capital
- Monitoring and evaluation of the organization and executive's performance
- Fostering the organization's reputation and legitimacy in the community
- Maintaining formal and informal accountability of the organization with its various stakeholders
- Recruitment and board development to ensure a strategic vision for the organization

The central value at the core of these key functions is accountability. Accountability requires that board members clarify expectations, codify the appropriate behaviors within their organizations, accept responsibility for the organization's activities and performance, and, most importantly, put in systems to answer for or sanction inappropriate behaviors and inefficiencies that could compromise the organization's mission. Beyond being responsible for the organization's actions, board members are ultimately accountable legally and morally for the organization's successes and failures.

Board Relationships

The relationship between board members and between board members and staff, particularly between the chair of the board and the executive, is delicate and complex. While open debate and respectful allowance for divergent opinions within the boardroom can contribute to healthy governance, no nonprofit wants to be involved in a public dispute between its board members, executive director, and staff. These public spats undermine the credibility of an organization and foster a climate of distrust within it. A recent example in the United States is the case of the Eagle Forum founded by Phyllis Schlafly in 1972. Schlafly was a staunch conservative who embodied a clear anti–marriage equality, antifeminist, and antiabortion agenda. The controversy stemmed from her endorsement of Donald Trump in the 2016 election, while Ted Cruz had already been endorsed by high-ranking staff in the organization. The board, including Schlafly's daughter, has tried to remove President Ed Martin, arguing that taking a political position could jeopardize the 501(c)(3) status of the organization; the conflict is now in the courts.

Both board and staff must be clear on expectations of each other. From the executives' perspective, effective board members must be accessible/available, be committed to the mission, have special talents and skills, attend meetings, be constructive problem solvers, have an understanding of niche, be flexible, be a resource developer, understand policy versus management, be selfless, have rapport with staff, and demonstrate representation/empathy (Kearns 1995, 346–349). These considerations could also apply to board members' views of effective executives. Conflict arises when there is a perceived misalignment between the two sides of the relationship.

Independent of the organization's actual mission, by defining clear roles and expectations from the beginning of that relationship, board members can avoid many problems. The responsibility for the relationship is shared among board members and the executive. On the one side, board members and the chair must be engaged, active, and attentive to the needs and activities of the organization without indulging in micromanagement of the executive director. On the other side, executives must communicate effectively with the board, be transparent about the challenges facing the organization, and always act with the best interest of the organization in mind. Putting personality conflicts aside, open and transparent communication will foster a positive relationship between the board and its executive. Achieving this delicate balance relies on important and necessary safeguards, such as whistleblowing policies, clear term limits for board membership, and regular evaluations of the staff, the chief executive, and the board. However, evaluations are not sufficient; enforcement mechanisms must be put in place to allow for change if problems are found. While not unique to the United States, the reliance on an extensive set of policies shaping the organization's internal behavior is somewhat characteristic of how rules, laws, and regulations shape the internal culture of an organization.

Board culture is largely shaped by a positive relationship with the executive. The most important characteristics of American board culture include the ability of board members to listen and treat others respectfully and to support creative initiatives (BoardSource 2017, 21). Based on a study of US nonprofits, Golensky (1993) suggests that there are four dimensions to the relationship between boards and their executives: Board-executive communication, executive assets (influence), board-executive congruence of vision, and board-executive role expectations. As she suggests, it is the interplay of these dimensions (as they do not operate in isolation) that will determine the quality of the relationships.

Organization of Meeting, Culture of Inquiry

Defining one culture of inquiry applicable to the US sector would be problematic, given the diversity of and within nonprofit organizations (which is, perhaps, itself unique). One commonality that emerges within the sector is the reliance on structured and clear rules of engagement between board members and their organization. BoardSource (2017) suggests that there are key elements that board members can adopt to foster effective meetings:

- Being prepared by reading the material in advance
- Focusing the meeting on strategy and policy rather than operational issues, which should be delegated to the executive leader
- Having clear agendas, good facilitation, and good time management
- Ensuring enough time is devoted to deliberation

Several tools can be used to optimize meetings, such as a consent agenda, under which noncontroversial items can be discussed under one agenda item, thus avoiding spending unnecessary time to approve each separate item. However, the use of this agenda strategy relies on the assumption that the agenda is distributed well before the meeting takes place and that board members read all the material provided in advance. Another tool used by some nonprofits in the United States is *Robert's Rules of Order*. First published in 1876, this is an exhaustive guide on how to run meetings. While complex, it offers clear procedures for passing motions, voting, registering dissent, and all other aspects of deliberation. The main drawbacks are its complexity and the need for expertise on its rules, which can prove a real challenge for resource-strapped organizations. It is important to note that these rules are merely a guide and that an organization's bylaws always take precedence. While not used in the United States alone, the reliance and popularity of these rules are indicative of a general culture here in which codes of conducts and rules are shaping the formal nature of meetings.

Board Evaluation and Monitoring

A simple Google search of *evaluation and nonprofit boards* reveals over 26 million results. However, given the sheer size of the United States' nonprofit sector, many of the resources readily available online are geared towards nonprofits in this country. There are two types of resources available to evaluate and monitor board performance: Self-assessments and formal evaluations. Board self-assessments are very popular, as they are low-cost solutions and especially welcome for small nonprofit organizations. They often constitute various checklists and questionnaires that promote self-reflection and learning within the organization. A 2015 survey of boards of directors of nonprofit organizations revealed that only 34% of organizations evaluated their boards annually and 36% never did (Larcker et al. 2015, 14). Because American nonprofit organizations are mostly run by volunteer boards, and since volunteer time is often limited, evaluating the board performance is not always deemed a priority in comparison to more pressing needs related to achieving the organization's mission. Since research has shown that board performance is linked to organizational performance (Brown 2005), it is important that boards consider evaluating their performance as an integral part of their responsibilities vis-à-vis their organization.

Increasingly formalized evaluations are part of a growing accountability industry composed of a myriad of consultants (Raggo 2014). BoardSource, for instance, even offers certification for governance consultants who are schooled in its consulting methodology. An important challenge for nonprofits is the mobilization of resources needed for independent board-evaluation assessments. Having an independent evaluation of board practices can be too onerous for small organizations with small boards. The proliferation of web-based resources has democratized the evaluation of board performance while providing an overwhelming amount of potentially useful information.

Accountability and Ethical Challenges

Because of the rule-oriented approach to US nonprofit governance and the requirements of financial disclosure by tax-exempt organizations, an important challenge to board governance relates to questions of accountability. The emphasis on financial transparency and record keeping, while desirable, has created an equivalence between fiscal accountability and general accountability to the organization's mission. Boards may find it easier to wrestle with black-and-white numbers on a page than to deal with the ambiguous gray areas that boards can face related to mission. If board members' main goal is to foster the organization's mission, a special attention should be put on the accountability relationships between the board and the organization's stakeholders, particularly the beneficiaries of these organizations. The board and the executive face the challenging task of balancing the needs of their organization's recipients and its *raison d'être* with the demands of their donors. Board members undertake the difficult task of ensuring the survival of the organization and its growth by ensuring renewed financial support from donors and putting the recipients at the center of their decisions. This is where a diverse board can foster a better representation of all the stakeholders in the organization. However, while increasing representation is a desirable goal, board members must consider the asymmetry of power between board members and ensure that broader representation does not lead to the tokenization of diversity within the board. To prevent such an occurrence, training and capacity building of new board members, especially those from historically marginalized groups, needs to be offered systematically to all board members.

In interviews with 152 executives of international nonprofits registered in the United States, respondents discussed several accountability problems, noting the lack of clear policies and discipline in following through with evaluation results (Raggo 2014). Anecdotal evidence suggests that there are many policies on the books, yet little effort is made to ensure that organizations learn from their mistakes, as the results of evaluations are rarely acted upon. To address this challenge, board members must be open to acknowledging mistakes made in the organization and by the board. Admission of error and acceptance that their organization will not always succeed despite the best of intentions is an important part of taking appropriate risks and making good decisions in the future. Cultivating an organizational culture where mistakes are punished without a learning opportunity will undermine the accountability relationships between the staff of an organization and the board members.

Trends

In the US context, the changing political landscape has important implications for boards and their organizations. An unprecedented level of mobilization within civil society organizations following the election of Donald Trump in 2016 and the series of controversies that have plagued his administration have created opportunities and challenges for US-based nonprofits. In 1954, Lyndon B. Johnson introduced the amendment that banned 501(c)(3) organizations from engaging in political activities (now known as the Johnson Amendment). During his 2016 campaign and early in his term, Trump suggested that he would get rid of this provision to allow churches to engage in political activities. While the December 2017 Tax Reform Bill did not include a repeal of the Johnson amendment, by increasing the standard deduction, it will limit the ability for tax payers to itemize charitable deductions thus potentially reducing the nonprofit sector's funding by at least 12 billion dollars (Rosenberg and Stallworth, 2017).

Repeal of the The Johnson Amendment would have clear implications for the work nonprofit organizations and their boards can and cannot engage in. Boards are often concerned about violating the Johnson Amendment, which could result in the organization losing its tax-exempt status. Some have argued that this provision limits free speech, and thus many in the nonprofit sector would actually welcome such a change if not restricted to religious 501(c)(3)s, as some have proposed. With an increasing polarized society over key issues such as abortion, immigration, and civil rights, board members are increasingly under pressure to actively engage in political debates and take public positions.

Other trends are towards smaller boards and fewer committees. As noted earlier, boards have declined from 19 to 15 members since 1994 (BoardSource 2017, 17). Over the same period the number of standing committees has declined from 6.6 to an average of 4.5. The most common committees are executive, finance or finance/audit, governance, and nominating (or governance and nominating) (BoardSource 2017, 19). Short-term needs, such strategic planning and CEO search, are often addressed through task forces. Most boards avoid mirroring the programmatic agenda of the staff in board committee structure.

Conclusion

In this chapter, we have provided you with a broad overview of board governance in the United States and have discussed the various considerations that apply to US-based boards. Whether diversity (or lack thereof), composition, structure, recruitment, or engagement, boards in the United States face important challenges that reflect the diversity of organizational culture and the population. Boards face an increasingly complex legislative environment coupled with a politically polarized society. This raises important accountability challenges for board members whose fundamental mission is to help their nonprofits in achieving their missions. To do so, they must consider how and why their boards are organized the way they are. They must be open to change, adaptable, and willing to learn from their mistakes. How the sector adapts to the changing political landscape will undoubtedly shape the next generation of board governance practices, which themselves will be shaped by diversity, immigration, and activism.

Case Study: Mesa Arts Center Foundation

Board engagement is critical to healthy boards and good governance. Lack of engagement can afflict all types of boards, but it is often a concern for boards that do not govern, such as advisory and fundraising boards, large boards, and boards that have not made the effort to understand the various motivations of their members. Below is a case study of Mesa Arts Center Foundation, the largest art center in the southwestern region of the United States, which successfully improved the level of engagement of its board of directors.

Because it is city owned and operated, the 10-year old center has a separate 501(c)(3) organization that raises funds for the center's programs and for other special purposes outside of the regular operational expenses that are covered by the city. Gifts for the programs of the center made through the foundation are tax deductible.

Tasked with raising funds for the center instead of governing, the foundation board did not feel a sense of ownership. Having a board of 33 (more than twice the size of the average US board) made it harder to foster the sense of connection between members that smaller boards enjoy. A larger board can better help with fundraising, however, having many more connections with the community.

In 2014 consultant Penelope Cagney was engaged to help the foundation increase the level of its board's engagement. The nine-month consultation was overseen by a small task force of the board. It began with an online BoardSource self-evaluation covering all aspects of governance, followed by 35 interviews specifically about engagement conducted with current and past board members and other key stakeholders. The resulting report was used to formulate the agenda for a board retreat in early 2015 that was focused on increasing engagement.

The retreat was designed to elicit suggestions from the board itself on how to increase engagement. Its ideas were evaluated, prioritized, and organized into a plan of action. Metrics were established to measure success: Stable revenue, better attendance of board meetings, less unplanned turnover, and greater satisfaction with the overall board experience.

Two years after the plan was set in place, Board Chair Cassidy Campana, a member of the engagement task force, says,

> What was key for us was having an honest conversation about why people join our board. The primary motive is of course to support our mission, but we also recognized that there are many other reasons why members serve on boards: to widen their business or social networks, to represent their company in the community, to continue a family tradition, or to improve skills. Knowing what was important to our members made it possible to make serving on the board a more fulfilling experience for them. We created a dashboard to help us monitor our progress, and I'm happy to report that we've achieved most of our priority objectives. Board members today look forward to and rarely miss meetings, turnover is minimal, and revenue has stabilized.
>
> ***Board Chair Cassidy Campana***

A few of the specific actions the board took include:

- Incorporating so-called mission moments regularly into board meetings (for instance, having artists come to meetings to perform or talk with the board)
- Providing regular opportunities for the board to socialize before and after meetings to encourage familiarity
- Organizing outside activities (tours, art studio experiences) to increase connection
- Breaking up into small roundtable groups at meetings (face-to-face, introverted board members feel comfortable in contributing to the discussion)
- Having more strategic dialogues in meetings

"It was useful to have a third party guide us through this process. Together we designed a consultative process that itself engaged our board," says Cassidy.

Jo Wilson, Task Force Chair, says that it was important to engage the staff (not just the CEO), as well as the board, because the relationship between staff and board is different for a nongoverning board (i.e. the board does not select the CEO and the CEO reports to the city, not the foundation). She also says that continuing the task force for a year ensured that the plan was followed. The task force also made sure that the topic of engagement was revisited in subsequent board retreats. The work has now been folded into that of the standing Board Development Committee.

> The foundation was only eight years old when we embarked on this project. We addressed the engagement issue early on in our organization's life, so that engagement would become ingrained into our board's culture.
>
> **Jo Wilson, Task Force Chair**

UNITED STATES REFERENCES

BoardSource. 2017. *Leading with Intent: 2017 National Index of Nonprofit Board Practices*. BoardSource.

Brown, W.A. 2005. "Exploring the association between board and organizational performance in nonprofit organizations." *Nonprofit Management and Leadership* 15, no. 3: 317–339.

Campana, Cassidy. 2017. Board Engagement at Mesa Arts Center. Received by Penelope Cagney on October 19, 2017.

Golensky, M. 1993. "The board-executive relationship in nonprofit organizations: partnership or power struggle?" *Nonprofit Management and Leadership* 4, no. 2: 177–191.

Herman, R.D., and D.O. Renz. 2000. "Board practices of especially effective and less effective local nonprofit organizations." *American Review of Public Administration* 30, no. 2: 146–160.

Ingram, R.T. 2015. *Ten Basic Responsibilities of Nonprofit Boards.* BoardSource.

IRS. 2017. Internal Revenue Manuals. Part 7: Chapter 25 Exempt Organizations Determinations. https://www.irs.gov/irm/part7/irm_07-025-003 (accessed December 28, 2017).

Larcker, D.F., N.E. Donatiello, B. Meehan, and B. Tayan. 2015. *2015 Survey on Board of Directors of Nonprofit Organizations.* Stanford Graduate School of Business; Rock Center for Corporate Governance.

LeRoux, K., and J. Langer. 2016. "What nonprofit executives want and what they get from board members." *Nonprofit Management and Leadership* 27, no. 2: 147–164.

Kearns, K.P. 1995. "Effective nonprofit board members as seen by executives and board chairs." *Nonprofit Management and Leadership* 5, no. 4: 337–358.

McKeever, B. 2015. *The Nonprofit Sector in Brief 2015: Public Charities, Giving, and Volunteering.* Urban Institute.

Pfeffer, J. 1973. "Size, composition, and function of hospital boards of directors: a study of organization-environment linkage." *Administrative Science Quarterly* 18, no. 3: 349–364.

Raggo, P. 2014. "Leaders' accounts: a study of transnational NGOs leadership views on accountability" (PhD thesis, Syracuse University). ProQuest Dissertations & Theses Global.

Renz, D.O. 2010. "Leadership, governance, and the work of the board." In *Jossey-Bass Handbook of Nonprofit Leadership and Management,* 3rd ed., edited by D.O. Renz, 125–158. Jossey-Bass.

Rosenberg, J. And P. Stallworth. "The House Tax Bill is Not Very Charitable to Nonprofits". *Tax Policy Center,* November 15, 2017. http://www.taxpolicycenter.org/taxvox/house-tax-bill-not-very-charitable-nonprofits (accessed January 2, 2018).

Trompenaars, Fons, and Charles Hampden-Turner. 1997. *Riding the Waves of Culture: Understanding Cultural Diversity in Business.* London, UK: Nicholas Brealey.

U.S. Census Bureau, 2012-2016 *American Community Survey 5-Year Estimates.* https://factfinder.census.gov/faces/tableservices/jsf/pages/productview.xhtml?src=CF (accessed January 2, 2018).

Wilson, Jo. 2017. Board Engagement at Mesa Arts Center Foundation. Received by Penelope Cagney on October 20, 2017.

CHAPTER **10**

From Reform of Governance to Transfer of Power

The Future of International Civil Society Organizations

Burkhard Gnärig

*This chapter focuses on the leading international civil society organiza-
tion (ICSOs)—the ones with impressive global brands, such as Amnesty
International, Greenpeace, and Oxfam; those with global budgets of over
US$1 billion, such as World Vision, Save the Children, and Caritas; and
those with a special niche, such as Transparency International, HelpAge,
and Sightsavers. We will look at organizations that are active around the
globe under one single name. Governing these organizations is a very
demanding challenge and identifying best practice in their governance is
an even more difficult one. Burkhard Gnärig, founder and CEO of the
International Civil Society Centre, a membership organization of many
of the largest ICSOs, explains why this is the case before advancing the
exploration of ICSO governance as far as possible.*

About 10 years ago my organization, the International Civil Society Centre, brought together, for the very first time ever, the chairs of
the major ICSOs. In preparation for their first meeting we asked them
what they wanted to discuss. The answer was surprisingly homogeneous:
Global governance. When we inquired further we found that they were
not interested in discussing the strengths and weaknesses of the United
Nations (UN) system: They wanted to review the global governance of
their own organizations. When the meeting finally took place, the chairs

231

were very excited to have the opportunity to talk to each other. As they had never met before, we started with a round of introductions, asking everybody to say a few words about themselves and make a brief remark about why they were so interested in discussing ICSO governance. The first chair started explaining how pleased he was to have the opportunity to learn about the governance of other organizations in the room, as he felt that his own organization's governance was not functioning very well. He ended, "To be honest, our governance is really flawed and I want to learn from you how to get it right." To everybody's surprise a roaring laughter filled the room and then chair after chair each gave his or her story demonstrating how ineffective his or her governance was. The most oft-mentioned examples were on governance decisions taking too long, decisions being based on the lowest common denominator, decisions not being implemented, and conflicts of interest between national chapters that paralyzed the decision-making of the whole organization.

We continued our meeting by analyzing the flaws of the existing global governance models and discussed ways to overcome the challenges. In the end, everyone went home excited and filled with ideas on how to improve their governance. When the following year's meeting approached we again asked the chairs what they wanted most to discuss. Once again, the answer was "global governance." Even today the issue of effective global governance is very high on most global chairs' agenda. But let's not be overly critical of their failure to resolve this issue: If we look at the UN, we have to admit that our governments have not resolved this challenge either.

In this chapter we will explore why effective global governance is so difficult to achieve and what it would take to make global governance more effective. We will make our journey in four steps: First we will look at the federated model that determines most ICSOs' governance. Second, we will look at ICSOs leaders' own analysis of their organizations' governance and learn about their approaches to governance change. Third, we will discuss key aspects of conducting governance reform. Finally, we will identify some of the cornerstones of ICSOs' transformation that will be required if they want to remain legitimate and relevant in the future.

ICSOs' GOVERNANCE MODEL OF CHOICE: INTERNATIONAL FEDERATIONS OF AUTONOMOUS NATIONAL ORGANIZATIONS

It is fascinating to see how similar the governance of most major ICSOs is, no matter whether they were founded in the middle of the nineteenth century (as the YWCA or the Red Cross were) or 100 years later (as CARE and Oxfam were); and no matter whether they are service providers (such as Save the Children and Plan International) or advocacy organizations (such as Amnesty International and Transparency International): Most of them are federations of national member organizations. What made so many ICSOs opt for the federated governance model?

How the Federated Model Emerged

The early development of many ICSOs was often both dynamic and chaotic, and founders were either not interested or unable to wield global control. Once the idea for a new organization had proven viable and effective, local and national organizations emerged quickly, with little interest in and often little need for international coordination. The world of the nineteenth and most of the twentieth centuries was determined within national boundaries, and international control of national affairs was seen as undesirable and virtually impossible. In such a world, international governance could only be conducted by representatives of nation-states: The League of Nations and later the UN, the World Bank and the other Breton Woods[1] institutions, the International Olympic Committee, FIFA (*Fédération Internationale de Football Association*), the Commonwealth, and the EU (European Union)— all of them composed by independent countries coming together to govern common issues. The federation made up of country representatives seemed to be the only international governance model on offer.

For decades the federated model served its purpose well, until the mid-1980s, when globalization created new threats and opportunities that made closer global coordination among national organizations that carried the same name a necessity. Often, the threats rather than the opportunities brought national organizations closer together. For instance, a major scandal in a national CARE, Oxfam, or Save the Children organization that would have been a local, or, in the worst case, a national challenge in the past, would now quickly spread around the globe, impacting the global brand and affiliates everywhere. Suddenly national organizations had to manage the risks of potential misbehavior of their sister organizations in other countries. In order to manage these risks certain standards on key issues, such as financial accountability, program quality, and child protection, needed to be established throughout all organizations carrying the same name. A second risk that affected several of the large ICSOs resulted from the fact that a number of their national affiliates were running parallel programs in the same developing country. Donors and host governments increasingly asked why these programs could not be brought under a single management to establish a single point of contact in each country, to save overhead costs, and to deliver better services. To avoid such criticism, the ICSOs concerned needed to strengthen their internal cooperation.

Together with these new risks came new opportunities: Donor governments and large foundations developed regional and global strategies and were looking for partners that could implement large programs on an international scale. International advocacy—towards the UN and its various organizations, towards the World Bank and International Monetary Fund, and towards the EU and other regional bodies— became a more important aspect of ICSOs' work, and a stronger global cohesion of national organizations under one global name provided better opportunities for being heard. As a consequence of these and other opportunities and threats, ICSOs strengthened their international governance. However, most did not question the federated model they had been using for decades. Given the existence of many independent national organizations, the choice of a federated structure seemed obvious. In fact, it was the only structure acceptable to the national organizations. They wanted to preserve their independence and limit the need to compromise with others to the bare minimum. Today, most ICSOs have federated governance models. Not all of them call themselves federations, however. Wanting to underline the independence of their national member organizations, some call themselves confederations and others alliances or networks.

The Advantages of the Federal Model

What is so attractive about the federated governance model? First, it perfectly accommodates the typical structure of many national CSOs. Around the world, governments have created similar legal and tax-exemption frameworks in which CSOs have to operate. Usually these require a CSO to be governed by an in-country board of directors. Usually the national board is legally responsible for the appropriate use of all resources collected in the country. The federated model is based on these provisions: It takes the national structure as the starting point and just adds an international board to the national ones.

Second, it mirrors the global governance of most international institutions. No matter whether we look at the UN, the World Bank, the EU, or the vast majority of other international institutions—all are composed of national governments who cooperate as far as it to their particular advantage, but not when their interests are not aligned with the institution's. Most of today's ICSOs were founded when this international architecture took shape—and they reflect the thinking that shaped our world of nations. The federated model of ICSO governance doesn't need much justification: It mirrors the way in which national governments work together.

Third, it provides national legitimacy. In a world still very much defined by the nation-state, being a "proper" British, Indian, or American organization with a fully empowered national board helps with raising funds and wielding influence. These positive features are mirrored by a number of negative ones.

The Challenges of the Federal Model

A federated-governance model is highly complex and very difficult for ICSOs to run. Imagine decision-making in a federation of 20, 50, or even 100 national affiliates, all with their own fully independent national board. In addition—not on top—there is a global board aiming to turn the enormous diversity of national interests of countries such as the United States, Fiji, Swaziland, Guatemala, and Japan into consistent global policies. As national boards are constituted under national law there are very limited means for the global board to take—and even less so to enforce—any decision against the explicit interest of a national board. This makes it very hard for many ICSOs to get anything done at the global level.

One of the consequences of federated governance is a tendency to avoid decisions in situations of diverging or even conflicting national or cultural interests. I remember how an international campaign against the corrective spank or smack employed by parents, teachers, or other authorities to discipline children did not take shape because some prominent supporters of one national affiliate believed in the maxim "Spare the rod, spoil the child"—that the occasional parental smack was a legitimate tool in the education of children. In the self-assessment of ICSO leaders below, we will see that taking quick decisions that are guided by global rather than national interests is an uphill struggle.

This struggle is made even more challenging by the lack of power at the global center. Usually called international secretariats or international offices (but rarely head offices), most global units are coordinating rather than leading the international organization. This powerlessness at the global level on the one hand stems from the fact that national affiliates—by charity law in most countries—retain all powers at the national level and on the other hand by the fact that most international secretariats depend on national affiliates' financial contributions.

Given these downsides at the level of international governance, the persistence of the federated model may surprise. The main reason for the continued dominance of the federated model is that it reflects very well the distribution of power between the national and global levels. I remember the visit of a CEO around the turn of the millennium, who asked for my advice in turning a national organization into an international one. Based on my personal experience with the federated governance of several ICSOs, I urged him to avoid the federated model. I suggested that he speak to any other CEO of a federated organization, who would most likely give him similar advice. He still decided to turn his unitary organization into a federated one. It looks as if the federated model of ICSO governance is practically unavoidable. However, in the face of the increasing need for consistent and effective international decision-making, ICSOs will have to find ways to allocate sufficient power to the global level.

THE SELF-ASSESSMENT: THE QUALITY OF ICSOs' GOVERNANCE

In April and May 2017 we distributed a governance questionnaire to the leaders of 32 of the world's best-known ICSOs. Representatives of 26 organizations, or 81%, filled in the questionnaire. This very good return, as well as a number of explicit requests to share our findings, indicates that there is considerable motivation in the sector to come to grips with the existing governance challenges.

All together we received 32 replies: 23 from CEOs and 9 from chairs. In most organizations only the CEO replied, but in some both the chair and the CEO filled in the questionnaire, and in a few only the chair participated in our review.

Facts About Participating ICSOs

85% of ICSOs have federated governance. We first asked about the governance structure of the ICSOs and found that two-thirds of the organizations (65%) have a general assembly or members meeting. All have an international board and 85% have a number of national boards. This confirms our understanding that the vast majority of ICSOs work on the basis of a federated governance model and face the challenge of aligning national governance with international governance.

69% of international boards are controlled by national representatives. We further wanted to know how their international governance is connected to their national affiliates. We found that nearly half of all international boards (46%) consist exclusively of representatives from national affiliates. In another 23% the majority of directors are representatives from national affiliates, and in 15% of the boards less than half of all directors come from national affiliates. Only 15% of participating ICSOs do not have any representatives of national affiliates on their international boards. Looking at these figures we can say that the international governance of the vast majority of ICSOs (69%) is controlled by their national affiliates.

International boards focus on supervision. We provided the leaders with the—slightly adapted—BoardSource list of the *Ten Basic Responsibilities of Nonprofit Boards* and asked them to tell us where these responsibilities were predominantly allocated in their organizations.

We found that only half of the responsibilities were predominantly exercised by international boards, who:

- Select the international CEO (94%).
- Support and evaluate the international CEO (91%).
- Provide financial oversight (81%).
- Ensure legal and ethical integrity (72%).
- Build a competent board (66%).

The five remaining responsibilities are allocated elsewhere in ICSOs' governance and management structures:

- Determine the vision and mission—mainly shared between ICSOs' general assemblies (47%) and international boards (47%).
- Enhance the organization's public standing—mostly a management (72%) task and much less one of the international board (41%).
- Ensure effective planning—even less important for the international board (31%) but very much the responsibility of management (75%).
- Ensure adequate financial resources—not a major responsibility of most international boards (28%), who are as much concerned as national boards (28%), while management is in charge (63%).
- Monitor and strengthen programs—even less seen as a responsibility of the international board (25%) but very much as a management (78%) task.

The Challenges of ICSOs' Governance

After collecting those basic facts about their organizations, we asked the leaders to give us their personal assessments of the quality of their organizations' governance.

Nearly half of international leaders see national governance as a challenge. This takes us to leaders' assessments of the quality of their organizations' governance. We asked first about their organizations' overall governance, then specifically about their international governance, and finally about their national governance. Given a choice of POOR, AVERAGE, GOOD, VERY GOOD, and EXCELLENT, 39% of the respondents consider their own organizations' governance overall to be AVERAGE, 28% consider their international governance to be POOR or AVERAGE, and nearly half (47%) see their national governance to be POOR or AVERAGE. This means that 4 out of 10 international leaders do not find their organizations' overall governance good, and they predominantly blame flaws in national governance for the situation.

Seventy-eight (78) percent think their organization is too slow in taking decisions. What will ICSOs' future governance reform focus on? Obviously, we don't know, but we have some indications from the replies to some of our questions. For instance: 31% of leaders think that their organizations are *often* too slow in taking decisions and 47% think this is *sometimes* the case, and 28% *often* experience decision-making as too cumbersome while 47% *sometimes* do.

Sixty-nine (69) percent see decision-making as overly compromised in the effort to balance national interests. In a significant number of organizations, decision-making is either *often* (31%) or *sometimes* (38%) too much focused on balancing national interests. One of the reasons for this may be that the organization is dominated by its largest national affiliate(s): 26% believe that this is *often* the case while 28% see it happening *sometimes*.

Sixty-five (65) percent of all ICSOs are reforming their governance or planning a reform. Given leaders' assessments of their own organizations' governance, reform seems to be a necessity in many ICSOs. And there certainly has not been a lack of trying: 88% of ICSOs have reformed their governance during the past 10 years, and 35% even have done it several times. Even more telling is the fact that two-thirds of all responding organizations (65%) are either engaged in the process of reforming their governance at present or plan to do so over the next two years. Overall we can say that ICSO leaders are less than enthusiastic about their organizations' governance, and that they have tried to improve their governance before and they will try even harder over the next few years.

If we take our results so far as a basis, future governance reform should make ICSOs' decision-making both faster and more effective. It should strengthen the basis for decisions that are in the best interests of the organization globally, rather than pursuing the national interests of the most powerful affiliates or seeking the lowest common denominator between diverging or even competing national interests.

The Direction of Governance Reform

What do ICSO leaders tell us about their intentions for governance reform? What do they plan to focus on? One area of potential improvements concerns the question, Who among the organizations' key stakeholders should be represented in ICSOs' governance?

Fifty-six (56) percent of ICSO leaders would like to increase the number of beneficiaries in their governance. The most significant change concerns the people ICSOs are aiming to serve. More than half of all leaders (56%) believe that beneficiaries should be *more* involved in their organizations' governance. The only other group a significant number of ICSO leaders would like to see *more* involved in their governance are external experts: 50% would like to bring additional experts into their governance. If ICSOs follow the guidance of our survey, they will increase the numbers of beneficiaries and experts in their governance while leaving the numbers of activists, national affiliates, and donors as they are.

Seventy-seven (77) percent want national affiliates to remain or be more involved in international governance. Asked to what degree representatives of their national affiliates should be involved in governance, 50% of respondents believe that national affiliates should stay involved at the *same* level, 27% think they should be even *more* involved, while 17% would like them to be *less* involved, and only 7% think they should *not at all* play a role in the organization's international governance. This is surprising given the replies to some other questions in our survey, which identify the strong role of national affiliates in the organizations' international governance as a major challenge. One possible explanation for this seemingly inconsistent view may be linked to the distribution of power in most ICSOs. Power is mainly rooted in income, and in most ICSOs money is earned by national affiliates, especially the ones in industrialized countries, rather than by the global entity. This means that governance that properly reflects the real power relations needs to have a strong involvement of the rich national affiliates.

Most ICSOs also depend on their national affiliates to implement the organization's programs and most other decisions of the international board. When asked whether their governance is "unable to secure implementation of its decisions," 13% of all respondents stated that this is *often* and 47% that this is *sometimes* the case. This takes us to 60% of organizations that experience a lack of cooperation in making their decisions a reality. Kicking their national affiliates out of the international governance would probably further reduce the odds of having board decisions implemented. Whatever the correct explanation, it is obvious most ICSOs cannot imagine running their international governance without strong involvement of their national affiliates. Thus, our earlier assumption that ICSOs will try to change their governance to make them less dependent on their national affiliates seems unrealistic.

We finally asked respondents for any comments they wanted to provide that completed the statement: We will/we should reform our governance in the following way. We also provided space for any other comments they wanted to make. Clustering the statements under those sections provides the following areas ICSO leaders want to focus on in reforming their governance:

Professionalization and effectiveness. Governance should be "less bureaucratic," more professionals should be involved, the right mix of skill sets should be secured, governance processes should be streamlined, and in some organizations the size of governing bodies should be reduced.

Accountability and transparency. Governance processes need to be more transparent—in general and specifically towards "those we serve"; roles, responsibilities, and accountability need to be better aligned; national affiliates should be more accountable to the organization as a whole; and accountability needs to be the basis of better performance evaluation and management.

Diversity in governing bodies. The composition of international boards should reflect the organization's global presence, there should be more board members from the Global South (experts and/or partner representatives), a better gender balance in governance is needed, and local ownership should be strengthened and the most marginalized should be included.

In conclusion: While leaders identify a range of aspects of their governance they want to reform, very few, if any, want to change their governance model as such. For the foreseeable future, we have to expect the federated system will remain the dominant model. On the other hand, given its obvious—and widely acknowledged—flaws, federated governance is not the most appropriate answer to increasingly pressing global challenges. Climate change, eradication of species, pollution of the oceans, scarcity of fresh water supplies, increasing competition for shrinking resources, dramatically growing international migration, terrorism, authoritarian government, shrinking civic space, and many other challenges demand consistent and effective global answers. Such answers can only be found with the benefit of humanity as a whole in mind. They can neither be determined by a handful of a few rich-country representatives nor by finding the lowest common denominator among all countries. Under these aspects federated governance cannot be the last word in conducting global affairs.

TOWARDS EFFECTIVE GLOBAL GOVERNANCE

As so many ICSOs are embarking on a new round of governance reform, let's discuss some critical aspects of a more effective global governance model for ICSOs. We will focus on four recommendations ICSO leaders should take into account when embarking on another round of governance reform:

1. Conduct governance reform with a strategic perspective.
2. Address the distribution of power.
3. Govern facilitation rather than intermediation.[2]
4. Govern growing complexity and accelerating change.

Conduct Governance Reform with a Strategic Perspective

Having been involved in several governance reform processes, in the various roles of CEO, board member, or outside adviser, I often found two patterns of seemingly instinctive behavior, both of which threaten the success of governance reform.

The first one is the endeavor to fix the flaws of the existing governance system. Many governance reforms start with a review of the strengths and weaknesses of the governance as practiced over the past three to five years. After identifying specific aspects that did not go well in recent times, the review usually provides some recommendations on how to resolve these challenges. Based on this analysis the board or the general assembly of the organization decides on the way ahead and another round of governance reform takes its course. What is going wrong here? The organization has decided to resolve some challenges of the past, and while the reform process takes its course—often lasting for several years—new challenges to the organization's governance arise. And all too often, shortly after the governance reform has been concluded, a new discussion about the organization's governance starts. I assume that many of the ICSOs in our survey that reformed their governance *several times* over the past 10 years have fallen into that trap. Change fatigue in many organizations is often due to that mistake having been made too often. In order to avoid this mistake, governance reform has to look at future demands rather than past shortcomings.

The second mistake often made in governance reform is to look exclusively inside the organization. Questions such as: How can we speed up decision-making? How can we avoid internal resistance to decisions? How can we secure smooth implementation of our decision? are often the only ones that are being asked. Such an approach fails to see that governance is only as effective as it enables the organization to fulfill its mission in the outside world. Governance that does not take its lead from the demands of the fast-changing environment in which all ICSOs operate today cannot be effective. I recommend starting with the question: What are the changing conditions under which we aim to fulfill our mission in the outside world? Based on the answers, the next question should be: What kind of governance would be best suited to fulfill our mission in the outside world?

Look to the future, look to the outside world.

Combining our replies to both mistakes in governance reform, we can say the guiding question for any governance reform should be: What kind of governance should we have in order to best serve our mission in the outside world over the coming five years? Or in brief: Look to the future, look to the outside world.

Address the Distribution of Power

One of the main reasons why ICSO's governance does not work very well is that it does not properly reflect the distribution of power in the organization. For instance, I have experienced several situations in which ICSOs agreed on decisions that were not wholeheartedly supported by some of the larger national affiliates. Usually the skeptical affiliates voted with the majority, as it was more comfortable than explaining and defending an opposing position, but then they did not act on the decision's implementation. What went wrong here?

Generally, ICSOs are very skeptical towards power: In their work they frequently experience how many governments, armies, armed movements, certain companies, and many others are abusing their power. Against this background, being powerful is usually perceived as negative in itself. Thus, ICSOs usually avoid addressing the elephant in the room: The question of where power resides in their own organization. They follow principles such as "one affiliate—one vote," preserving the illusion that all affiliates are equal. In organizations in which the richest affiliate may have 100 times the budget of the poorest one this is an unrealistic assumption: The allocation of power is not reflected in the governance. It only manifests itself in the implementation of decisions: The powerful affiliates decide whether a vote of the international board is going to be implemented or not. A governance structure reflecting the distribution of power would give the larger affiliates a veto right, and at the same time oblige them to implement all decisions that are taken at the international level. Governance reforms that do not properly reflect the distribution of power in the organization will fail to provide the basis for effective decision-making and implementation.

Sadly, aligning governance to the distribution of power fails in a situation in which power is not allocated where it would be most useful in achieving the organization's mission. This is possibly the single biggest challenge most ICSOs face. As discussed earlier, most ICSOs were shaped at a time when they could pursue their missions predominantly at the national level. Meanwhile, globalization demands many more decisions at the global level, and the empowerment of the individual through digital technology mandates more decisions be taken at the local or even individual level. Thus, power should flow from the national level in both directions, towards the global and towards the individual. In fact this power shift in ICSOs has been happening over the past decades and continues to occur at present, but at too slow a pace. Therefore, aligning governance with where power resides at present will not make the organization much more effective in its international work—but actively shifting power would.

ICSOs will have to find ways to shift a significant part of the power of the (rich and usually Northern) national affiliates to the local and global levels. If they fail at doing this, they will also fail at fulfilling their global missions—and they will lose their appeal to the next generation of donors and activists. Governance reform on its own will not produce this power shift. For instance, inviting some more beneficiaries to join an ICSO's board does not shift power to the local level in a governance system in which the rich affiliates still decide whether they will finance and implement the international board's decisions. History tells us that the powerful rarely give away any of their power if they are not being forced to do so. So, the question is whether the boards and CEOs of rich and powerful national affiliates in the Global North will be willing to empower their local partners and beneficiaries and their global decision-making bodies. Should such a miracle happen and power shift to where it delivers maximum benefit, it would not be too difficult to establish a governance system that frames power in a very legitimate and effective way.

Govern Facilitation Rather Than Intermediation

Most of the largest ICSOs are facing significant changes to their traditional role as intermediaries between donors and recipients of aid. When organizations such as Save the Children, Oxfam, CARE, and many others were founded, they served as indispensable intermediaries between donors, usually in the Global North, and recipients, usually in the Global South. Without ICSOs, donors and recipients could not possibly find each other—nor did they have a common basis of communication, let alone cooperation. With the emergence of the digital world this situation has changed fundamentally. All potential donors and the vast majority of potential recipients have access to the Internet. They can find each other through web-based searches or on one of the aid and cooperation platforms that have been set up by a new generation of digital CSOs.

This means that donors and beneficiaries can come together virtually, communicate with each other, and collaborate without the help of a traditional ICSO. And increasingly they do so. With the completion of the spread of the Internet to the poorest and remotest parts of our planet, which will happen over the next 10 years, and the rise of a new generation of donors who have grown up with the Internet and are used to communicating globally, the traditional role of ICSOs as intermediaries will fade away—or at least become much less important. The vast majority of donors will give through highly efficient and much cheaper Internet-based platforms to the people they want to support. And many recipients will be very happy to get rid of often-patronizing Northern-based ICSOs and work directly with individuals and institutions who want to support them.

Governance reform, which aims at securing ICSOs' future, will have to take these changes into consideration. If my organization can no longer play the role of intermediary and can no longer expect to live from the related income, is there a different role we can play—and what governance will that role demand? I believe that there are a number of important tasks ICSOs can and should pursue. For instance, they should swap their role as intermediary for a role as moderator in the communication and cooperation between donors and recipients. For instance, there often will be culture and language differences between donor and recipient that need to be overcome. ICSOs, with their vast experience and presence in the field, could help. There will be a continued need for advocacy for a more just and sustainable way of organizing our societies: ICSOs have the capacity and knowledge to do this. We don't have the room here to explore ICSOs' potential future roles any further, but two important consequences from the loss of the intermediary role seem to emerge: First, the power of intermediaries, resulting from the fact that they were indispensable for any cooperation between donors and recipients, will shrink. And second, the large incomes ICSOs drew from their work as intermediaries will shrink accordingly. This means that ICSOs will have to learn to pursue their missions with less money and less power. They will not only have to find new roles for themselves, but they will also have to acquire a new legitimacy.

I cannot imagine that all of this will be possible with ICSOs' present governance structures, processes, and personnel.

Govern Growing Complexity and Accelerating Change

Global governance necessarily means governing complexity. It means governing different cultures, languages, ways to see the world, and ways to express one's views. It means governing small and large, rich and poor, and powerless and powerful elements and actors. It means governing in a world that grows in complexity at breakneck speed while sticking to its old ways of governance that were developed in times of much less complexity and much slower change. A few years ago I was asked to advise one of the leading ICSOs on governance reform. They had identified the lack of speed in their decision-making as one of their key challenges. Often external events demanded an immediate response from the organization, but their decision-making processes across their extensive global structures took so long that once they had developed a solid and widely shared position the world had already moved on and there was no longer any interest in what the organization had to say.

ICSOs that want to be seen as leading global influencers need to find ways to organize their governance and management in such a way that they are able to produce quick, relevant, and competent statements on behalf of the whole organization within a few hours rather than days, weeks, or months. As the world demands an ever-faster pace in decision-making, it also becomes more complex by the day. No longer can any single person or group credibly claim to hold all information necessary to run a billion-dollar ICSO that operates worldwide. This means that decision-making has become much more decentralized. The people who are directly affected by a decision need to have much more influence in making the decision, and, wherever possible, take the decision themselves.

Leadership teams that are strategically established to cover a wide range of skills and represent a diversity of personal backgrounds and views secure a more solid basis for decision-making in complex and often inconsistent situations. At the same time they need to be set up to take decisions quickly, as the outside world no longer tolerates lengthy decision-making processes. Such teams will require very different leadership skills. Rather than being the one undisputed head of the team leading from the front, future leaders will be able to share leadership across the team and see themselves as facilitators and coaches rather than final decision makers.

Lately we can observe the first examples of shared leadership at the CEO level, but ICSOs are still far away from a systematic approach to shared leadership across the whole organization. Whether ICSOs will come up with governance and management approaches that allow them to quickly tackle complex situations in a fast-changing environment will very much define their future scope and relevance.

CORNERSTONES OF ICSOs' TRANSFORMATION

If our observations and assumptions are correct and

- The shift from ICSOs' role as intermediaries to a role as platform provider and facilitator,
- Power shifts from the national towards the global and local levels and from governance towards management and stakeholders,
- And the demand for faster and better quality decisions and their immediate and consistent implementation

turn into vastly uncontested necessities, ICSOs will have to fundamentally transform themselves in order to meet these requirements and thus remain legitimate and relevant. The following to-do list for ICSO leaders contains some of the critical strategic actions they will have to undertake in order to transform the role, the setup, the power distribution, and the governance of their organization:

Build a platform organization with widely shared power and responsibility. Today's pyramidal governance and management structures will hopefully be replaced by platform-based structures and effective networks with powers and responsibilities much wider spread. Future ICSOs will moderate and facilitate activities on these platforms but not unilaterally determine and control them. Governance under these circumstances needs to be much more modest and serving than ICSO governance today.

Drive strategic decisions in both directions: Bottom-up and top-down. Top-down decision-making will no longer be the dominant way of running a global organization. Key decision-making will have to flow in both directions, up from the grassroots and down from the global level, while decisions of minor strategic importance will be taken at the level where they are most relevant.

Empower local and global actors across the organization. While in most ICSOs today 80–90% of all strategic decisions are taken by national affiliates—either by national boards or by international ones that are dominated by national representatives—legitimate and effective governance of the future will demand a more balanced distribution of power among the local, national, and global levels. Thus, a major power shift from the national level to the local and the global levels is required.

Limit formal governing bodies to their supervisory role. Given the existence of dozens of national boards and one global board, all working in parallel within the same ICSO, and given many boards' tendency to stray beyond their supervisory roles and take executive decisions, it is easy to see that many ICSOs are overgoverned and undermanaged. Effective ICSOs of the future will restrict their boards to a supervisory role and shift all executive decisions to the management and all overarching strategic decisions to the organizations' wider stakeholder community.

Empower executives at all levels of the organization. Given the need for fast and competent decisions in a highly complex world, more and more decisions will have to be taken by the professionals who do the work. Decision-making within local, national, regional, and global teams strictly determined by their competencies and duties will reduce the risk of failure. Recruiting the right staff and management will be even more important, and building diverse and well-functioning teams will be key. Leadership will become even more a coaching, rather than a directing, role.

Involve stakeholders in setting the ICSO's vision, mission, and strategy. As ICSOs are transforming themselves from closed and siloed entities into open and cooperative platforms, their direction will be set by a much wider group of stakeholders. Digital communication allows everybody to contribute to discussions and decision-making, and ICSOs' key stakeholders will expect to be given the right and opportunities to be involved.

Promote diversity among decision makers on all levels. Participation in governance, management, and stakeholder-based decision-making and running of the organization has to reflect the composition of the ICSO's global community. Discrimination based on gender, ethnicity, religion, or other reasons is not acceptable, and ICSOs have to actively promote diversity at all levels of their work.

Bringing together the different strands of thought in this chapter, we can say:

- ICSOs are generally not happy with their governance. Most of them are either conducting governance reform at present or plan to do so in the next two years.

- However, their leaders' assessments of governance shortcomings and their plans for change don't look bold and strategic enough to overcome the flaws of today's federated governance and comply with the demands of the outside world.
- The allocation of powers in today's ICSOs does not reflect the needs of a globalized world populated by self-confident individuals and communities. Any governance reform that hopes to succeed has to be based on a consistent reallocation of powers.
- A significant power shift from national affiliates to both local partners and the global center is required.
- On another level, power has to shift from governance to management on one hand and the wider stakeholder community on the other.
- ICSOs' national affiliates, and specifically their boards, cannot be forced to give away power. If they lack strategic insight and refuse to share their power, the ICSO will quickly loose its global legitimacy and relevance and will be replaced by other, more adaptable organizations.

Predicting the future is always difficult, and it remains to be seen whether my expectations become true. However, the question of whether we will continue to govern our global affairs in multinational federations with a small number of national representatives holding all the power or whether we will find forms of governance that balance the "my country first" approach with a "my family first" and a "humanity's future first" reaches way beyond ICSOs. It is also the question posed to the UN and many other global entities. And whether we will find a convincing answer to this question or not will not only shape ICSOs' future but the future of much more powerful and important international institutions, and, ultimately, the future of humanity.

NOTES

1. The Bretton Woods conference, formally known as the United Nations Monetary and Financial Conference, was the gathering of 730 delegates from all 44 Allied nations at the Mount Washington Hotel, situated in Bretton Woods, New Hampshire in the United States, to regulate the international monetary and financial order in 1944 after the conclusion of World War II.
2. Many ICSOs still serve as intermediaries between donors, usually in the Global North, and recipients, usually in the Global South. This role is becoming obsolete as the Internet enables donors and recipients to find each other and work together.

CHAPTER **11**

The Future

Penelope Cagney

It seems fitting to conclude with some thoughts about the future for boards within the larger context of society and the civil sector. Let's consider what the implications for NGOs might be given the following scenarios:

The gap between the wealthy and the middle class continues to widen.

Ultrarich funders increasingly drive the philanthropic agenda.

Reaction to some of the negative effects of globalization forces some nations increasingly inward and international concerns grow increasingly less important to them. Others, enjoying an increase in prosperity, turn outward and claim a role on the global stage.

The pace of technological innovation continues to accelerate and revolutionize our ways of thinking and doing things.

In rethinking organizations and leadership, new models for governance are required.

Let's look at each of these in turn.

WEALTH INEQUALITY

Economist Thomas Piketty warns, "... the inequality of returns on capital as a function of initial wealth, can lead to excessive and lasting concentration of capital ... fortunes can grow and perpetuate themselves beyond all reasonable limits and beyond any possible rational justification in terms of social utility" (Piketty 2013, 443). A growing concentration of wealth in the hands of a few will influence civil society. Already we are seeing very wealthy private funders tackling problems that government can't or won't, and as a result, they could set the philanthropic agenda for everyone (Callan 2017). "This isn't the government collecting taxes and deciding which social problems it wants to solve through a democratic process," said Eileen Heisman, chief executive of the National Philanthropic Trust, in an October 20, 2017 article in the *New York Times* (Gelles 2017). "This is a small group of people, who have made way more money than they need, deciding what issues they care about."

PROACTIVE PHILANTHROPY

Not only are philanthropists more directly setting the agenda, they are taking things into their own hands. An example is India's Shiv Nadar, founder of HCL Technologies, who is concentrating his efforts on education and has created his own schools. They are not content to funnel their philanthropy through nonprofit middlemen and are creating their own organizations to address select societal problems.[1] Their commitments are to causes, not to organizations.

Some funders are even questioning the role for nonprofits as program creators and implementers—intermediaries between funder and fundee. There are nonprofits such as GiveDirectly that are simply putting money into the hands of beneficiaries and letting them decide how best to use it. Nonprofits may end up administering programs that are perceived as unnecessary, and the boards at their helm slip into obsolescence.

REACTION TO GLOBALIZATION

Disappointed in the dream of prosperity promised by globalization, some nations are turning inward and disengaging from the world's problems. On the other hand, the global interest of other nations, newly prosperous, has grown. However, meeting challenges of vast scope, such as natural disasters and climate change, requires a united international front if there is to be any hope of resolution. We will see more direction for the sector as a whole coming from new players in global philanthropy.

TECHNOLOGICAL INNOVATION

Technology has already transformed the world of nonprofit governance. Today's boards make use of board portals, file sharing, task management, and dashboards; they access Big Data to inform their decision-making and planning, and they convene virtually. BoardSource's 2015 *Leading with Intent*, a biannual survey of thousands of boards, reported that 66% of international organizations had at least one virtual meeting in 2014 and a full 78% of international organizations allowed for virtual participation. But it is not just international organizations:

- 41% of national and 8% of local organizations had a virtual meeting.
- 68% of national and 59% of regional/multinational organizations allowed for meeting by teleconference (BoardSource 2015, 19).[2]

Boards must keep abreast of technological changes. Technology will provide tools to facilitate their governing business, but it will also challenge them with the changes the future will bring to their organizations.

While very wealthy donors may be driving the agenda from the top, it's also true that social media has also made philanthropy more democratic by making information more available and by making giving easier around the globe. Technology is also instrumental in the emergence of new kinds of organizations.

TOMORROW'S ORGANIZATIONS

Tomorrow's successful organizations may be exponential, defined as "one whose impact (or output) is disproportionately large—at least 10 times larger—compared to its peers because of the use of new organizational techniques that leverage accelerating technologies" (Ismail 2014, 18). We are just beginning to see the profound changes that disruptive technologies will bring.

Yesterday's corporations, matrixes built on simple arithmetic formulas involving labor and ownership of capital assets, are inflexible—the penalty for the economies of scale that have been the basis of their competitive advantage. These organizations required a rigid hierarchical structure driven by financial outcomes instead of realization of mission; linear thinking instead of indirect, creative, and lateral thinking; and internal innovation, rather than accessing innovation resources from outside.

Tomorrow's corporations will travel light. Exponential companies access resources that you don't have to own (technology, staffing, physical facilities, etc.) and recognize information as the greatest asset. They see the massive capital and labor-intensive investments of yesterday as potential millstones around their corporate necks. Two comparisons of new versus old types of organizations are Airbnb versus hotel chains with massive investments in real estate and labor, and Uber versus cab companies with their huge pools of cars (Laloux 2014, 252).

Some ideas about nonprofit organizations originated with corporations. Command-and-control was the leadership model for old-style hierarchies. This traditional style generally involves the accumulation and exercise of power by the few at the top of the pyramid.

Tomorrow will require new kinds of organizations and new kinds of leaders. Leaders with the right characteristics are critical because organizations cannot evolve beyond their level of leadership (Laloux 2014, 252). Some leaders have already left the old command-and-control model behind. Steve Jobs claimed that Apple was run like a start-up: "We always let ideas win arguments, not hierarchies (Reestman 2011)." The top leaders of organizations that have achieved the highest evolutionary level have tamed their egos (Laloux 2014, 252). The leaders of tomorrow are humble.

SERVANT LEADERSHIP

First described by Robert K. Greenleaf as a viable model for leaders of modern organizations, servant leaders share power and put the needs of people and communities first, helping people develop and perform as highly as possible. Similarly, in *Good to Great*, a Level 5 Leader is one who "builds enduring greatness through a paradoxical blend of personal humility and professional will." (Collins 2001, 20). Servant leadership is not new. This concept is timeless—a feature in many religions—but it is also a very contemporary idea with potential for wide applicability (Trompenaars and Voerman 2010). The servant leadership model has had long success in Asia and other places (Liden 2012). Think Nelson Mandela and Ghandi. An outstanding example from the philanthropic world is India's Tata family and the companies that they own: "The oldest for-profit social enterprise in India is Tata Steel at Jamshedpur. They built schools, hospitals, places of worship, created a sustainable environment and then said in all humility: 'we also make steel.'" (See Chapter 2.)

> Humility ... opens you up to the ability to deal more realistically with the world. It's no longer about who's right; it's about what is accurate. (Hess 2017)

This type of leadership may emerge as a viable model for board leaders.

NEW APPROACHES TO GOVERNANCE

Boards may rethink the way that they conduct their business, including taking a fresh look at the traditional fiduciary and strategic work of the board. *Governance as Leadership: Reframing the Work of Nonprofit Boards* (Chait, Ryan, and Taylor 2004) newly defines the work of the board as taking place in three modes: Fiduciary, strategic, and generative. Simply stated, it is a creative means of gaining helpful perspective in framing the problems of the board before planning begins and before the board tackles financial concerns. This approach can boost governance and board decision-making to higher ground.

Another recent idea is that governance does not reside solely in the board. Community-Engagement Governance™, an innovative model proposed by Judy Freiwirth, PhD, is designed to distribute governance throughout the organization rather than concentrating it in the hands of a few at the top (Freiwirth 2014). As noted earlier, the old pyramidal command-and-control style of leadership no longer fits an emerging paradigm.

Participants in Freiwirth's study of this model report that governance decision-making in this model enables them to make more efficient decisions, and because key stakeholders are involved in the decision-making processes, the resources and knowledge of all become available for quicker, more effective decisions.

CONCLUSION

The only thing we know for certain is that the world we have today will not be the one we have tomorrow. But we do know this: Leaders will be needed as much as ever, and they must be quipped to guide the way. As boards around the world create governance models that really work for them, in the process we may also discover ways of governing that will elevate the performance of boards everywhere.

REFERENCES

BoardSource. 2015. *Leading with Intent: A National Index of Nonprofit Board Practices*. BoardSource: 19.

Callan, David. 2017. "As government retrenches, philanthropy blooms," *New York Times*, June 20. www.nytimes.com/2017/06/20/opinion/jeff-bezos-bill-gates-philanthropy.html?smid=tw-share (accessed November 4, 2017).

Chait, Richard P., William P. Ryan, and Barbara E. Taylor. 2004. *Governance as Leadership: Reframing the Work of Nonprofit Boards*. Wiley.

Collins, Jim. 2001. *Good to Great*. Harper Collins.

Freiwirth, J. 2014. "Community-Engagement governance: engaging stakeholders for community impact." In *Nonprofit Governance: Innovative Perspectives and Approaches*, edited by C. Cornforth and W.A. Brown, 183–209. Routledge.

Gelles, David. 2017. "Giving away billions as fast as they can." *New York Times*, October 20.

Hess, Edward. 2017. *Humility is the New Smart: Rethinking Human Excellence in the Smart Machine Age*. Berrett-Koehler.

Ismail, Salim. 2014. *Exponential Organizations*. Diverson Books: 18.

Laloux, Frederick. 2014. *Reinventing Organizations*. Nelson Parker.

Liden, Robert C. 2012. "Leadership research in Asia: a brief assessment and suggestions for the future." *Asia Pacific Journal of Management* 29, 205–212.

Piketty, Thomas. 2013. *Capital in the Twenty-First Century*. Belknap Press.

Reestman, Tom. 2011. "Ideas, not hierarchy: on Steve Jobs supposedly making all Apple decisions." *Small Wave* (blog). www.thesmallwave.com/2011/08/28/ideas-not-hierarchy-on-steve-jobs-supposedly-making-all-apple-decisions (accessed November 4, 2017).

Trompenaars, Fons, and Ed Voerman. 2010. *Servant-Leadership Across Cultures*. McGraw-Hill.

NOTES

1. Via Twitter in June 2017, Amazon's founder, Jeff Bezos, currently the world's richest individual, in an interesting twist to setting an agenda for his philanthropy, solicited the general public's input on what he should support. He has not, at the time of this writing, established a foundation. See Wingfield, Nick. 2017. "Jeff Bezos Wants Ideas for Philanthropy, So He Asked Twitter," New York Times.
2. See Ellen Hirzy's BoardSource 2016 publication, *Virtual Meetings Untangled*, for guidelines for best practices on conducting these kinds of meetings.

FURTHER READING

Cornforth, C. 2014. "Nonprofit governance research: the need for innovative perspectives and approaches." In *Nonprofit Governance: Innovative Perspectives and Approaches*, edited by C. Cornforth and W.A. Brown. Routledge.

Coventry, Louise. 2017a. "Navigating dualities: a case study of organisational governance in Cambodian civil society." In *International Development: A Global Perspective on Theory and Practice*, edited by Paul Battersby and Ravi Roy. Sage.

Coventry, Louise. 2017b. "Want to improve governance? Context matters." *Nonprofit Quarterly* Spring: 55–58.

Frank, Robert. 2017. "At last, Jeff Bezos offers a hint of his philanthropic plans." *New York Times*, June 15.

Hirzy, Ellen. 2016. *Virtual Meetings Untangled*. BoardSource.

Morozov, Evgeny. 2016. "Rockefeller gave away money for no return. Can we say the same of today's tech barons?" *Guardian*, October 15. www.theguardian .com/commentisfree/2016/oct/15/mark-zuckerberg-philanthropy-rockefeller (accessed November 4, 2017).

Ostrower, F., and M.M. Stone. 2010. "Moving governance research forward: a contingency-based framework and data application." *Nonprofit and Voluntary Sector Quarterly* 39, no. 5: 901–924.

Appendix

10 BASIC RESPONSIBILITIES OF NONPROFIT BOARDS (SUMMARY)[1]

1. Determine mission and purposes, and advocate for them.
2. Select the chief executive.
3. Support and evaluate the chief executive.
4. Ensure effective planning.
5. Monitor and strengthen programs and services.
6. Ensure adequate financial resources.
7. Protect assets and provide financial oversight.
8. Build and sustain a competent board.
9. Ensure legal and ethical integrity.
10. Enhance the organization's public standing.

THE SOURCE: 12 PRINCIPLES OF GOVERNANCE THAT POWER EXCEPTIONAL BOARDS[2]

1. *Constructive Partnership.*

   Exceptional boards govern in constructive partnership with the chief executive, recognizing that the effectiveness of the board and chief executive are interdependent. They build this partnership through trust, candor, respect, and honest communication.

2. *Mission Driven.*

   Exceptional boards shape and uphold the mission, articulate a compelling vision, and ensure the congruence between decisions and core values. They treat questions of mission, vision, and core values not as exercises to be done once, but as statements of crucial importance to be drilled down and folded into deliberations.

3. *Strategic Thinking.*

   Exceptional boards allocate time to what matters most and continuously engage in strategic thinking to hone the organization's direction. They not only align agendas and goals with strategic priorities, but also use them for assessing the chief executive, driving meeting agendas, and shaping board recruitment.

4. *Culture of Inquiry.*

Exceptional boards institutionalize a culture of inquiry, mutual respect, and constructive debate that leads to sound and shared decision-making. They seek more information, question assumptions, and challenge conclusions so that they may advocate for solutions based on analysis.

5. *Independent-Mindedness.*

Exceptional boards are independent minded. They apply rigorous conflict-of-interest procedures, and their board members put the interests of the organization above all else when making decisions. They do not allow their votes to be unduly influenced by loyalty to the chief executive or by seniority, position, or reputation of fellow board members, staff, or donors.

6. *Ethos of Transparency.*

Exceptional boards promote an ethos of transparency by ensuring that donors, stakeholders, and interested members of the public have access to appropriate and accurate information regarding finances, operations, and results. They also extend transparency internally, ensuring that every board member has equal access to relevant materials when making decisions.

7. *Compliance with Integrity.*

Exceptional boards promote strong ethical values and disciplined compliance by establishing appropriate mechanisms for active oversight. They use these mechanisms, such as independent audits, to ensure accountability and sufficient controls; to deepen their understanding of the organization; and to reduce the risk of waste, fraud, and abuse.

8. *Sustaining Resources.*

Exceptional boards link bold visions and ambitious plans to financial support, expertise, and networks of influence. Linking budgeting to strategic planning, they approve activities that can be realistically financed with existing or attainable resources, while ensuring that the organization has the infrastructure and internal capacity it needs.

9. *Results Oriented.*

Exceptional boards are results oriented. They measure the organization's progress towards mission and evaluate the performance of major programs and services. They gauge efficiency, effectiveness, and impact, while simultaneously assessing the quality of service delivery, integrating benchmarks against peers, and calculating return on investment.

10. *Intentional Board Practices.*

Exceptional boards purposefully structure themselves to fulfill essential governance duties and to support organizational priorities. Making governance intentional, not incidental, exceptional boards invest in structures and practices that can be thoughtfully adapted to changing circumstances.

11. *Continuous Learning.*

Exceptional boards embrace the qualities of a continuous learning organization, evaluating their own performance and assessing the value they add to the organization. They embed learning opportunities into routine governance work and in activities outside of the boardroom.

12. *Revitalization.*

Exceptional boards energize themselves through planned turnover, thoughtful recruitment, and inclusiveness. They see the correlation between mission, strategy, and board composition, and they understand the importance of fresh perspectives and the risks of closed groups. They revitalize themselves through diversity of experience and through continuous recruitment.

NOTES

1. Ingram, Richard T. 2015. *Ten Basic Responsibilities of Nonprofit Boards*, 3rd ed. BoardSource.
2. BoardSource. 2005. *The Source: Twelve Principles of Governance That Power Exceptional Boards*. BoardSource.

Glossary

There is no universal agreement about much of the nonprofit sector's terminology (or even what we call the sector—variously described as voluntary, third, or public benefit). The following definitions are offered as a guide to aid in the reader's understanding of this text.

board of directors; trustees   The board is a governing body of a nonprofit or for-profit corporation; it has special legal and ethical responsibilities to and for the organization (BoardSource 2016). Its members are most often referred to as *directors* or *trustees*. These terms are often used interchangeably, but there can be situations in which there is significant difference. In the United States, a trust may be organized so that there are several trustees on the board, each with specific duties or responsibilities. Trustees may not be legally required to act as a group or to consult with one another about anything. They may never even meet. Members of a board of directors, however, may all share the same responsibilities and need to meet to carry them out appropriately.
Sometimes the law dictates the term to be used. Regional (e.g., US state) laws may suggest or require the use of one term or the other, or specify duties or responsibilities differently depending on which term is used. There are some organizations in which the bylaws even call for an organization to have both sorts of governing bodies, with different powers or roles (National Center for Charitable Statistics 2002). In most US states, trustees of a charitable trust are held to a higher standard than directors. For example, while a board director will generally only be liable for gross negligence, a trustee may be held responsible for acts of simple negligence—meaning that even acting in good faith, a trustee may be liable for a negligent act while a board director will not be (Charity Lawyer 2016).

charity   A charity is a nonprofit with the purpose of benefiting the greater public. A charity's goals and aims are to improve the quality of life for the greater community. The legal definition of a charitable organization varies depending upon where it operates. Regulation, tax treatment, and the way in which charity law affects charitable organizations also vary. For example, an INGO can be a registered charity in the United Kingdom but can be considered an NGO in another country. In the United Kingdom only those bodies registered with the Charity Commission can call themselves charities. British charities receive certain tax advantages, but also receive more oversight in their affairs and must make annual report to the commission. Charities in Canada must be registered with the Charities Directorate. Charities in Singapore must be registered with the Charities Directorate of the Ministry of Community Development, Youth and Sports.

civil society   Civil society is diverse in nature and composition. The history and cultural context for civil society may vary greatly from country to country or region to region, and therefore a universally applicable definition is elusive. The World Bank has adopted this definition: "The term civil society [is] to refer to the wide array of non-governmental and not-for-profit organizations that have a presence in public life, expressing the interests and values of their members or others, based on ethical, cultural, political, scientific, religious or philanthropic considerations" (World Bank n.d.). In some Central European countries, *civil society* is a concept that relates to civic values (Marshall 1994).

CSOs (civil society organizations)   The World Bank defines civil society organizations (CSOs) as a "wide of array of organizations: Community groups, non-governmental organizations (NGOs), labor unions, indigenous groups, charitable organizations, faith-based organizations, professional associations, and foundations" (Civil Society Team and World Bank 2007, 1). Under some definitions the term can even include for-profit entities (Marshall 1994). Within this sector, this book focuses on CSOs, which some also refer to as NGOs. Other common terms are *nonprofit* and *not-for-profit*. Some may not be inclined to use the latter terms, as they describe organizations for what they are not instead of for what they are. For the book's purposes, we will not focus on the experiences of labor unions, trade unions, or political parties.

Global North, Global South   The Global North is home of the G8 and four of the five permanent members of the UN Security Council. The Global South is Latin America, Africa, and developing Asia, including the Middle East. The term *Global North* often refers to apparently rich northern countries that give aid, while *Global South* refers to ostensibly poor southern countries that receive it.

governance BoardSource defines governance as "the legal authority of a board to establish policies that will affect the life and work of the organization and accountability for the outcome of such decisions" (BoardSource 2016).

ICSOs (international civil society organizations) Also known as international NGOs (INGOs), ICSOs constitute a subset of NGOs in which federations or coalitions of NGOs with multiple geographic sites coordinate their programming at the global level. The official definition of *international NGO* was established on February 27, 1950, by Resolution 288 (X) of the Economic and Social Council (ECOSOC). ECOSOC is one of six principal organs of the United Nations System established by the UN Charter in 1945. These kinds of organizations are discussed in Chapter 10.

NGOs (nongovernmental organizations) NGOs are a subset of CSOs. NGOs are highly diverse groups of organizations engaged in a wide range of activities that take different forms in different parts of the world. There are an estimated 10 million NGOs worldwide (Nonprofit Tech for Good and Your Public Interest Registry 2017). *Origins.* The term *nongovernmental organization* was first coined in 1945, when the UN was created.[1] The UN allowed certain approved and specialized international NSAs (nonstate agencies, or nonstate actors) to observe at its assemblies and at some of its meetings. *Classifications.* There are many different classifications of NGO characteristics in use. The most common aspects focused on are orientation and level of operation. An NGO's *orientation* refers to the focus of its mission and programming, encompassing humanitarian aid, human rights, and environment agendas. An NGO can also be categorized according to its *level of operation*, or geographic scope of operation (i.e., local, regional, national, or international). In some countries NGOS may have charitable status, in others, not necessarily (e.g., the United States). *Variations.* Various alternative or overlapping terms for NGOs are in use (BoardSource 2016). There are national terms related to the legal form of organization (such as GONGO, or government-organized

NGO, in China). Other variations include (Differencebetween.net 2017; YourStory 2015):

- DONGO: donor-organized NGO
- ENGO: environmental NGO
- QUANGO: quasi-autonomous NGO
- TANGO: technical assistance NGO
- GSO: grassroots support organization
- MANGO: market advocacy organization
- BINGO: big (or business-friendly) NGO
- TNGO: transnational NGO

Other variations are specific to particular languages or language groups; for example, in Spanish, French, Italian, and other Romance languages, *ONG* has the same meaning as *NGO* (e.g., Organización no gubernamental [Spanish] *or* Organizzazione non governativa [Italian]). NGOs may also use particular domain extensions (for instance, *.org*, the abbreviation for *organization*, is commonly used in North America for NGOs, although any person, organization, or brand can use the designation). The extension *.ngo*, the abbreviation for *nongovernmental organization*, is most popular in Asia, while *.ong* is the Latin language-based abbreviation for *nongovernmental organization*. Both .ngo and .ong are only available to nonprofits, NGOs, and charities. The extension *.ong* is most popular in Latin America and Europe.[2]

nonprofits; not-for-profits (NPOs)   Broadly defined, the term *nonprofits* can apply to just about type of organization, private or public, from which the owners cannot draw profits or dividends. Nonprofits can generate surplus revenue, but that money must stay within the organization and be used for mission purposes and not distributed to stockholders. NPOs may not necessarily benefit the greater public, and among them are many commercial trade unions, professional associations, and foundations. There are many locally defined types of nonprofits, for instance, PBIs (public benevolent associations) in Australia and IPCs (institutions of a public character) in Singapore.

In Australia, PBIs are charitable institutions that have as their main purpose relieving poverty or distress. This is one of the categories (or "subtypes") of charity that can register with the Australian Charities and Not-for-Profit Commission (ACNC). PBIs include some hospitals and hospices, and some disability-support and aged-care services (see Chapter 4).

In Singapore, IPCs are nonprofit entities that are able to issue tax-deductible receipts for qualifying donations to donors, and are subject to the regulation of fundraising and the conduct of fundraising appeals by charities (see Chapter 3).

Policy Governance®   Also known as the Carver model, Policy Goverance® is an integrated set of concepts and principles that describes the job of any governing board. It outlines the manner in which boards can be successful in their servant-leadership role, as well as in their all-important relationship with management. Unlike most solutions to the challenge of board leadership, its approach to the design of the governance role is neither structural nor piecemeal, but is comprehensively theory based (PolicyGovernance.com).

REFERENCES

BoardSource (website). 2016. "Glossary of nonprofit governance." www.boardsource .org/wp-content/uploads/2017/01/Glossary-Nonprofit-Governance.pdf (accessed November 7, 2017).

Charity Lawyer (website). 2016. www.charitylawyerblog.com/2016/04/24/nonprofit-jargon-buster-directors-vs-trustees (accessed October 29, 2017).

Civil Society Team and World Bank. 2007. *Consultations with Civil Society*. 1.

Differencebetween.net (website). 2017. "Difference between NGO and non-profit organizations." www.differencebetween.net/business/difference-between-ngo-and-non-profit-organizations (accessed October 29, 2017).

Marshall, Gordon, ed. 1994. *Concise Oxford Dictionary of Sociology.*

National Center for Charitable Statistics. 2002. www.ccsweb.urban.org/PubApps/ nonprofitfaq.php?i=15&c=67 (accessed October 29, 2017).

Nonprofit Tech for Good and Your Public Interest Registry. 2017. "25 facts and stats about NGOs worldwide." www.techreport.ngo/previous/2017/facts-and-stats-about-ngos-worldwide.html (accessed November 7, 2017).

Policy Governance.com (website). n.d. http://www.carvergovernance.com/index .html(accessed December 28, 2017).

Wikipedia (website). "Non-governmental organization." n.d. www.en.wikipedia.org/wiki/ Non-governmental_organization#cite_note-3 (accessed December 28, 2017).

World Bank (website)."Defining Civil Society." n.d. www.web.worldbank.org/ WBSITE/EXTERNAL/TOPICS/CSO/0,,contentMDK:20101499~menuPK: 244752~pagePK:220503~piPK:220476~theSitePK:228717,00.html (accessed December 28, 2017).

YourStory (website). 2015. "NGO vs. NPO." https://yourstory.com/2015/10/ngo-vs-npo (accessed October 29, 2017).

NOTES

1. Wikipedia (website). "Non-governmental organization: History." n.d. www.en .wikipedia.org/wiki/Non-governmental_organization#History (accessed December 28, 2017).
2. Nonprofit Tech for Good (website). 2015. www.nptechforgood.com/2015/05/17/4-reasons-why-your-nonprofit-should-register-ngo-and-ong (accessed November 7, 2017).

About the Contributors

Bekay Ahn, CFRE, has been working in the nonprofit sector for 20 years as an author, lecturer, teacher, speaker, and fundraising consultant. He is the founder and principal of the International Council for Nonprofit Management, where he provides strategic counsel to nonprofit and corporate clients, primarily in the areas of organizational development, team building, philanthropy, strategic planning, and nonprofit management and leadership. Bekay has founded and initiated several organizations and institutions, including the Honor Society of Charity of Korea, Asia Philanthropy Awards, and the Society of Philanthropy. Bekay teaches the Certified Fund Raising Executive (CFRE) course that certifies professional fundraisers. He is currently a leading faculty member teaching philanthropy and fundraising at Hanyang University in Seoul, Korea. A passionate writer and educator, Bekay has published six books on fundraising, philanthropy, and related topics.

    Penelope Cagney has more than 30 years of experience helping nonprofits succeed in governance, fundraising, and planning. She has taught fund development, strategic planning, governance, and communications at the Arizona State University Nonprofit Management Institute and at the School of the Art Institute and Columbia College in Chicago, and she was a distinguished visiting professor at American University in Cairo, Egypt. She is the coeditor of the 2015 Skystone Partners Research Prize winner and cause planet.org Best Books of 2015 awardee *Global Fundraising: How the World is Changing the Rules of Philanthropy* (Wiley/AFP 2013). The Chinese language version of the book will be published by the Shanghai University of Finance and Economic Press in 2018. She is also the author of *Nonprofit Consulting Essentials: What Every Nonprofit and Consultant Needs to Know* (Jossey-Bass/Alliance of Nonprofit Management 2010). Penelope serves on the board of the Association of Fundraising Professionals (AFP) International Foundation. Penelope serves on the Wish Fund Committee for Make-A-Wish International. She is also credentialed as a Certified Fundraising Executive (CFRE).

Consuelo Castro has a law degree from the *Universidad Nacional Autónoma de México* (the National Autonomous University of Mexico) and in international relations from the *Universidad Iberoamericana* (Iberoamerican University). Consuelo is founder of the *Centro de Enlace y Desarrollo para OSC* or *Cenlade* Liaison and Development Center for CSOs). She worked at the *Junta de Asistencia Privada para el Distrito Federal* (Mexico City Private Assistance Board) from 2014 to 2016, and from 1994 to 2014 at the *Centro Mexicano para la Filantropía* or *Cemefi* (Mexican Center for Philanthropy) as legal director. She has served on several boards, such as Habitat for Humanity Mexico. She has participated as a speaker at international events and trainer in various subjects, such as good governance practices, legal issues, and strategic planning for nonprofit boards in countries such as Brazil, Bolivia, Costa Rica, Paraguay, and Peru. Consuelo is a consultant on legal and fiscal issues and governance of nonprofit organizations in Mexico and has helped to incorporate several of them. Consuelo works to ensure a legal framework for the growth of philanthropy. She has actively participated in initiatives such as the Federal Law for Promotion of Civil Society Organizations in Mexico. She has also promoted the reform of various federal and local fiscal tax incentives for human rights and environmental organizations. Consuelo Castro has also written various articles and publications on nonprofit organizations.

Tariq Cheema, founder of the World Congress of Muslim Philanthropists, is a renowned social innovator and philanthropist who has devoted his life to making the world a peaceful, equitable, and sustainable place for all. The World Congress of Muslim Philanthropists is a global network of affluent individuals, corporations, foundations, governments, and officials from academia dedicated to advancing effective and accountable giving. His recent trendsetting efforts towards institutionalizing Muslim philanthropy have earned worldwide acclaim. Dr. Cheema ranks among the 500 most influential Muslims impacting the world today.

Louise Coventry is a part-time PhD candidate at RMIT University, Melbourne, who lives in Ho Chi Minh City, Vietnam. A passionate advocate for an inclusive society and social justice, Louise also works as an organizational development consultant with civil society clients across Southeast Asia. Louise holds degrees in social work, psychology, and community management. Her dissertation explores the governance of CSOs in Cambodia.

Noshir H. Dadrawala is the CEO of the Centre for Advancement of Philanthropy, a nonprofit company offering compliance-related advice to nonprofits and corporate social initiatives in India. His career spans over three decades in the social sector working with a diverse range of organizations, from large established national and global organizations to corporate and family grant makers to start-ups. His expertise in the sector is widely recognized, as is his deep understanding of compliance within the philanthropy sector. His current international affiliation includes serving as a director on the board of the International Centre for Not-for-Profit Law. Previously he was on the boards of Worldwide Initiatives for Grantmaker Support and the Asia Pacific Philanthropy Consortium. He also serves as a trustee on several boards in India, including the Forbes Foundation, the Everest Industries Foundation, Happy Home and School for the Blind, and the Bombay Community Trust. Noshir has authored several resource books, has been a speaker at many local and international conferences, and serves as a guest faculty member at leading business schools in India.

Naila Farouky, CEO of the Arab Foundations Forum (AFF), has more than 20 years of experience in project management, media production, and strategic communications. Naila Farouky is a Peabody Award-winning executive who has built a career across several continents. In 2014, Naila assumed the role of CEO for the AFF, a regional, membership-based association of foundations and philanthropic entities working across the Arab region. Prior to taking on her role at AFF, Naila spent 13 years at the iconic Sesame Workshop (the company that produces Sesame Street) in New York. She holds a bachelor of arts in psychology from the American University in Cairo. During her affiliation with the John D. Gerhart Center for Philanthropy and Civic Engagement at the American University in Cairo, Naila coauthored a scan narrative on philanthropic giving in post–January 25th revolution Egypt.

Burkhard Gnärig, for nearly three decades, has been leading different civil society organizations including terre des hommes, Greenpeace, and Save the Children. Burkhard is one of the co-founders and the first Executive Director of the International Civil Society Centre, a nonprofit organization helping international civil society organizations (ICSOs) to improve the effectiveness and efficiency of their work.

Besides being a CEO, Burkhard has been board chair or board member of organizations in Germany, Italy, Switzerland, India, Korea, and Japan. Burkhard provides advice on international leadership, governance, and management to many of the major ICSOs including Amnesty International, CARE, Greenpeace, Oxfam, Plan, Transparency International, World Vision, and YWCA. In 2015 Burkhard published *The Hedgehog and the Beetle*, a book on disruption and innovation in the civil society sector.

Alan Hough, PhD, is a sometime academic, sometime consultant, and sometime practicing board member in Australia. He was a senior research fellow at the Australian Centre of Philanthropy and Nonprofit Studies at the Queensland University of Technology, and has published on theories of governance, board-monitoring practices, and board involvement in strategy. As a consultant, Alan has worked on governance and strategy with organizations across the full range of Australian NGO organizations. More recently he has worked as a consultant assisting NGO and for-profit disability service providers prepare for Australia's new National Disability Insurance Scheme. Alan has served as a practicing board member of organizations working on HIV/AIDS, mental health, and peer support. He keeps an eye out for the quirky and unexpected in organizational life.

Miho Ito earned an undergraduate degree from Northwestern University and an MBA and an MA from Southern Methodist University. While in the United States she held positions such as artistic coordinator at the San Antonio Symphony and manager of fundraising activities for the Walt Disney Concert Hall at the Los Angeles Philharmonic. After returning to Japan she founded Arts Bridge, an organization that offers fundraising consulting and event-planning services. She is currently serving as the executive director of Music Dialogue, a chamber music organization.

Krishan Mehta, PhD, has been a fundraising professional in Toronto, Canada for almost 20 years. He has held a number of both senior development and marketing positions at Ryerson University, Seneca College, and the University of Toronto. He has been an instructor in Ryerson's fundraising management program since 2009 and in Carleton University's graduate program in philanthropy since 2017. In 2015, Krishan earned his PhD from the University of Toronto, where he studied the charitable activities of high–net worth immigrants in

Canada. He served as the president of the AFP's Greater Toronto chapter from 2016 to 2018 and was the cochair of two government-funded AFP projects for over five years, the first being a conference series on philanthropy and emerging donor groups and the second a fellowship program for inclusive fundraising leaders. Krishan has published various book chapters, articles, opinion pieces, and reviews on nonprofit volunteering and philanthropy, and he is a frequent speaker on a range of fundraising topics, from diversity and inclusion to ethics and new models of giving.

Oma Lee is a policy expert specializing in philanthropy, charity, and social businesses in China. She is a senior analyst at the China Philanthropy Research Institute, one of China's foremost think tanks working on philanthropy and charity research. Her work involves pushing policy and policy implementation to advance China's charity and foreign NGO laws. She previously worked in international legal development in China.

Yinglu Li is the director of the Center for Charity Law at the China Philanthropy Research Institute. She is also a senior analyst at the China Global Philanthropy Institute and a consultant for the China Charity Alliance on charitable trusts. She is an expert on China's legal policies on charities and charitable trust systems. She was the chief editor of the Expert Proposal on the China Charity Law and was also heavily involved in the drafting and compilation of the legal interpretations of China's first Charity Law. She was also in charge of drafting the Administrative Measures for Charitable Trusts of Beijing Municipality, the first detailed charitable trust rules in China. She regularly consults for charitable organizations, trust companies, and law firms.

Usha Menon is the founder of Usha Menon Management Consultancy, an international training and coaching consultancy service that works exclusively with social-impact sectors across Asia. Specializing in nonprofit governance, leadership, fundraising, and philanthropy, Usha brings a wealth of multicountry experience, expertise, and insights garnered over the past 30 years. Usha Menon's clients include international, regional, and local social-impact entities; UN organizations; INGOs; associations; social enterprises; economic think tanks; capacity-building organizations; government departments; and academic, arts, and health institutions, all of whom have benefited from the training, mentoring, and consultancy provided by Usha. Usha has transformed the performance of many nonprofit boards across Asia and designed and curated the Nonprofit Directors Program, which caters to the learning needs of board members. She has also developed the curriculum for and been on the core faculty of a variety of governance and leadership programs in universities across Asia, including programs at the Lee Kuan Yew School for Public Policy at the National University of Singapore, the postgraduate development management course at the S. P. Jain Institute of Management and Research in India, and the mosque leadership development program at MUIS Academy in Singapore, among others. She is one of Asia's leading nonprofit bloggers and posts sector insights and observations regularly through her blog *Asian Insights*, many of which are translated by capacity-building entities in Japan, China, and Germany.

    Valerio Melandri is a consultant, trainer, and educator in fundraising. He is a professor at the University of Bologna and director of the Master in Fundraising Program (www.master-fundraising.it), the only postgraduate fundraising program in Europe. Melandri is a visiting professor at Columbia University in New York City, where he teaches international fundraising at its School of International and Public Affairs. He is founder and president of the Philanthropy Research Centre (www.philanthropy.it), a center for research, training, and consultancy based in the Faculty of Economics in Forlì at the University of Bologna. He is chairman of the organizing committee for the Fundraising Festival (www.festifaldelfundraising.it), the largest event for fundraising in Italy and the fifth most attended in the world. He has participated in over 40 national and international conferences over the past year, presenting in Italian or English. He has published various books on philanthropy, the most recent of which is *Melandri Fundraising: Creating A Stronger Donor Relationships to Sustain Your Nonprofit for the Really Long Haul* (Civil Sector Press, 2017).

    Mike Naholi Muchilwa is the CEO of Innovative Concepts and chairs the Kenya Association of Fundraising Professionals. He has over 25 years of experience in governance, organization development, resource mobilization, strategic and business planning, entrepreneurship development, and fair trade. Mike has worked with organizations such as Agriprofocus, SERRV, the World Fair Trade Organisation (WFTO), and KICK. He has also worked as a consultant to the subsidiary of a leading Dutch consultancy firm, DHV, for five years. Mike has founded several organizations, including Kick Trading, the Kenya Federation of Alternative Trade, and WFTO Africa. Mike has trained the board and management of various organizations on governance. He has sat on the boards of various organizations and managed others, giving him a strong perspective on CSO governance. He holds a degree in economics from the University of Nairobi. He has also written two books, *The Job of Getting a Job* and *The Side Hustle——Running a Business Besides Your Job*. Along with other global consultants, he contributed to the award-winning philanthropy book *Global Fundraising: How the World is Changing the Rules of Philanthropy*, and the award-winning *Diversity and Philanthropy: Expanding the Circle of Giving*.

Garth Nowland-Foreman has had a lifetime of working in, with, and for NGOs, and has an insatiable curiosity for finding out stuff. He is currently director of the LEAD Centre for Not-for-Profit Leadership (specializing in governance consulting and training) and has been the chair or a board member of numerous NGOs (local, national, and international; large and small; service-provider, advocate, and member associations). For 18 years he taught graduate programs on NGO management part time in Aotearoa New Zealand and the Pacific. He also chaired the first intersectoral efforts to measure the size and economic impact of the NGO sector in Aotearoa New Zealand as a part of the Johns Hopkins International Comparative Nonprofit Sector Project. Garth has been an advocate for study of the sector and has written widely, particularly on issues of NGO funding and accountability.

Paloma Raggo, PhD, is an assistant professor of philanthropy and nonprofit leadership at the School of Public Policy and Administration at Carleton University in Ottawa, Canada. Her current research follows three streams: International NGO/nonprofit governance, global philanthropy, and online teaching. She has received a grant from the Social Sciences and Humanities Research Council of Canada to investigate accountability challenges at various decision-making levels in an INGO as a follow-up to her doctoral work at the Maxwell School of Citizenship and Public Affairs at Syracuse University. At Carleton University, she has taught graduate courses on nonprofit governance and leadership, the globalization of philanthropy, and philanthropic and nonprofit research methods. From 2011 to 2013 she served as the associate director of the Institute for Qualitative and Multi-Method Research at Syracuse University. Her research has been published in *Nonprofit Voluntary Sector* and the *Journal of Nonprofit Education and*

Leadership. She has authored several book chapters on international NGOs and accountability. She is currently working on a book to be titled *Leadership and Accountability in International NGOs* (under contract).

Darmawan Triwibowo has more than 15 years as a development worker, managing development projects for various international non-profit organizations in Indonesia and abroad. His scope of work covers a wide range of responsibility in project management, including program planning, monitoring and evaluation, capacity building for partner organizations, advocacy and campaigns, and networking. He was involved in various campaigns and advocacy projects on key global development agendas, such as economic inequality, extractive industry transparency, and aid effectiveness. He earned his master's degree in public policy and administration from the University of Missouri in St. Louis, and is currently serving as the executive director of the TIFA Foundation and as a member of the Open Society Foundation in the Asia-Pacific region.

Masataka Uo is the founder and CEO of Japan Fundraising Association, a nationwide network that promotes philanthropic giving and social-impact investment in Japan, and the founder and CEO of Fundrex, a leading consulting company that provides strategic development and donor-database consulting for more than 150 nonprofits and social businesses. He is also the vice chair of the Japan National Advisory Committee for the G-8 Social Impact Investment Task Force (which became the Global Social Impact Investment Steering Group [GSG] in 2015) and the vice president of the Japan Volunteer Coordination Association.

Marilyn Wyatt is a coach and mentor to nonprofit boards. She has worked with CSOs in more than 30 countries and is the author of the widely used *Handbook of NGO Governance*. Before launching her own practice she was director of international programs in Europe and Asia at BoardSource. She has previously worked as director of communications at the Aspen Institute; as a US Foreign Service officer with postings to Warsaw, Prague, and Washington; and as a communications specialist for the USAID in Pakistan. Marilyn began her career as senior editor working for the 1984 Olympic Games in Los Angeles. Marilyn has a PhD in comparative literature from Johns Hopkins University and a BA with a major in English from Cornell University. She has served on the boards of many organizations, including the Czech Fulbright Commission, the American School in Warsaw, the International School in Prague, Developments in Literacy (Pakistan), and the Vaclav Havel Library Foundation.

Index

Page references followed by *fig* indicate an illustrated figure; followed by *t* indicate a table.